DEATH TO DEATH

DEATH TO DEATH

*A Detailed Study Which Illuminates the Many Flaws of the
Death Penalty and Argues for Its Demise*

ROBERT V. DOLAN, MD

ISBN: 0692605827
ISBN 13: 9780692605820
Library of Congress Control Number: 2015921353
Robert V. Dolan, Fullerton, CA

CONTENTS

PROLOGUE

My first interest in writing this book came during a social event when I joined a small group of people who were discussing the death penalty. One individual was adamantly prodeath, primarily because he did not want to have to pay for "those people on death row" for the rest of their lives. I mentioned that I had read somewhere that, compared with sentencing a murderer to life in prison, committing someone to death row was more expensive, but no one in the group believed me, and I was not so sure myself. That prompted my research into the subject, and I found my recollection about the monetary costs (let alone the costs on all other levels) was indeed the case—and to a far greater extent than one would imagine. That fact was only one of many issues leading to my conclusion that the capital-punishment system, as it functions today in the United States, is very seriously broken.

The intent of this book is to touch on the most salient issues but not completely cover them, because the latter endeavor would require several tomes by multiple authors and thus is not even in the realm of practicality. Hopefully, the size of this volume makes it readily available to all readers.

When discussing murderers or other criminals, I almost exclusively use masculine pronouns. This is not intended to exclude women from these considerations (although while there are females who have committed murder and other heinous crimes, males do so in far greater numbers). But, practically speaking, identifying in one gender eliminates tedious repetitions of "he or she" and "she or he."

In referencing professionals in the area of psychiatry and psychology, I often use the term "psychiatrists" alone. This is not done to minimize the importance of psychologists but to avoid the repetition of mentioning both groups, again for the benefit of seamless reading. For the same reason, in discussing the area of anesthesiology in regard to lethal injection, reference is made almost exclusively to anesthesiologists, but it should be understood that this includes nurse anesthetists as well.

Though I have had input from multiple sources, the ultimate responsibility for opinions in this book is mine. My wish is that the reader evaluate these opinions, agree or disagree, and hopefully come to some conclusions about this topic, which affects us all in many ways. Capital punishment is an issue we do not think about very frequently, and we almost completely rely on legal professionals for the way it functions. The issue is that it is still *our* process, one that has become massively dysfunctional, and *we the people* need to reconsider our social, ethical, and financial responsibilities.

ACKNOWLEDGMENTS

Although the opinions and factual information are ultimately mine, I have been blessed with input from numerous people of different disciplines. They supported me, gave me information, traded ideas with me, and outright taught me so many things. The first, of course, is my wife, Marianne, who has put up with me, supported me, helped me with the organization of the book, and even did some proofreading. My daughters, Kate Brahm and Jennifer La Grange, and son, Matt, supported this endeavor in many ways, all the way from the technical to grammar corrections. Terri Dolan, my daughter-in-law, proofread the entire manuscript, provided help in organization, and made grammatical corrections. A talented good friend, Pete Williams, is a retired trial attorney who personally defended five death-penalty defendants and supervised the defense of eighty more as the head deputy of the Law Offices of the Los Angeles County Public Defender, where he practiced from 1970 to 1990. In that capacity, he became part of the capital-punishment system and learned the practical function of all its intricacies.

Dr. David Sheffner, a renowned forensic psychiatrist, was kind enough to educate me in numerous ways as to the relationship between psychiatrists and lawyers and the boundaries between that both must cross. In addition, his discussion of the capabilities and functioning of the delusional mind helps elucidate the inadequate and somewhat irrational use of the legal term "insanity." Dr. Linda Meza, a psychologist who specializes in death-penalty cases, was very helpful in explaining exactly how a psychologist can function within the courtroom. Author Julie Davis was incredibly free with her time and very helpful in the area of the practicalities of book authorship and publication. Clinical psychologist Dr. Jo Ann Brannock reviewed most of my material on insanity, offering some constructive and helpful suggestions and criticism. Dick Ackerman, attorney and former Republican state senate leader in California, was a valuable source for many legal questions and political implications therein. His wife, Linda, performed the function of cracking the whip when she thought I was getting lax. Retired orthopedist Dr. Jack Parker steadily supplied information he found during the course of his extensive reading. Author Mike Oates Jr. contributed by sharing his experiences of the realities involved in publicizing and publishing.

I extend a special note of recognition for the support from my son Michael, who passed away in 2011. When I first got the idea of putting this all together, it was through his support that I really got started. Had he still been with us and able to offer from his brilliant mind, this endeavor would have been done quicker and would have been much better. This, of course, is only one of the many ways I miss him, but without his prodding, I would not have begun this project, and it is to him that I dedicate this book.

KEY REFERENCES

There are several books and publications that I have relied on heavily and would recommend to anyone who wants to probe more deeply into these issues. The first is Stuart Banner's book titled *The Death Penalty: An American History*, an interesting account of the origins of our death penalty in colonial times and how it has evolved since, to become what it is today. Philip Dray, in his book *At the Hands of Persons Unknown: The Lynching of Black America,* catalogs the history of lynching in the United States with an emphasis on black Americans in the South and also its use in the West as the sole means of any kind of justice system. Dr. Robert Hare's book *Without Conscience: The Disturbing World of the Psychopaths among Us* is a probing and complete analysis of the mind of the psychopath, written by the premier expert on the subject of psychopathy. Complementing that work is an article in *Scientific American Mind* by Kent Kiehl and Joshua Buckholtz titled "Inside the Mind of a Psychopath," which also probes into the workings of this pathology and even references some attempts at treatment. The most complete and definitive reproducible analytic report is from the National Research Council's Committee on Deterrence and the Death Penalty, titled "Deterrence and the Death Penalty."

A man with considerable experience in the area of the death penalty and a real feel for the system's inadequacies is Professor Robert Blecker, a pro-death-penalty protagonist, with whom I found myself agreeing on many fronts even though we, ultimately, came to directly opposite opinions on capital punishment. His book *The Death of Punishment: Searching for Justice among the Worst of the Worst* is an expression of his philosophy and views on the subject.

Many of the facts and figures in this book come from statistical analyses by the Death Penalty Information Center (DPIC), an anti-death-penalty group that provides information online. Three "bibles"—the Constitution of the United States, the *Diagnostic and Statistical Manual of Mental Disorders* (*DSM-5*), and the California Penal Code—provided foundations with factual materials and definitions.

REVISIONIST INTRODUCTION

I received my first concepts of how a death sentence was carried out from the movies, in which condemned individuals were usually executed quickly, if not immediately. I still remember the final scene in the 1953 film *The Robe*. Jay Robinson, as Caligula, in a horrible nasal voice, sends Marcellus (played by Richard Burton) and Diana (portrayed by beautiful actress Jean Simmons) to their immediate deaths for the "crime" of being Christian. Marcellus and Diana march out into the clouds, the last move they will make on this earth.

Today, in real life, things would be a little different. Roman prosecutors would have gotten Diana to turn state's evidence and freed her immediately. Caligula would indeed have sentenced Marcellus to death, but at the same time, Marcellus's attorneys would arrange for his transfer to a cell on death row and start the appeals process. The good emperor Caligula would have had to hock one of his famous pleasure barges to handle his side of the court costs. Oh, wait. He would have had to sell both barges, because the way we do it, if the criminal does not have the wherewithal to handle his legal costs, we cover for him. Meanwhile, the proceedings would cause Marcellus so much stress that he might develop coronary artery disease and have to undergo bypass surgery. That expense would require the emperor to sell one of his villas. This final ignominy would be the blow that causes Caligula to pass out, go into a coma, and die. Marcellus would live on, only to succumb finally to death at age ninety-eight while working out on a prison treadmill. Marcellus's estate might then sue on the grounds that he was improperly supervised while exercising and win a large award, which would completely destroy Caligula's family financially. To pay the bills, they would have to take jobs as oarsmen on a trireme, which would have been making continuous runs to and from Egypt.

Chapter 1

WHAT DEATH PENALTY?

The problem is that, for the most part, we really do not have a death penalty. The answer to the question of what is right with the system is much shorter than the answer to the question of what is wrong with the system.

There are fifteen thousand murders a year in the United States, and less than fifty executions per year (thirty-nine in 2013, thirty-five in 2014, and twenty-eight in 2015), which means that about 0.2 percent of murderers are executed each year. On the rare occasion that executions do occur, they are usually long after initial sentencing.

The process exhausts the legal system in terms of court time, expenses, and professional personnel. The expenses are enormous. Capital trials are much more expensive than noncapital trials, and this is even more exaggerated in the penalty phases. It is far more expensive to house someone on death row than in the general population, and then comes the appeals process, which can drag on for a seeming eternity, all the while costing huge amounts of money.

Although they might gain some satisfaction if there is an eventual execution, victims' families suffer over and over again during the tedious procession of legal maneuverings.

A murderer can avoid the death penalty if he chooses the "right" location to commit the crime—for example, a state that has already eliminated capital punishment. The result is that two identical crimes can be handled very differently, depending on factors that have nothing to do with the crime itself. Even in areas where the death penalty is still on the books, jurisdictions and prosecutors pursue capital punishment with varying levels of vigor. The decision of when and if to seek the death penalty can depend on such variables as how the involved legal professionals feel about the death penalty in general and in regard to a particular case. The qualities of a defendant's attorneys contribute enormously to his ability to avoid the death penalty, and there are often obvious advantages in the courtroom for the rich and famous. In addition, states have varying aggravating and mitigating considerations that can significantly affect outcomes, again with the dynamic that the same crime can have a much different outcome depending on something as irrelevant as location.

This country receives criticism from many nations that have eliminated the death penalty. In fact we are the only developed country—what we call a "first-world" nation—in the West that still has the death penalty. Although other nations' opinions should not completely guide our actions, this factor plays a major role when nations refuse to extradite murderers back to the United States because of the possibility of a death sentence. Other nations accuse us of human-rights violations, pointing out our continuing use of the death penalty as well as the large number of people we have in one form of incarceration or another.

There still exists the possibility of executing an innocent person, and this fear has long been a powerful argument for abolitionists.

There also exists a real possibility that a convicted individual can obtain redemption and turn his life around, even with the potential of his influencing the lives of others headed down similarly errant pathways. There is an argument that, especially since it takes so long to finally come to the rare execution, we are killing a changed person and not the one who committed the crime.

There is always the question of whether or not we should take into consideration the mental or social status of the murderer. Was his upbringing so bad that those factors encouraged him toward negative pathways that were far more unlikely routes for people who had much better chances in life? Whether you agree with this or not, it becomes an important issue, particularly in the penalty phase of capital trials.

Racial inequalities remain an issue with the institution of capital punishment, although this problem was much worse in the past.

The death penalty can be a real political football. If a politician with some clout wants to appear tough on crime, his support of the death penalty is an obviously powerful tool. A politician's stand on capital-punishment issues has affected many an election.

There has been an almost knee-jerk reaction from the standpoint of political philosophies in which conservatives, by and large, are "supposed" to be for capital punishment and liberals against it. There is, however, a developing wave of understanding by which people of both persuasions are realizing the terrible flaws within the system and coming to the conclusion that we need something better.

There are ethical and social arguments for and against the death penalty. Some argue that having a death penalty demeans our national ethos, whereas others feel it is a powerful tool we can use in the cause of our national morality. Religious arguments seem to balance out in this debate because some religious people and groups feel the death penalty is intrinsically wrong, while others hold that it is a necessary and righteous tool against evil.

Because this issue seems to strike very visceral responses on both sides, the role of capital punishment as a deterrent has long been a subject of debate, often with great virulence. Although some people support the idea that the death penalty is an effective deterrent, the majority of experts in the field think there is essentially no deterrent effect, especially in the way it is practiced today. There is the argument that the death penalty would act as a real deterrent to crime if it were practiced in an efficient and expeditious manner in which most capital murder cases resulted in a death sentence and executions were carried out rapidly. However, that is hardly the way we do it, and most people would likely agree that the current state of our capital-punishment system cannot possibly serve as a weapon.

The Gallup poll of 2015 indicates that 63 percent of Americans feel that people who've committed heinous crimes should be eliminated and, to that end, still support the death penalty. However, more and more people realize that the capital-punishment system is so flawed that it is no longer the way to accomplish the goal of removing a murderer from society. A life sentence without possibility of parole (or LWOP—life without parole) accomplishes this goal in a much more realistic, honest, and efficient manner.

Although there are about fifteen thousand murders a year, we execute fewer and fewer convicted criminals—so few, in fact, that in 2015, the number was down to twenty-eight. Nationally about thirty-two hundred people are on death row, and the numbers continue to grow, although fewer are added to that census every year. According to Death Penalty Information Center (DPIC) statistics from 1977 to the present, there has been a progressive decline in the numbers of death sentences as well. There were two peaks—in 1994 and 1996—when 315 death sentences were handed down in each of those years, but such sentences have since diminished to the point that there were only eighty in 2011 nationwide, making it the first year when fewer than one hundred were so sentenced, and that number is down to seventy-nine in 2012 and 2013. At our current decreasing rate of execution, if we were to sentence no one else to death, it would take over one hundred years to empty all of our death rows without considering the much larger number who would die of natural causes. The reality, of course, is that the ranks will grow, and we will never eliminate our death-row populations, meaning that receiving a "death sentence" is really a "life sentence" with the rare exception of those few unlucky individuals we finally get around to killing.

About 60 percent of Americans still say they favor having the death sentence, but it appears that, for the most part, we are not really willing to carry it out. And when we do, it is usually so far down the temporal line that the long delays tend to mute any impact it might have on the public and the family and friends of the victim. When we sentence someone to death, it is because we feel the criminal's crime was so terrible that he should be eliminated from this earth, and we make a promise to carry out that act of condemnation.

One expected result is that the execution offers some element of closure and vindication for family and friends of the victim, but for the most part, that does not happen because we fail to deliver on our promise and instead offer them prolonged frustration and emotional pain. We put families and friends through a living, frustrating hell in which execution gets thwarted time and time again as they relive the horrors of the crime. Though there are exceptions, most family members and friends want to see the murderer executed, but we often fail to deliver on that promise.

Kay Brenneman addressed a crowd in Modjeska Park in California, the location where she celebrated her son's twelfth birthday over thirty years ago. Unfortunately that proved to be the last birthday her son ever celebrated. On August 25, 1981, he entered an apartment complex in Anaheim to solicit customers for his paper route and was never seen alive again. Two days later police arrested Robert Jackson Thompson for the murder, also charging him with kidnapping and sexual abuse, and two trials later a jury sentenced him to death.

Mrs. Brenneman wanted to see Thompson executed for this horrible crime, exhorting the recent assemblage in Modjeska Canyon to remember her son, stand strong on crime issues, and support provictim and anti-crime legislation. Unfortunately, Thompson died of a heart attack while on death row in San Quentin in 2006, and Mrs. Brenneman's only real solace was that she outlived her son's murderer. Since most Americans support the death penalty, they likely would agree with her and want to see her son's murderer executed. But with the current state of our capital-punishment system, this case went the way most death-penalty cases do, the murderer living a long life and dying of natural causes. Thompson died a quarter of a century after his arrest and, at the time of his death, was still in the process of fighting his sentence.

What we did was spend a lot of money and lie to this mother, who expected us as a society to do what we said we would do—execute her son's murderer. There is no sense of enthusiasm for capital punishment because, more than a weapon for justice, it is a mockery to us, our legal system, and most of all, the families of murder victims.

Chapter 2

FOUR EXAMPLES, FOR EXAMPLE

These cases all demonstrate many failures of our capital-punish-ment system. A criminal's rampant cruelty and audacious dis-regard for justice do not result in execution but in a life prolonged by legal maneuverings. Questionable decisions and outright errors in judgment and sentencing highlight multiple frailties of the death penalty.

RODNEY ALCALA
We now have sentenced Rodney Alcala to death three times. He was charged with the kidnapping and murder of twelve-year-old Robin Samsoe on June 20, 1979. His most recent trial was in 2011, fully thirty-one years after the first jury arrived at the same conclusion.

In 1964 the US Army discharged Rodney Alcala for what was called a "nervous breakdown," and at the time, military psychiatrists indicated he had an antisocial personality disorder. Later other psychiatrists added on to his psychological profile that he had a narcissistic personality disorder and borderline personality disorder.

His first known violent act, in 1968, was luring an eight-year-old into his apartment, where he raped her and bludgeoned her with a steel bar. Fortunately an observer called police, and they arrived in time to save the little girl, but they did not apprehend Alcala, who fled out the back door. Alcala went to New York, where he functioned under the aliases "John Berger" and "John Burger." He murdered Cornelia Crilley, a twenty-three-year-old flight attendant, whose battered body was found in her New York apartment on June 12, 1971.

Alcala took a job as a camp counselor in New Hampshire, where two children who attended the camp saw his face on a post-office poster and reported this to the authorities. He was arrested and sent back to California to stand trial for the rape and attempted murder of the young girl. By that time, however, her family had relocated her to Mexico and refused to allow her to participate in the trial. Because the primary witness was unavailable, the prosecuting attorneys were unable to obtain a conviction of Alcala for rape and attempted murder. They settled for an assault conviction for which Alcala served thirty-four months and was then paroled after showing signs of rehabilitation.

Two months later Los Angeles police arrested him for assaulting a thirteen-year-old girl, who had accepted a ride to school from him. He was tried, convicted, and paroled after two more years in prison. His parole officer then allowed him to travel to New York, where he killed Ellen Jane Hover, the twenty-three-year-old goddaughter of Dean Martin and Sammy Davis Jr. On June 15, 1977, she told friends she was going to meet with a photographer, and she was never seen again. A year later her remains were found on the John D. Rockefeller Estate in Westchester County.

Alcala returned to Los Angeles, where he presented himself as a photographer, convincing hundreds of young women and men to pose for him, usually in sexually explicit manners. During this period he went on a killing spree that took the lives of Jill Barcomb, Georgia Wixted,

Charlotte Lamb, and Jill Parenteau. Police have obtained the photos from Alcala's photography sessions for review and, with the public's assistance, are trying to determine if any of the people photographed were victims as well.

In 1978, in the midst of his killing spree, Alcala appeared on television's *The Dating Game* on ABC, and he was charming and clever enough for bachelorette Cheryl Bradshaw to select him as her date, but she refused to go out with him because she found him to be "creepy."

On June 20, 1979, Alcala kidnapped and killed twelve-year-old Robin Samsoe, and the next month, he was arrested for her murder. In 1980 a jury found him guilty, and Alcala was sentenced to death. However, the California Supreme Court later reversed the decision for the fact that the Orange County jury was improperly informed of his criminal record since the prosecution mentioned Alcala's previous sentence and incarceration for molestation.

Alcala was therefore retried in 1986, and again he was convicted and sentenced to death. A witness in the first trial was too frail to appear at the second trial, but her testimony was read to the jury. A federal district court later overturned that conviction on the basis of the fact that the original testimony was read and the witness had not appeared in person.

DNA, blood, and fingerprint evidence linked Alcala to the murders of the other four women, all murdered in horrible fashion and whose cases were included together in the third trial, in 2011, in a little-used process called "bundling." Once again the jury found him guilty, and Alcala was sentenced to death. This case had several bizarre twists, however, in which Alcala, who supposedly has a high IQ, represented himself in court. During the trial he interrogated and took testimony from Marianne Connelly, Robin's mother, who at that time was sixty-six years old.

Despite his apparent extensive preparation for the trial, his own defense was very frail and at times inane, and at no time was he a match for senior prosecutor Matt Murphy, whose calm, well-thought-out profes-sionalism easily convinced the jury Alcala belonged on death row.

New York authorities sought the extradition of Alcala for the two mur-ders in that state, and on February 7, 2012, a judge decided he could be sent back, but because the defense team was preparing another death-penalty appeal in California, the judge stayed the ruling until the usual extradi-tion appeal was settled. New York finally was able to extradite him, and Alcala pleaded guilty to a grand jury indictment for the murders of Cornelia Crilley, twenty-three in 1971, and Ellen Hover, twenty-three in 1977, and was sentenced to twenty-five years to life. Instead of launching a defense as he had done in the past, Alcala told the judge he was pleading guilty to the New York murders so he could go back to California to continue pursuing his appeal of his third death sentence in the Robin Samsoe case. It is worthy of note that he presented no defense prior to the convictions for the other four women he killed or during his trial for the Samsoe case.

At present the Alcala defense is working on more appeals in the California system, while he continues to sit on death row.

Retired Judge Donald McCartin has expressed outrage over the fact that people he felt were unqualified overturned the verdict of the sec-ond trial, over which he presided. He phoned special reporter Frank Mickadeit of the *Orange County Register* to express his feeling that Alcala was precisely the reason California should abandon capital punishment. It is very distressing that Marianne Connelly had to endure at this third trial what she has been going through for thirty years because of the flawed capital-punishment system. During his career Judge McCartin sent nine men to death row, and as one might expect, none has been executed.

LESSONS FROM RODNEY ALCALA

Rodney Alcala has played the system expertly for decades and knows he can continue to do so, even to the point of almost nonchalantly pleading guilty to the New York murders so he can go back to California to continue the charade there. A classic psychopath—he has no regard for anyone or anything other than himself. Throwing out his first two murder convictions had nothing to do with whether or not he was guilty, but on issues most would think are so peripheral and unimportant that they should be disregarded. In the first one, why *shouldn't* the panel know about Alcala's previous history, especially when the assault on the eight-year-old girl had been so savage? And in the second reversal, what was so wrong about reading the testimony since the witness was unable to appear? His innocence has never been an issue. The absurdity of our justice system in this pursuit is the issue.

ALBERT GREENWOOD BROWN

Albert Brown was convicted of murder on February 4, 1982, in the case of the rape and strangulation murder of Susan Louise Jordan, a fifteen-year-old high-school girl who was on her way to class in Riverside, California. Brown, posing as a jogger, abducted her and dragged her into an orange grove. He raped her, used her shoelaces to strangle her, and then took her identification and schoolbooks. He later phoned her mother and coldly stated, "Hello, Mrs. Jordan. Susie isn't home from school yet, is she? You will never see your daughter again. You can find her body on the corner of Victoria and Gibson." He made a similar call to the Riverside Police Department, and officers found the body at that location.

Brown's history is of some interest in that he had a previous conviction for the rape and strangulation of a fourteen-year-old girl, who had just returned home after finishing her paper route. He observed the house and waited until everyone left and then entered to await his prey. When the girl entered the house, Brown overpowered her, choked her until she was unconscious, and then raped her in her mother's bedroom. Fortunately she survived. On May 4, 1978, Brown was convicted of rape with force and sentenced to four years in state prison. On June 14, 1980, he was paroled after serving less than two years and went to work at a car company, where he washed cars for a living.

After hearing the murder case of Susan Jordan, the jury needed only three hours to find Brown guilty, and he was subsequently sentenced to death. Then began the appeals process through which his defense motioned habeas corpus to the US Court of Appeals for the Ninth Circuit in San Francisco, arguing that Brown received ineffective counsel at the time of his defense and also that his sentence was cruel and unusual, thus violating his Eighth Amendment rights.

In February 2006, Judge Jeremy Fogel halted the execution of convicted murderer Michael Morales because of complaints about the old execution chamber and problems associated with performing a lethal injection within it. In response, the state of California renovated the facility to the tune of $853,000 so executions could be carried out properly. Brown's sentence was to be carried out in that new facility. Judge Fogel offered Brown a choice of method of execution, which included the gas chamber or either of the intravenous approaches—a single dose of sodium thiopental or a three-drug cocktail. Brown refused to make a selection by the deadline of September 27, 2010, and his attorneys argued he was unprepared to make such a choice because of his "obvious neuropsychological deficits." The defense attorneys then made a last-ditch appeal for clemency to Governor Schwarzenegger along with a request to commute the sentence to life imprisonment without parole. The governor denied this request, but he delayed the timing of the execution to nine o'clock at night on September 30 to give the appeals court more time to review the case. The appeals court ordered the judge to revisit the case, because California law specifically states that the judge could only ask the inmate to choose between the gas chamber and lethal injection, but not the method of injection. Judge Fogel admitted that his offer was ill-advised and halted the execution to address the defense's arguments of cruel and unusual punishment. At this point the defense also requested the case be reviewed on grounds that Brown had suffered child abuse and that this should have been brought up at the trial.

The California Supreme Court denied the prosecution's appeal to carry out the execution by September 30. The appeals court noted that the prison supply of Sodium Pentothal expiring October 1 also pointed to the fact that adequate amounts of the drug would be available January 2011, and thus, the execution was put on hold, and it remains, at the time of this writing, in a limbo status.

LESSONS FROM ALBERT BROWN

Albert Brown's case is also over three decades long with no end in sight. The two-year sentence for rape and attempted murder of a fourteen-year-old girl was inadequate enough to keep him off the streets, where he committed the rape and murder of a fifteen-year-old high-school girl. Brown was to be next in line for execution, and the state of California constructed a new $850,000 facility to replace the old one, which was considered to be no longer adequate. However, his termination has been delayed by his defense team's use of the "cruel and unusual" maneuver, his inability to select a preferred method of execution, and an inadequate supply of Sodium Pentothal. The Pentothal issue is now eliminated, since the use of the drug has for the most part been discontinued in favor of the single-drug use of pentobarbital. Nevertheless, there are enough issues on the table to ensure that Brown will someday die of natural causes.

Many people criticize the appeals process and the toll it takes on victims' families. Emotional wounds have little chance to heal since family members have to relive the horror of the crimes at every appeal and endure repeated disappointments every time justice is thwarted. Susan Jordan's sister, Karen, criticized the repeated delays of Brown's trial with this statement: "The appeals process in California is nothing more than a never-ending war of attrition against justice and the rights of victims and their families."

This case also brought up the issue of how politicians make use of their stance on the death penalty to promote their own careers. In the political overtones to this case, Albert Brown's attorneys suggested that the move to execution was promoted because of the race for governor between Jerry Brown and Meg Whitman. Both sides denied this accusation, but Attorney General Brown pushed to resume capital punishment after the new protocols in regard to lethal injection were adopted. However, there is no record of his mentioning this case specifically, nor any documentable indication that either candidate was attempting to appear "tough on crime" by voicing support of Brown's execution or for upholding the death penalty.

BRIAN NICHOLS

Brian Nichols was on trial for a brutal assault on his former girlfriend. He was in the Fulton County Courthouse in Atlanta, Georgia, on March 11, 2005. He was preparing for the trial by changing into civilian clothes, and in so doing, sheriff's deputy Cynthia Hall removed his handcuffs. Nichols then took her by the arm, attacked her, and hit her in the face so hard that she sustained severe neurologic injuries. He then went in search of Rowland Barnes, the judge who presided at his trial. Nichols entered courtroom 8-F through a door that allowed him to come up behind Judge Barnes, who was hearing a civil trial. Nichols shot the judge in the back of the head, killing him instantly. He looked for the prosecuting attorneys, and when he could not find them, he picked out court reporter Julie Brandau as his next victim and shot her in the head as well.

Nichols apparently went searching for his former girlfriend in the witness room, but he did not find her because she had not yet arrived at court. Sergeant Hoyt Teasley had just entered the building when he spotted Nichols fleeing out of the courthouse down several flights of stairs.

Sergeant Teasley pursued, despite the fact that he had no time to put on his bulletproof vest or get his radio, a means through which he might have gotten a better idea of how dangerous this suspect was. When they got outside, Nichols fired at Teasley and shot him in the abdomen, causing a fatal hemorrhage.

Nichols proceeded to terrorize many people in the area and carjacked several different vehicles during his escape. US Immigration and Customs Enforcement agent David Wilhelm was working on his new, partially unfinished home when Nichols shot and killed him and stole his wallet, money, and car.

At two o'clock in the morning on March 12, Nichols approached Ashley Smith in the parking lot of her apartment complex. He pointed his gun at her and forced her into her apartment unit. During the next several hours, she was able to calm him down and gain his confidence. Eventually he let her drive off by herself. She called 911, and this led to his arrest by the Gwinnett County Police Department SWAT Team. Smith detailed her clever and heroic actions in her book *Unlikely Angel: The Untold Story of the Atlanta Hostage Hero.*

During his interrogation, Nichols described in detail his crimes and freely admitted his guilt. He felt he was a soldier on a mission against a judicial system that was unfair to African Americans. Fulton County District Attorney Paul Howard described Nichols as "someone who was proud of what he had done—that he did not show remorse."

The case gained national and even international attention, as members of the French media joined the cadre of over a hundred reporters who attended the events of Nichols's trial for the killing spree. Fulton County had a reputation as being against capital punishment, and for that reason, the entire legal apparatus moved very slowly and cautiously every step of the way. First the local judges recused themselves on the basis that they could not be impartial due to their relationships with the victims. Superior Court Judge Hilton Fuller took the case, but he also stepped down because he also felt, after investigating the case, that he could not be impartial. Before he stepped down, however, he suspended the case indefinitely because of financial issues. Facing a severe budget crunch, the state public defender's office cut off funding to Nichols's lawyers. The Georgia General Assembly even got involved, passing a law that allowed the state to pay for only two attorneys in a defense case.

After all the delays, the case finally went to trial. The panel was selected over a nine-week period during which over 240 prospective jurors were interviewed. The prosecution amassed over three hundred potential witnesses and used seventy-four of them in the case. This was considered a "slam dunk." Numerous witnesses had observed the crimes, and the defendant had not only confessed but also described the details of his crimes. District Attorney Paul Howard sought the death penalty because of the heinous nature of the crimes and the total disregard for the lives of officials and private citizens.

Nichols had been on trial for a vicious attack on his former girlfriend in which he, armed with two pistols, had broken into her apartment, tied her hands and feet, and threatened to pour lighter fluid all over her, burn her to death, and then take his own life. During seven terrifying hours, he raped her, threatened her, and warned her that if she told anyone about this incident, he would kill her and her family, even if he had to go to prison for a long time. This incident, his demeanor, and the statements he had made during his confession led the defense team to disclose that they wanted to defend Nichols on the basis of mental-health issues, and on September 22, 2008, they entered a plea of not guilty by reason of insanity. This plea, as is usual, was rejected, and a little over two weeks later, on November 7, 2008, the jury found Brian Nichols guilty of all fifty-four counts against him. Georgia law demands that the jury must come to a unanimous decision for a death sentence, and since the jury failed to reach unanimity, the judge sentenced Nichols to multiple life sentences without the possibility of parole and added hundreds of years of incarceration for the other fifty-plus charges.

LESSONS FROM BRIAN NICHOLS

The Brian Nichols case contains many of the same issues within the Alcala and Brown sagas, but it also highlights issues of money, race, and geography.

Nichols and Money

One of the most striking things about this case is the squandering of money in a community that could not afford such a luxury. The trial itself, not including the payouts to the victims and their families, ran up costs of over $5 million, and the proceedings had to be delayed at one point for budgetary reasons—it was breaking the county bank! There was no real question of guilt or innocence. The man was guilty, and his defense team would have entered such a plea and avoided a trial entirely had the prosecution been willing to accept a LWOP sentence. Instead, under a lot of pressure from the public to seek the death penalty because of the enormity of the crime, prosecutors decided to make this a capital case. Even so, the prosecution knew they were facing a venue that was vigorously anti–death penalty, and so they proceeded with utmost care, resulting in special efforts that contributed to incurring huge expenses. Nevertheless, they were unable to obtain the death penalty and settled for a life sentence, a result they could have obtained without a trial at all and at minimal expense.

Nichols and Race

Another important issue raised in this case is that of race, as Nichols claimed he considered himself a soldier against a judicial system that was unfair to African Americans. However, his actions seemed to be the product of spontaneous behavior and not the result of a mission to correct social wrongs, but he did make that statement, possibly with the hope that he might obtain sympathy from jurors, particularly since eight African

Americans were on the panel. All of this is, of course, conjecture, and we have no idea whether his statement had any effect on the jury at all, but it introduces the issue of race, which has been—and still is—a huge consideration in the American death-penalty system.

Nichols and Geography

One issue that affects our system is the capricious nature of different geographic locations. Some states have no death penalty at all, while others pursue it with varying degrees of enthusiasm. The particular location where this case took place was one in which the mood of Fulton County was strongly anti–death penalty, and this affected not only how the prosecution approached the case but also, very possibly, the result of the case. Would the outcome have been different if this case were tried in a locale where people and authorities were strongly pro–capital punishment? The problem with the patchwork approach to punishment across the United States is that the same crime can be treated differently depending on where it is tried.

C. T. WILLINGHAM

Cameron Todd Willingham was at home alone with his three daughters in Corsicana, Texas, two days before Christmas in 1991, when fire broke out. Willingham claimed the smoke was so thick he could not get to the girls, and sadly, all three children perished. Although one investigator's opinion was that the fire was accidental, the majority of investigators were of the opinion that the fire was due to arson. Ultimately Willingham was convicted and sentenced to death for the crimes of arson and murder. Many court challenges were pursued, but Texas executed Willingham in 2004.

Since his execution several experts have challenged the original findings, and strong opinion among them is that there was no evidence for arson. Willingham's family sought an inquiry to present new evidence of his innocence before a court of law. The Texas Third Court of Appeals demanded the judge be recused from the case, and the legal approach to the question remains, therefore, somewhat in limbo. The family requested the Texas Forensic Science Commission (TSFC) also review the case, and that process is still ongoing.

The review process has been clouded by the not necessarily unexpected political and philosophical debates and challenges capital-punishment issues so often invite. The anti-death-penalty forces, including members of the American Civil Liberties Union (ACLU), feel there has been stonewalling of the postexecution investigation. Political commentator Rachel Maddow kicked off the political football by doing a piece on MSNBC early in the Republican primary, outlining the case and leaving viewers with the conclusion that airing the details could have had a detrimental effect on Governor Rick Perry's reelection campaign. On the other hand, there's the possibility that, as Kaye Bailey Hutchinson—former US senator from Texas—has suggested, this whole investigation was merely a stratagem of the anti-capital-punishment people to discredit the death penalty.

The TSFC investigations led to suggestions for various improvements in future forensic investigations of fires, and its investigators are inquiring into the one-thousand-plus arson-related imprisonments in Texas at this time. However, we are left with the possibility that an innocent man might have been executed. This case strikes at one of the cardinal arguments against the death penalty—the killing of an innocent person—and leaves us with an unsettling sense that we might have done just that. Who knows where this might have led? Maybe Willingham would have been exonerated and released—or maybe not, but at least the public would have had the opportunity to review the newer materials and opinions and given him the chance for what appears to be a reasonable reexamination of the case. Obviously this is a moot point, since we have already executed Mr. Willingham.

LESSONS FROM C. T. WILLINGHAM

The C. T. Willingham case involves several areas of speculation, but most notably it raises very important issues around the death penalty. The possibility that this case involved the murder of three children elevated it to a higher emotional level, which might contribute to the arguably understandable need to find a way to assuage painful emotions by exacting a harsh punishment. The more recent findings, by apparently more sophisticated techniques and agencies, raise serious doubts as to whether Willingham's case involved arson at all and ultimately point to the possibility that this was a tragic misapplication of justice. The case also emphasizes the need to be wary of what we deem expert opinions since, in this case, at the time of deciding conviction and sentencing, the only "professional" information might well have been flawed. Though unfounded, the issue was brought up that the entire move to question the accuracy of the original experts might have been a move by the anti-death-penalty people to make a statement. Rivals of Governor Perry, armed with the later information that disproved arson, kicked the ubiquitous political football onto the field, claiming Perry's support of the sentence was motivated by his political ambitions of trying to look "tough on crime." Whenever we see something go wrong, we have a natural tendency to find out why it went wrong and then pin the blame on someone. Though Willingham's execution might have been a mistake, at the time, the information available led to the conclusion that he was guilty of arson and murder, and thus the governor's decision to support his execution.

These cases all point out the blundering inefficiency of our death-penalty system, and probably the worst part is that, of all of these examples, the only person we executed might well have been innocent.

Chapter 3

A BRIEF HISTORY OF CAPITAL PUNISHMENT

O ne question you might ask yourself is "Where did we get the idea of capital punishment in the first place?" Societies have made use of the death penalty from time immemorial, but the earliest recorded documents are tablets that represent the Mesopotamian Code of Ur-Nammu, which was written in the Sumerian language between 2100 BC and 2050 BC. Interestingly most crimes were punished by monetary fines, and death was recommended only for rape, robbery, adultery, or murder. This is of some interest because it indicates these earliest known approaches to the death penalty were more "progressive" than those in many later civilizations in which death was the prescription for punishing a wide variety of crimes.

The most famous records that documented a civilization enforcing the death penalty were in the Code of Hammurabi. During his rule in Babylon as king from 1795 BC to 1750 BC, Hammurabi wrote an extensive code of laws covering wide swaths of jurisprudence, including the death penalty, which was put into effect for many offenses, some of which were a little unusual. One example was in regard to home construction.

If a builder were to construct a house that proved to be faulty, its collapse resulting in the death of the owner, the builder would be subjected to death. If, in addition, the son of the owner of the home were killed in this manner, the son of the homebuilder would to be put to death—yes, the son, who might have had nothing to do with his father's faulty construction project.

The concept here was an attempt to equate punishment and crime. This might well have been the foundation for the concept of "an eye for an eye," *lex talionis*, which the Israelites embraced in the Mosaic laws and is mentioned in the book of Leviticus of the Bible. Interestingly, however, throughout the history of jurisprudence, the concept *of lex talionis* has been used on both sides of the equation of fairness. On the one hand, this concept dictates that the level of punishment is to be harsh enough to match the severity of the crime, and on the other, it protects against excessive punishment, and this latter, lesser-known application of the concept has been used to protect against overzealous prosecution. Remember Portia in Shakespeare's play *The Merchant of Venice* and how she saved her lover? Her argument was that the pound of flesh her lover owed for defaulting on a loan had to be only and exactly a pound, and not a drop of blood. Since the court had decided that the default was equal in value to a pound of flesh, Portia was demanding true *lex talionis*.

From there capital punishment was present as a means of punishment in many civilizations and cultures down to the Greeks and Romans, and it seems as though all the methods of execution involved significant physical pain. They included crucifixion, drowning, brutal beating, burning alive, and impalement, among many others. In his book *Execution: The Guillotine, the Pendulum, the Thousand Cuts, the Spanish Donkey, and 66 Other Ways of Putting Someone to Death*, author Geoffrey Abbott describes some of the gruesome ways in which societies have eliminated criminals, leading to the conclusion that these methods are limited only by the human imagination—often at its most sadistic levels. It is important to review the gamut of methods of execution that have been used in the past to understand the progression toward almost entirely pain-free methods.

One of the more unusual stories to come out of this book was that of the "brazen bull," a device invented by an Athenian artist named Perillus. This was a life-size, hollowed-out replica of a bull constructed of bronze, a material selected because of its ability to heat up quickly. The condemned person was placed inside a trapdoor in the back, and a fire was started under the bull to create horrible torment for the victim. Perillus constructed flutes within the nostrils of the bull so the screams of the victim could be heard outside as the lowing sound of a bull, supposedly for the enjoyment of those observing the execution.

The irony for Perillus is that he became the first victim of his creation. He had taken his device to Phalaris, the tyrant of what is now Agrigento. Phalaris was so appalled by this hideous device that he tricked Perillus into becoming its first victim. He asked Perillus to enter the cavity of the bull and to make the sounds of someone being tortured so he might appreciate the "music." He then had his men lock Perillus in the bull and set the appropriate fires underneath. When Perillus was nearly dead, they extricated him from the bull and killed him by throwing him off a cliff.

Unfortunately, this gruesome device went on to be used against many Christian martyrs, male and female, young and old. The ultimate irony for Phalaris was that the populace finally rose up against the tyrant and subjected him to the same ghastly death in the brazen bull.

Abbott also describes several other methods of execution, some of which, though terrible in every way, show the ingenuity of the designers, who had to be depraved just to consider these devices.

Methods of execution became more and more limited, and by the tenth century in Britain, hanging was the sole means of carrying out the death penalty. It is of some interest that this really was something of an abolitionist movement, and we see in retrospect that it was quite significant for the times. In the case of Britain, it was William the Conqueror's refusal to allow anyone to be executed for any crime except in times of war. That often comes as a surprise to the amateur historian, because most do not assume someone called "the Conqueror" would be connected with such a benevolent piece of legislation. His reasons for this seemingly altruistic move might be rooted somewhere other than in benevolence, but we do not know that for certain. King Henry VIII reversed the trend, however, as his administration oversaw many executions for a variety of crimes. Under his reign the repertoire of methods became more extensive, adding to the mix—to name a few—boiling, beheading, and drawing and quartering.

By the eighteenth century, over two hundred crimes were punishable by death, and many were relatively minor offenses. There is a fairly famous example of the textile workers known as the Luddites, who, in the years 1811 to 1816, while protesting against job-eliminating machines, destroyed some knitting frames. The group derived its name from a historically vague figure named Ned Ludd, who supposedly destroyed such a frame in 1779 in a fit of insanity and rage. In response, Parliament passed the Frame Breaking Act, which made the breaking of knitting frames an act punishable by death. We do not know if anyone was actually hanged, but the name "Luddites" lives on in our lexicon as people opposed to advances in technology.

Because of the inappropriateness of the death penalty as punishment for many of the crimes, juries tended not to convict people of lesser crimes, and this led to reforms of the British jurisprudence system in regard to capital punishment. The reforms included eliminating over a hundred crimes from the roster of offenses punishable by death.

British colonists who settled America brought with them many "things British," including a legal system that upheld the death penalty. At that time, capital punishment was the penalty for a wide range of offenses from murder, treason, manslaughter, and rape to robbery, burglary, arson, counterfeiting, and theft. In the seventeenth and early eighteenth centuries, there was essentially wholesale support of capital punishment for these offenses. There were no prisons at this time, and the concept of lesser punishments had not yet taken firm root, so the death penalty was used against all kinds of offenses.

There were no significant voices against the death penalty until some opposition began to emerge in Europe, where respected intellectual writers brought up some very significant objections. Notably Voltaire and some members of the English Quaker movement, such as John Bellers and John Howard, gave mobilization to the abolitionist movement.

Cesare Beccaria provided the most powerful stimulus against capital punishment in his 1764 "An Essay on Crimes and Punishment." He was opposed to the death penalty, except for cases in which the individual was a threat to the government as in the form of a revolution. He presented two seemingly disparate arguments, both of which have been echoed by many interested people over the years. On the one hand, he argued that the death penalty was pernicious to society, a concept that mirrors the current thought processes in which people feel the death penalty is at least beneath us as a civilized society and at most immoral or unethical. On the other hand, he argued that the death penalty was only a momentary punishment and that a better deterrent would be a lifetime of confinement and hard labor in which one functioned as a beast of burden, an idea largely based on his arguments that the punishment should fit the crime. Though he was opposed to the death penalty, his position was far from one of leniency for murderers. His was the first really strong voice for the abolitionist movement, and he influenced a lot of powerful people in Europe. Austria and Tuscany abolished the death penalty because of Beccaria's influence.

In this country Thomas Jefferson tried to revise Virginia's death-penalty laws by introducing a bill that would limit capital punishment to a penalty for crimes only of murder and treason. This bill tanked by only one vote.

Another influential opponent of the death penalty was Dr. Benjamin Rush, a signer of the Declaration of Independence. He felt the death penalty had no deterrent effect whatsoever, and he was actually on the other end of the spectrum in that he believed the death penalty produced a brutalizing effect that caused an increase in criminal behavior overall. William Bradford, Philadelphia attorney general at the time, was one of Rush's disciples, and he later became the US attorney general. Largely due to his influence, Pennsylvania, in 1794, repealed the death penalty for every offense except first-degree murder.

In the early nineteenth century, there was a movement in which people came to the realization that many crimes that were previously deemed grounds for the death penalty really did not warrant such a harsh punishment. During this period many states reduced the number of crimes punishable by execution and built state penitentiaries.

Although there was very little opposition to capital punishment in the early part of the nineteenth century, there is some evidence that people had some misgivings about it. In the introduction to his excellent book *The Death Penalty: An American History*, legal historian Stuart Banner presents the story of Stephen Clark. In the summer of 1820, Stephen set fire to a barn, and the fire spread to several other houses. No one was hurt, and Stephen had no previous criminal history and came from a well-respected family.

Several requests were made for the governor to grant clemency on his behalf, but they were denied. One local newspaper pointed out that the crime had caused a great deal of suffering, indicating that the mercy of clemency shouldn't trump the need for justice. So in the spring of 1821, Clark was hanged in Salem, Massachusetts. The procedure carried along with it the usual armed guards and sheriffs, as well as representatives from the clergy, who prayed with young Stephen and addressed the sizable crowd, calling them all to penitence and urging them to avoid vice for the rest of their lives.

Stephen was hardly the figure of a brutish criminal as he was a very slight, pale sixteen-year-old. He was obviously terrified throughout the entire procedure, unable to speak to the crowd when requested to do so. He had trouble climbing the gallows and had to lean on a minister to maintain an erect posture at one point. Deputies tied his hands behind him and placed the cowl over his head and then the noose around his neck. Shortly thereafter the trapdoor of the execution platform was opened, and Clark fell to his death.

Though he had been treated sternly by the governor and other authorities, as well as by the press, Clark's postmortem was much more sympathetic. Supportive poetry arose, and for several decades, he was remembered with sympathy. Although no great abolition movement occurred in those days, there was evidently serious sympathy for some figures subjected to capital punishment, particularly in this case, in which the victim was such a frail, terrified, and immature individual.

Political theorist John Stuart Mill, in 1868, felt capital punishment should be reduced only to crimes of murder.

Politician Horace Greeley, in 1872, commented that death penalty sanctioned revenge and that the spectacle of the execution itself caused increases in violence. He further argued that the process actually weakened the horror of bloodshed, much in the way we currently discuss violence in the media as having an effect of numbing people, particularly our youth, to violence. He also drew attention to the probability of innocent deaths and the result that jury members might tend to let the guilty off as they became aware of the potential to convict the innocent. He also cited the possibility of finding people innocent after they had been executed, and he drew attention to the absurdity of that situation and the frustration of families of the executed. After all what good is it to be proven innocent after one has been executed? Does concern for the criminals also stimulate what Greeley called "a pernicious sympathy" for them? It seems many arguments we see today against capital punishment were articulated by Greeley over a century and a quarter ago.

Lawyer Robert E. Crowe, in 1925, argued for the deterrent effect of the death penalty as he felt capital punishment should be maintained as a safeguard for the public. He also argued against trends for sympathy toward the murderer in a hanging to the extent that people actually forgot the plight of the murdered. This conceit persists, particularly in the penalty phase of capital-punishment trials, in which the defense team often refers to the plight of the criminal, the difficult times in his past, and the abuses he suffered.

One of the most vehement American voices against capital punishment was that of highly respected Clarence Darrow, whose law practice involved his defending over a hundred murder suspects in the Chicago area. In his writings he often discussed the fact that people he defended for murder had, so to speak, the cards stacked against them. He was a strong proponent of the concept that because murderers grew up in such terrible environments, they were motivated to do things the rest of civilized society would find abhorrent. He described all this in his 1928 book *Attorney for the Damned*, in which he further argued that capital punishment only appeased the mob's emotions of hatred and revenge, and that it was no deterrent.

Perhaps one of the most important recent events that might lead to the abolition of the death penalty is the decision by the American Law Institute (ALI) to withdraw the section of the Model Penal Code that deals with capital punishment because of the "current intractable institutional and structural obstacles to ensuring a minimally adequate system for administering capital punishment." The ALI, founded in 1923, now consists of four thousand lawyers, judges, and law professors of the highest qualifications, and its function is to evaluate and revise principles of the law that have long influenced American jurisprudence and more recently international legal systems as well. Ironically, the 1962 ALI recommendations on how to eliminate arbitrariness in capital cases led the Supreme Court in 1976 to reinstate capital punishment in the case of *Gregg v. Georgia*.

The ALI did not completely come out against capital punishment in its recent action, but in 2009 its members voted against revising or replacing the section that deals with the various aspects of capital punishment, further voting to withdraw that section from the Model Penal Code.

The institute's final conclusion reads as follows:

> The foregoing review of the unsuccessful efforts to constitutionally regulate the death penalty, the difficulties that continue to undermine its administration, and the structural and institutional obstacles to curing those ills forms the basis of our recommendation to the Institute. The longstanding recognition of these underlying defects in the capital justice process, the inability of extensive constitutional regulation to redress those defects, and the immense structural barriers to meaningful improvement all counsel strongly against the Institute's undertaking a law reform project on capital punishment, either in the form of a new draft of § 210.6 or a more extensive set of proposals. Rather, these conditions strongly suggest that the Institute recognize that the preconditions for an adequately administered regime of capital punishment do not currently exist and cannot reasonably be expected to be achieved.

The ALI therefore establishes that the current capital-punishment system is unworkable and unfixable. Since the ALI, the largest and most influential group of legal minds in the country, concludes that the capital-punishment system is broken beyond repair, the only logical action is to abolish it completely.

As a general rule, the history of capital punishment in the United States has been one of gradual diminution in frequency and indication. Early on, execution was the only punishment for a wide variety of offenses, but gradually, these indications were removed, and we are left with execution as a means of punishment for only murder or, more rarely, treason. The last other indication was struck down when the Supreme Court decided capital punishment was inappropriate for the rape of a minor. The establishment and expansion of prisons allow us to use incarceration in our sentencing, whereas the only prior option for serious crimes was death.

A most interesting aspect of capital punishment is the fact that even though, especially in the past, the vast majority of Americans supported the death penalty, people were reluctant to take part in the actual execution process, and this resulted in very few people willing to be "the executioner." The English used professional executioners, but we did not adopt this part of the process. Instead we passed this obligation on to sheriffs, who often were very reluctant to take part. To encourage other people to perform this grisly task, authorities arranged for various modes of payment that often included whiskey as part of the package, which may well have served as a bracer to carry out the job. In other cases prisoners who were facing death were given the choice of executing other prisoners to obtain relief from their own executions.

Today we have several different individuals taking part so no one person is the executioner. Lethal injection is orchestrated in many steps that require many active participants to play different roles. Even in firing squads, by which multiple individuals fire at once, one member fires a blank round so squad members do not know who really did the killing. The Japanese, one of the few remaining first-world peoples still practicing the death penalty, have their own solution to avoiding individual ownership of the grisly task of execution. They still use hanging as the primary means of execution, but it is done as a nonpublicized event in an isolated environment involving several participants. The condemned person stands over a switch-operated trapdoor. At the appropriate time, several guards activate switches, but only one is the mechanism by which the trapdoor opens. In this way the guards, who by law may not refuse to participate, do not know who the real executioner is, much in the way we spread out the task in firing squads and the multiple steps of lethal injection.

Early on, hanging was the primary method of execution in America. It was intended to be a swift, relatively painless death, but this goal was often not obtained. At first, the prisoner, with the noose around his neck, was taken to a tree where he was made to climb a ladder. The end of the rope was tied to a tree limb, and then the ladder was "turned out." The problem was that the sudden tightening of the noose around the neck was not rapid enough to produce an instantaneous, painless death. This method often provided a gruesome, slow asphyxiation or even a complete failure, so the process had to be repeated. Later developments in the hanging industry included the prisoner being placed in a horse-drawn wagon, the noose applied from a tree to his neck, and then the horses spurred to a rapid acceleration forward. Unfortunately, this method too often proved to be ineffective in the goal of obtaining a swift death because the vertical drop was inadequate, and the process was slow, so the impact on the condemned person's neck was not sudden enough.

Execution technology took a big step forward with the invention of the trapdoor, or gallows. Boston began using this method in 1694, and the British adopted this new development several decades later. Certainly the trapdoor system had its foibles, but it was a large improvement over past methods. The concept was that the sudden and fairly lengthy drop would cause instant death by fracturing the area of the second and third cervical vertebrae and instantly separating the spinal cord. This fatal injury became known as the "hangman's fracture." Though it had the desired effect of instant death much more frequently than did more primitive methods, there were still many episodes in which instant death did not occur and the prisoner instead died of asphyxiation while kicking and struggling.

In part because of the often-ineffective hanging process in which observers had to watch someone slowly struggle to die a truly miserable death by asphyxiation, a sham execution process was developed. Although there is no indication this was done very frequently, there are some documented cases. Elizabeth Ranier had a baby out of wedlock at a time in early America when this was such a terrible disgrace that she was driven to kill her newborn baby. She was sentenced to stand in the gallows with a noose around her neck for half an hour but was not executed. This process was sometimes accompanied by other punishments, most often lashing. This spared citizens the horror of a public execution, which would have been even worse in this case, for example, because the victim was a woman. In this way people could still attend the ceremonious makings of a hanging, and this whole process would hopefully have a deterrent effect on the crimes for which the criminal was sentenced.

The clemency system was another process that contributed to the diminution of the number of executions carried out. In the eighteenth century, New York governors granted clemency to over half of those who received death sentences. There were, however, no guidelines for governors to follow in the granting of clemency, so people with the right friends had much better chances of receiving this benefit. Payments, of course, were also probably part of the process whereby clemency was provided, and apparently slaveholders were known to pay for clemency for their slaves. In other cases, criminals were offered clemency if they agreed to testify and provide evidence against associates in a process very similar to the current avenue of plea bargaining.

Expressions of penitence by criminals was another method by which the numbers of executions actually diminished. John Green was sentenced to death for blasphemy, but he blamed his conduct on his drinking and admitted to his alcohol abuse. He argued that his altered state of mind caused him to blaspheme and that he would not have done so had he been sober. There is no real evidence he was ever executed, so his defense was perhaps successful.

PUBLIC EXECUTIONS IN THE UNITED STATES

In colonial times executions were somber, solemn, or religious, and very well attended. They were characterized by long sermons from the clergy and comments from other people, including the condemned person, whose messages were usually along the lines of remorse and penitence. The Reverend Cotton Mather was famous for his spellbinding participation in these events. Sermons remained a significant part of the procedure, well into the nineteenth century and even into the twentieth century in some areas of the country.

Some believed capital punishment and the execution process had a deterrent effect on the general public, offered penitence for the condemned, and fulfilled the need for retribution. There was also a commonly held philosophy of a natural human tendency toward evil and that failure to punish a crime would spread guilt to the entire community.

People were very interested in these proceedings, turning out in large numbers. Gradually, however, public execution scenes became less somber and religious and turned into raucous, drunken affairs characterized by rowdy behavior of all sorts.

Largely because of the deterioration of the spectacle of a public execution, officials decided it best to move the events inside prisons, where a very few select people would observe. Invitees were usually VIPs of some sort or family members. Most observers were men, as it was considered very unladylike for women to be part of the audience. The general public, however, remained intensely interested, and newspaper reporters seized this opportunity to become the sources of information for a large group of very engaged readers.

Executions in the modern era remain in small venues, within specific prisons and with limited audiences. Our method of execution has, of course, changed to lethal injection, and the promulgation of information has now expanded to include modern technologies that allow the interested audience to be widely expanded even to the international level.

ELECTRIC CHAIR (1921-PRESENT)

Because of the inconsistency of hanging as a means of painless death, in 1886 the New York legislature appointed a commission to search for a better method of execution. The use of electricity in general was becoming widespread, and with that progress came incidents of injury and death. So the concept of using electricity to affect a rapid, painless death arose, and New York consulted experts in the field of electricity, including Thomas Edison, who opposed capital punishment but participated in the evaluations because he felt electricity had the potential of causing an immediate, painless death. Experiments on stray dogs demonstrated that they could be killed in what seemed like a painless, rapid fashion. In January 1888, the commission issued its report and, after comparing electrocution to thirty-four methods without the use of electricity, concluded that New York should adopt this modality of execution. New York arranged for three of its state prisons to be fitted with the needed equipment.

The state wished to purchase Westinghouse generators, but George Westinghouse, in a move that would later be replicated by drug companies over the lethal injection issue, refused to sell them for that purpose. The state went ahead and bought used generators in preparation for its first execution by electric chair. The state sentenced William Kemmler, who was convicted of murdering his girlfriend, to be the first man electrocuted and scheduled a date in June 1889. Shortly before the proposed date, Kemmler's lawyers filed a petition to block the execution on the grounds that it was cruel and unusual punishment. The legal battle went all the way to the US Supreme Court, which concluded that electrocution would not infringe on Kemmler's legal rights.

The initial execution did not go smoothly as problems with the equipment caused a malfunction that required a second jolt, which also went poorly because the electrodes were improperly placed. Bloody sweat appeared on the man's face, and this caused a certain amount of revulsion among some members of the audience. The electric chair did, ultimately, accomplish its goal, and authorities realized technical errors had caused the problems and sought to improve them. Within a year the state executed four men in one day without incident, and the era of the electric chair began.

Although many states, particularly in the West, did not adopt this mode of execution, enthusiasm for electrocution swept most states in the East as it was perceived a far more humane method of execution than hanging. Experience with the new method dictated that the people who performed these executions had to be experts in the field. This factor, plus the expense of the equipment, demanded locations for execution be centralized. So executions were taken away from the locales in which the crimes were committed and moved to state penitentiaries specifically outfitted for the task.

GAS CHAMBER (1921–PRESENT)

Around the same time electrocution was being incorporated, some proponents considered using poisonous gas for execution. Indeed, it had been used in the 1870s to exterminate unwanted dogs. As increased experience in the use of electrocution led to a goal of humane execution, interest in poisonous gas as an option markedly diminished until Nevada, which had never adopted electrocution and still relied on hanging or firing squad, decided to use it in 1921. Despite a minor glitch, the first execution, of a Chinese immigrant named Gee Jon, went smoothly as he appeared to die peacefully.

Several states, particularly in the West—often where electro-cution had not been adopted and hanging was still the main means of execution —followed Nevada's lead and instituted the gas chamber. In general things went smoothly, but reports of prolonged deaths caused opposition to the gas chamber, and thus began the endless quest for a more humane, painless method of execution.

LETHAL INJECTION (1982–PRESENT)

The continuing quest for a more painless and humane method of execu-tion led Oklahoma state examiner Dr. Jay Chapman to delve into the concept of lethal injection, and on May 11, 1977, he presented the combi-nation of drugs now known as Chapman's Protocol. This is a three-drug combination of anesthetic agent, paralytic agent, and cardiac suppressant, and it became the standard method of execution in the United States. From the beginning the specific drugs that have been used in combina-tion are, in sequence, sodium thiopental (Sodium Pentothal), which puts the individual to sleep, pancuronium bromide, which causes paralysis of the musculature, and potassium chloride, which causes instant death by stopping the heart. On December 7, 1982, Texas became the first state to use the lethal injection technique, to execute convicted murderer Charles Brooks Jr.

Most would agree that this new approach is far more humane and less painful than electrocution, the previous most commonly used method. Still, several issues have arisen in regard to the intravenous method, caus-ing postponement and even cancellation of executions, and exacerbating the polarization between pro- and anti-death-penalty factions.

The first is related to the controversy as to whether this technique causes cruel and unusual punishment for the convicted, an argument based on the pain and suffering that can be involved in establishing a satisfactory intravenous route of delivery. An example of this is the case of Romell

Broom, who was sentenced to death for the mid-1980s kidnapping, rape, and stabbing to death of a fourteen-year-old girl. On September 15, 2009, the state of Ohio started the execution, but the process failed because of the inability of two nurses, after eighteen attempts, to obtain a viable intravenous port. The misadventure was terminated at that point. Discussions of the cruel and unusual nature of this failed procedure have resulted in the fact that Broom remains on death row with no scheduled execution date and will probably remain there for the foreseeable future.

The second issue around cruel and unusual punishment involves the question of potential ineffectiveness of the anesthetic, which, initially, was exclusively Sodium Pentothal, with which the condemned is still awake but paralyzed and subjected to cardiac arrest. Dr. Leonidas Koniaris wrote an article that appeared first in British medical journal *The Lancet*, in which he questioned the adequacy of anesthesia in the American lethal injection system. Although there was no documentable evidence for it, he argued that the condemned prisoner could suffer during the procedure. He mentioned, among other concerns, the fact that there is no continuous monitoring as there is during a surgical procedure. The main thrust of his argument, however, involved the blood samples taken in the postmortem setting in which he found what he thought to be inadequate levels of Sodium Pentothal. This sparked considerable controversy and arguments—mostly refuting the assertion—from several sources. The most notable argument was based on blood samples taken after the execution of serial killer Michael Ross in the immediate postmortem time frame and at subsequent intervals. These results indicate that Pentothal continues to be absorbed in the postmortem period, and so blood levels taken at later times do not reflect what blood levels would have been while the condemned was still alive.

Despite the fact that most experts refuted its premise and held that the levels of anesthesia were adequate during the time of the execution, *The Lancet* article had some profound effects in the United States, particularly in the case of Michael Morales, who was scheduled for execution in California on February 21, 2006. Concerns about the need for surgical-level monitoring of the anesthesia led US District Court Judge Jeremy Fogel to a ruling that would require that a doctor perform the execution procedure. Two hours before the Morales execution was to take place, representatives of the state of California notified the US Court of Appeals for the Ninth Circuit that they could not comply with the judge's ruling. The execution was suspended indefinitely and later led to a complete cessation of capital punishment in California, since it is generally agreed that physicians are ethically prohibited from participating in executions and, therefore, no one can carry out such a procedure.

Although this catch-22 is really not a legal moratorium, it effectively acts as one because it establishes requirements that cannot be fulfilled and plays the role of an equally realistic barrier to execution. The great irony of this important development is that it was based on what is probably a flawed article in a foreign medical journal. Although most professionals agree that there is little or no chance of any significant pain during the course of an execution, it is still impossible to know for sure, and for that reason, the issue of undue pain causing cruel and unusual punishment remains a debatable issue.

In 2010 Judge Fogel lifted the so-called moratorium, and California was then free to proceed with intravenous lethal injections using Sodium Pentothal. In August 2010, the state was prepared to use its new facility for the execution of Alfred Greenwood Brown when another obstacle appeared in the form of lack of availability of Pentothal, which is a story unto itself.

It appears that the only company producing Sodium Pentothal was the Illinois-based Hospira. Largely because of the company officials' objections to its use in executions, they stopped making the sedative in the United States but attempted to ramp up production in its Liscate, Italy, plant. Because of the chance that there still could be shipments to the

United States, the Italian Parliament stepped in and demanded that the company completely discontinue the exportation of the drug to America because of the possibility that it could be used for executions, since Italy and the entire European Union are against the death penalty. In a manner similar to foreign countries reluctant to extradite a murderer back to the United States if there is a chance he will receive the death penalty, Hospira refuses to ship the drug to the United States.

Since Sodium Pentothal is an older drug that has been replaced by many other drugs for almost every other of its surgical purposes in the United States, the market is small, but some institutions in England still want to use it, and that could create a market for the Italian plant. Brokers have already attempted to obtain the drug from England to be sent to the United States, but thus far this avenue has met with minimal success.

Various states have begun using other drugs, thereby overcoming the seemingly easily surmountable issue of the Pentothal shortage. On December 16, 2010, the state of Oklahoma executed John David Duty, who was sentenced to die for the strangulation of his twenty-two-year-old cellmate in 2002. Pentobarbital was substituted as the first element in the three-drug cocktail, and the procedure apparently went smoothly.

In two separate cases, Ralph Baze and Thomas Clyde Bowling Jr. were each convicted of murder in Kentucky. Their attorneys argued that the three-drug lethal injection procedure would cause undue pain and suffering and therefore constitute cruel and unusual punishment, thus violating the Constitution. The Supreme Court took the case and on April 16, 2008, decided that the three-drug combination did not violate the Constitution. All the judges agreed with the decision, with the exception of Justices Ruth Bader Ginsburg and David Souter. An interesting aside was the opinion of Justice Clarence Thomas, who concluded that a system of execution violates the Constitution only if it is deliberately designed to inflict pain. He therefore agreed with the decision but on a different basis.

This decision, essentially, lifted the moratorium on the intravenous system of execution, since the Supreme Court justices felt it did not violate the Constitution. Since virtually all states that carried out executions via intravenous methods used the same procedures and drugs, this effectively lifted the moratorium across the country.

There has been discussion for some time that a single-drug intravenous approach might offer more benefits in terms of eliminating pain and discomfort. On December 8, 2009, the state of Ohio carried out the first execution using Sodium Pentothal as a single drug in the execution of Kenneth Biros, a convicted murderer. Apparently the only reported problem in the procedure involved difficulty in establishing an intravenous route, but once that was established, the execution was completed in only ten minutes.

The state of Ohio thus had demonstrated that the single-drug approach offered some real benefit, so the state overcame the unavailability of Sodium Pentothal on March 10, 2011, by substituting pentobarbital in the execution of Johnnie Baston, who was sentenced for the 1994 murder of Chong Mah in Toledo, and this apparently proceeded without any reported mishaps.

There have been a few variations on the theme, but pentobarbital has for the most part replaced Pentothal and usually as a single drug. In 2013 and 2014, of the seventy-four executions performed, forty-seven (63.5 percent) made use of pentobarbital as a single drug. Fifteen (20.3 percent) used pentobarbital as the first of a three-drug protocol, and eleven (14.9 percent) used a three-drug approach using midazolam as the anesthetizing agent. Two (2.7 percent) used a two-drug technique combining midazolam and hydromorphone. Only one (1.4 percent) was by electrocution during that time span, when the state of Virginia executed Robert Gleason in 2013.

The pharmaceutical companies that supply these agents have acted on their strong feelings against the death penalty by refusing to sell medications to states that might use them for execution. How much of these feelings come from their own sensitivities and how much is from external pressure from anti-death-penalty opinion of course is not known. Nonetheless, the states have found themselves in the peculiar position of having to "sneak around" to acquire execution agents. They have tried brokers, compounding pharmacies (which are authorized to mix different medications and elements usually for a patient's specific needs and are less tightly regulated), and other surreptitious approaches to obtain the required medications. The Drug Enforcement Administration (DEA) investigated Georgia's supply of thiopental and found the state had purchased it through questionable means. The source was London-based pharmaceutical supplier Dream Pharma, an entity that reportedly operated from the back of a driving school in England. Because of the questionable nature of the purchase of this thiopental, the DEA confiscated Georgia's supply. Apparently Georgia-based Correct Health also obtained thiopental from the same source, selling it to Kentucky and Tennessee authorities. The DEA tracked down these supplies, as well, and seized them from both Kentucky and Tennessee.

Further complicating the supply lines for execution drugs was the move by Denmark-based Lundbeck objecting to the use of its product, pentobarbital, for the purpose of executions. These obstructions have led some states to use other combinations, such as midazolam and hydrocodone.

The latest major story involves the case of Joseph Wood, who was sentenced to death for the 1989 murders of his estranged girlfriend and her father. Because of drug companies' refusal to provide the medications for the purposes of execution, the state of Arizona could not obtain the usual lethal cocktail of agents and planned to use a combination the state of Ohio had successfully used—anesthetic, midazolam, and hydromorphone, which is a pain medication. The state refused to reveal the manufacturers and batch numbers for these agents but reported that they were approved by the Food and Drug Administration (FDA) and had the proper expiration dates. Lawyers for Wood demanded to know the source, claiming the defendant's lack of access to this information violated his First Amendment rights of access to public proceedings. A US district court sided with the state, but the defendant's lawyers took it to the US Court of Appeals of the Ninth Circuit in San Francisco, where a three-judge panel agreed with the defense that the defendant had the right to know the source of the execution drugs.

The case then went to the US Supreme Court, which rejected this tactic as it has before in similar cases. This case had already been the recipient of significant media exposure because of the drug issues and appeals made by the defendant's attorneys, but it was catapulted even further into the headlines because the execution did not go as smoothly as planned, taking one hour and fifty-seven minutes from start to finish. During this period, Wood gasped and snorted many times, and this was quite uncomfortable for observers.

There was, of course, the expected response that this was a botched execution, even though officials insisted Wood was not awake during this prolonged procedure. According to the *Arizona Daily Star*, the victim's daughter, Jean Brown, said, "You don't know what excruciating is. Excruciating is seeing your dad lying in a pool of blood." Her husband, Richard, stated that Wood got the punishment he deserved.

Governor Jan Brewer issued a statement: "I am concerned by the length of time it took for the administered drug protocol to complete the lawful execution of the convicted double murderer, Joseph Wood. While justice was carried out today, I directed the Department of Corrections to conduct a full review of the process. One thing is certain, however, inmate Wood died in a lawful manner and by eyewitness and medical accounts he did not suffer. This is in stark comparison to the gruesome, vicious suffering that he inflicted on his two victims—and a lifetime of suffering he has caused their family."

CLAYTON LOCKETT

The state of Oklahoma executed Clayton Lockett on April 29, 2014. The defendant was already a four-time convicted felon, now facing death for the gruesome murder of nineteen-year-old Stephanie Neiman. In 1999 Ms. Neiman had the terrible misfortune of arriving at a friend's home that was being robbed by Lockett and his colleagues. The men subdued her, tied her down, raped her, and beat her with a pistol. Afterward they shot her with a shotgun, took her outside, and buried her alive—she did not survive.

Because of the unavailability of the usual drugs, the state moved to use midazolam as the first of the three-drug cocktail, which also included vecuronium bromide, a muscle relaxant with anesthetic properties, and potassium chloride, an agent that causes cardiac arrest when injected. Florida previously administered this same three-drug combination without incident but with five hundred milligrams of midazolam, whereas Oklahoma used only one hundred milligrams, a dose thought to be adequate as it is many times greater than what is used as an anesthetic in surgery. In its refusal to verify why that combination of drugs was chosen and how they were obtained, Oklahoma hid behind secrecy laws to prevent the public from knowing more than simply which three drugs were used. Reportedly the state purchased the drugs through its petty cash system, making the transaction essentially untraceable and unchallengeable.

The proceedings did not go smoothly from the beginning. Lockett tried to cut himself in the morning, and because he refused to go along peacefully, authorities used a Taser to subdue him and bring him to the execution chamber. Authorities placed the IV in Lockett's groin and covered the area so the public would not see it. Unfortunately, this also prevented authorities from seeing it, and at some time during the proceedings, the IV came out of the vein. How much of the medications he received is not really known. The first drug was administered at 6:23 p.m., and the condemned man was declared unconscious at 6:33 p.m. But *after* being declared unconscious, he raised his head and said, "Oh, man, I'm not—" The execution was halted after about twenty minutes, and he was declared dead at 7:06 p.m., presumably because of a heart attack. He apparently experienced some writhing and convulsing, and one of his attorneys was reported to have said, "It looked like torture."

Of course we find it reprehensible to cause the death of an individual who is totally helpless and defenseless, especially when reports come back that he might have been awake for part of the procedure. We feel much better about it when the condemned does not show any signs of consciousness or pain.

Still, this case documents all the elements that are wrong. We have been trying to use lethal injection for many years and still have not gotten it right. Of course anti-capital-punishment entities, such as pharmaceutical companies that refuse to sell the appropriate drugs, cause states to experiment but really only to a limited degree. In this case Oklahoma used a hundred milligrams of midazolam, a drug with which the state had less experience. More likely, however, it was the inadequacy of the intravenous ports that caused this case to go so poorly. That, of course, brings us to the personnel issue. Had there been experienced medical people to deliver the IV, the process probably would have been much smoother. Since no medical professionals will participate, we are left with people far less adequately trained to establish an IV.

So here we have a snapshot of some of the frailties of our lethal injection system. Many drug companies are opposed to it, refusing to deliver the appropriate medications. People who are recruited to administer the drugs are inadequately trained. States have taken to keeping quiet about the sources of the drugs and the dosages administered.

There is more, however. Those who previously felt *lex talionis* is part of our capital-punishment system have learned that this is far from the case. People were shocked and horrified by the sufferings Lockett had to endure, and watching anyone die is certainly an emotionally trying experience for most.

Contrast, however, Lockett's death with that of his victim. First of all Ms. Neiman was a total innocent, and Lockett certainly was not. Her horrifying ordeal of humiliation, terror, and pain—with the realization her death was imminent—went on for hours. One irony in this case is that authorities were so careful to hide the IV site, Lockett's groin, to assure his privacy that they were unable to see it was not working. Ms. Neiman was granted no such consideration of modesty but instead suffered total embarrassment as part of her humiliation and suffering. Lockett might have been awake for seconds or even minutes during his execution, but Stephanie suffered for hours at his hands. Lockett had a chance to prepare for his death in any way he chose; Stephanie Neiman did not. She had no chance for final words with her parents, family, and friends.

It seems we have lost our compass, because we are so concerned about the possibility of discomfort for the killer, while we forget about the terror and death of the victim. Criminologist Cesare Beccaria understood this centuries ago when he said that being put to death is too easy for killers.

ROCKY ROAD FOR STATES

Who is the bad guy here? We have the ridiculous situation of the DEA coming down on states because of "illegal" or at least questionable means of obtaining drugs, resulting in concerns about the quality of these agents. Therefore, an agency of the federal government has joined the anti-capital-punishment chorus by making it even more difficult for states to obtain the necessary agents. This is hardly the way one would think an accepted legal activity of government should have to function. Since other branches of the federal government attack states for various issues, including the way the drugs are obtained, the states resort to illegal tactics for these activities. The incredible result is that the practical process of capital punishment in the United States is at least bordering on being carried out through criminal means.

While most executions go smoothly and as expected, enough have been described as botched to cause, in reaction, delays and temporary moratoria that have resulted in holding off executions at least on a temporary basis. For instance, on December 13, 2006, the state of Florida executed Angel Diaz, but the procedure did not go smoothly and required a second round of medications. There were serious concerns that Diaz might have awakened and suffered some pain during the thirty-four minutes—instead of the expected ten—the procedure lasted. Two days later Governor Jeb Bush suspended all executions, and he appointed a commission to study the humanity and constitutionality of lethal injection.

States are now painted as "bad" for the illegal ways they obtain the drugs, "irresponsible and uncaring" for moving to new lesser-tested medications, and "incompetent" because of cases that have gone poorly.

One development that has occurred as a result of the problems with lethal injection is a consideration for returning to previous methods of execution.

UTAH

Things are a little more concrete in the state of Utah, where Representative Paul Ray of Clearfield is calling for the use of firing squads if the state cannot obtain the required drugs by thirty days before a scheduled execution. An interim panel of legislators approved this concept by a nine-to-two vote, and it was presented to the full body of lawmakers when they convened for their annual session in January 2015.

On March 10, 2015, Utah legislators passed the bill to allow firing squads for executions when the appropriate drugs are not available. This, of course, is totally undesirable in the realm of unintended consequences.

Because drug companies and the professionals who could easily perform the lethal injection technique have all decided their ethical and moral obligations are such that they cannot participate in the procedure, Utah is preparing to resort to a more primitive means of execution. The scene itself of a darkened enclosure piled with sandbags on the side and a sturdy metal chair onto which the condemned is strapped stands in stark contrast to a gurney that is more like a preoperative surgical area than an execution chamber. Granted, IV positioning and setup of lethal injection are really nothing but a façade for the same act of execution in contrast to the proposed beneficial effects of a surgical procedure, and in that way, it does lend itself to a more satirical aura.

OKLAHOMA

In the wake of Clayton Lockett's seemingly shoddy death by lethal injection, Oklahoma Representative Mike Christian suggested the state consider previously used methods, including firing squad, electrocution, and hanging. He has since introduced the concept of execution by nitrogen-induced hypoxia, and spurred on by the possibilities that lethal injection might be ruled unconstitutional and that the required drugs unavailable, the Oklahoma Senate gave final unanimous legislative support for a bill that employs nitrogen gas in the execution process if appropriate medications are not available. Governor Mary Fallin signed it into law on April 17, 2015.

The basic idea is that nitrogen replaces oxygen in the bloodstream, so the condemned die of asphyxiation without undue pain because the nitrogen, since it is inert and nontoxic, does not cause unwanted reactions. Whether this is really true is not known, and death-penalty opponents, such as former Georgia Supreme Court Chief Justice Norman Fletcher and Oklahoma Representative Emily Virgin, oppose it on that basis. On the other hand, the author of the bill, Mike Christian, claims the method is "foolproof."

REGRESSION AND INNOVATION

The sad state of our capital-punishment system has caused states, such as Utah and Oklahoma, to regress to more barbaric methods of execution and to delve into the future of untested methods. These are remarkable developments since we know a properly administered and fully sanctioned lethal injection process can be done with absolute minimum discomfort and without the element of tragic theater, and death by lethal injection is currently on the books for all states that enforce the death penalty. Since there has been such turmoil over what should be a straightforward lethal injection process, one can only imagine how much objection and delay might result from alternative methods. Certainly lawyers will object to the more traumatic methods, such as electrocution or firing squad, and the "cruel and unusual punishment" card will likely come out when trying to affix a gas mask or confine the condemned to a small space for delivery of what is supposed to be a painless agent such as nitrogen.

TWO REASONS FOR NONPARTICIPATION

Since the participation of competent professionals (doctors, nurses, or technicians) would essentially eliminate the glitches that give lethal injection a bit of a black eye, the question is why these health-care workers refuse to do so. There are two classic explanations for the reasons physicians (and others who agree with them basically for the same reasons) will not participate in legal executions. The first refers to dicta laid down by medical societies, and the second points to the requirements to which physicians are obligated through the Hippocratic oath.

MEDICAL SOCIETIES' PROHIBITIONS

The first major reason for physicians' refusal to participate in legal execution is the prohibition laid down by medical societies. The major document in this regard is that of the American Medical Association (AMA), and other societies rely on and refer to that opinion on capital punishment for their membership. The following is taken directly from the AMA Code of Medical Ethics:

Opinion 2.06—Capital Punishment

An individual's opinion on capital punishment is the personal moral decision of the individual. A physician, as a member of a profession dedicated to preserving life when there is hope of doing so, should not be a participant in a legally authorized execution. Physician participation in execution is defined generally as actions which would fall into one or more of the following categories: (1) an action which would directly cause the death of the condemned; (2) an action which would assist, supervise, or contribute to the ability of another individual to directly cause the death of the condemned; (3) an action which could automatically cause an execution to be carried out on a condemned prisoner.

Physician participation in an execution includes, but is not limited to, the following actions: prescribing or administering tranquilizers and other psychotropic agents and medications that are part of the execution procedure; monitoring vital signs on site or remotely (including monitoring electrocardiograms); attending or observing an execution as a physician; and rendering of technical advice regarding execution. In the case where the method of execution is lethal injection, the following actions by the physician would also constitute physician participation in execution: selecting injection sites; starting intravenous lines as a port for a lethal injection device; prescribing, preparing, administering, or supervising injection drugs or their doses or types; inspecting, testing, or maintaining lethal injection devices; and consulting with or supervising lethal injection personnel.

The following actions do not constitute physician participation in execution: (1) testifying as to medical history and diagnoses or mental state as they relate to competence to stand trial, testifying as to relevant medical evidence during trial, testifying as to medical aspects of aggravating or mitigating circumstances during the penalty phase of a capital case, or testifying as to medical diagnoses as they relate to the legal assessment of competence for execution; (2) certifying death, provided that the condemned has been declared dead by another person; (3) witnessing an execution in a totally nonprofessional capacity; (4) witnessing an execution at the specific voluntary request of the condemned person, provided that the physician observes the execution in a nonprofessional capacity; and (5) relieving the acute suffering of a condemned person while awaiting execution, including providing tranquilizers at the specific voluntary request of the condemned person to help relieve pain or anxiety in anticipation of the execution.

Physicians should not determine legal competence to be executed. A physician's medical opinion should be merely one aspect of the information taken into account by a legal decision maker such as a judge or hearing officer. When a condemned prisoner has been declared incompetent to be executed, physicians should not treat the prisoner for the purpose of restoring competence unless a commutation order is issued before treatment begins. The task of reevaluating the prisoner should be performed by an independent physician examiner. If the incompetent prisoner is undergoing extreme suffering as a result of psychosis or any other illness, medical intervention intended to mitigate the level of suffering is ethically permissible. No physician should be compelled to participate in the process of establishing a prisoner's competence or be involved with treatment of an incompetent, condemned prisoner if such activity is contrary to the physician's personal beliefs.

Under those circumstances, physicians should be permitted to transfer care of the prisoner to another physician.

Organ donation by condemned prisoners is permissible only if (1) the decision to donate was made before the prisoner's conviction (2) the donated tissue is harvested after the prisoner has been pronounced dead and the body removed from the death chamber, and (3) physicians do not provide advice on modifying the method of execution for any individual to facilitate donation.

This document is incredibly clear and requires no footnotes or lengthy explanations. The AMA's stand on physician participation in legal execution is that physicians should not take any active part at all in the process.

OATHS

Since the second reason for physician refusal to participate in executions refers to the Hippocratic oath, it is of some interest to review what is contained in the original oath as well as replacements that have evolved to be more consistent with modern practice. These are taken directly from documents supplied by the Association of American Physicians and Surgeons and include the original oath followed by samples of more recent variations and other oaths as well. Note that the bold treatment of text is for emphasis of particular passages.

The Oath of Hippocrates of Kos, fifth century BC

I swear by Apollo the physician, by Aesculapius, Hygeia, and Panacea, and I take to witness all the gods, all the goddesses, to keep according to my ability and judgment the following oath:

To consider dear to me as my parents him who taught me this art; to live in common with him and if necessary to share my goods with him; to look upon his children as my own brothers, to teach them this art if they so desire without fee or written promise; to impart to my sons and the sons of the master who taught me and to the disciples who have enrolled themselves and have agreed to the rules of the profession, but to these alone, the precepts and the instruction. **I will prescribe regimen for the good of my patients according to my ability and my judgment and never do harm to anyone. To please no one will I prescribe a deadly drug, nor give advice which may cause his death.** Nor will I give a woman a pessary to procure abortion. But I will preserve the purity of my life and my art. I will not cut for stone, even for patients in whom the disease is manifest; I will **leave this operation to be performed by specialists in this art.** In every house where I come I will enter **only for the good of my patients**, keeping myself far from all intentional ill-doing and **all seduction**, and especially from the pleasures of love with women or with men, be they free or slaves. All that may come to my knowledge in the exercise of my profession or outside of my profession or in daily commerce with men, which ought not to be spread abroad, I will keep secret and never reveal. If I keep this oath faithfully, may I enjoy my life and practice my art, respected by all men and in all times; but if I swerve from it or violate it, may the reverse be my lot.

Declaration of Geneva of the World Medical Association, adopted 1948, amended 1966 and 1983

I solemnly pledge myself to consecrate my life to the service of humanity;

I will give my teachers the respect and gratitude which is their due;

I will practice my profession with conscience and dignity;

The health of my patient will be my first consideration;

I will respect the secrets which are confided in me, even after the patient has died;

I will maintain by all the means in my power, the honor and the noble traditions of the medical profession;

My colleagues will be my brothers;

I will not permit considerations of religion, nationality, race, party politics or social standing to intervene between my duty and my patient;

I will maintain the utmost respect for human life from its beginning even under threat and I will not use my medical knowledge contrary to the laws of humanity;

I make these promises solemnly, freely and upon my honor.

Oath drawn up and approved by the Supreme Soviet of the USSR in 1971, with one addition (on nuclear war) in 1983

Upon having conferred on me the high calling of physician and entering medical practice, I do solemnly swear:

To dedicate all my knowledge and strength to the preservation and improvement of the health of mankind and to the treatment and prevention of disease, and to work in good conscience wherever it is required by society;

To be always ready to provide medical care, to relate to the patient attentively and carefully, and to preserve medical confidences;

To constantly perfect my medical knowledge and clinical skills and thereby in my work to aid in the development of medical science and practice;

To refer, if the patient's better interests warrant it, for advice from my fellow physicians, and never myself to refuse to give such advice or help;

To preserve and develop the noble traditions of Soviet medicine, to be guided in all my actions by the principles of Communist morality, and to always bear in mind the high calling of a Soviet physician and my responsibility to the people and to the Soviet state.

Recognizing the danger which nuclear weaponry presents for mankind, to struggle tirelessly for peace, and for the prevention of nuclear war.

I swear to be loyal to this oath as long as I live.

A Modern Hippocratic Oath, written in 1964 by Dr. Louis Lasagna, Academic Dean of the School of Medicine at Tufts University

I swear to fulfill, to the best of my ability and judgment, this covenant:

I will respect the hard-won scientific gains of those physicians in whose steps I walk, and gladly share such knowledge as is mine with those who are to follow;

I will apply, for the benefit of the sick, **all measures which are required**, avoiding those twin traps of overtreatment and therapeutic nihilism.

I will remember that there is art to medicine as well as science, and that warmth, sympathy, and understanding may outweigh the surgeon's knife or the chemist's drug.

I will not be ashamed to say "I know not," nor will I fail to call in my colleagues when the skills of another are needed for a patient's recovery.

I will **respect the privacy** of my patients, for their problems are not disclosed to me that the world may know. Most especially must I tread with care in matters of life and death. If it is given me to save a life, all thanks. But **it may also be within my power to take a life; this awesome responsibility must be faced with great humbleness** and awareness of my own frailty. Above all, I must not play at God.

I will remember that I do not treat a fever chart, a cancerous growth, but a sick human being, whose illness may affect the person's family and economic stability. My responsibility includes these related problems, if I am to care adequately for the sick.

I will prevent disease whenever I can, for prevention is preferable to cure.

I will remember that I remain a member of society, with special obligations to all my fellow human beings, those sound of mind and body, as well as the infirm.

If I do not violate this oath, may I enjoy life and art, respected while I live and remembered with affection hereafter. May I always act so as to preserve the finest traditions of my calling and may I long experience the joy of healing those who seek my help.

The Oath of the Healer written in 1991 by Louis Weinstein, professor of Obstetrics and Gynecology, University of Arizona, Tucson, Arizona

In the eyes of God and in the presence of my fellow students and teachers, I at this most solemn time in my life do freely take this Oath, whereby I shall pledge to myself and all others the manner in which I shall live the rest of my days.

I shall be ever grateful to my teachers who have planted the seeds of knowledge, which I shall nurture forever. I thank them for allowing me to see the importance of learning and realize that lifelong study is critically important to becoming a Healer.

I realize that on this day, I become a physician for all eternity. I shall strive to be a person of good will, high moral character, and impeccable conduct. I shall learn to love my fellow man as much as I have learned to love the art of healing.

I shall always act in the best interest of my patient and shall never allow personal reward to impact on my judgment. I shall always have the highest respect for human life and remember that it is wrong to terminate life in certain circumstances, permissible in some, and an act of supreme love in others. I shall never promise a cure, as only death is certain, and I shall understand that preserving health is as important as treating disease. When a patient for whom I have been caring dies, I shall have the strength to allow him or her to die with dignity and in peace.

I shall have as a major focus in my life the promoting of a better world in which to live. I shall strive to take a comprehensive approach to understanding all aspects of life. To become the Healer I wish to be, I must expand my thinking and practice from a system of episodic care to one of a preventive approach to the problems of mankind, including the social ills of malnutrition and poverty that plague the world in which we live.

I am not a God and I cannot perform miracles. I am simply a person who has been given the rights and responsibilities to be a Healer. I pledge to myself and all who can hear me that this is what I shall become.

An Oath that "Bears the Name of Hippocrates"

I do solemnly swear, by whatever each of us holds most sacred That I will be loyal to the Profession of Medicine and just and generous to its members That I will lead my life and practice my art in uprightness and honor That into whatsoever house I will enter: it shall be for the good of the sick to the utmost of my power, my holding myself far aloof from wrong, from corruption, from the tempting of others to vice That I will exercise my art solely for the cure of my patients, and will give no drug, perform no operation for a criminal purpose, even if solicited; far less suggest it That whatsoever I shall see or hear of the lives of my patients which is not fitting to be spoken, I will keep inviolably secret These things do I swear. Let each of us bow the head in sign of acquiescence. And now, if I will be true to this, my oath, may good repute ever be mine; the opposite, if I should prove myself forsworn.

Since we often hear the argument that taking a life is against the Hippocratic oath, which is part of the original oath written by an unknown author about a hundred years after Hippocrates died, how does the oath medical students take at the time of graduation fit into all this? The essence of the more modern oaths is really an admonition for an ethical appreciation of what a doctor's life is truly all about. When the graduating medical student takes an oath, he or she reads it aloud or repeats recitations of the graduation ceremony's celebrant. It is not something the student has pored over and had his or her lawyers evaluate. Students do not sign anything and have not really committed themselves to anything other than being good professionals. "The Hippocratic oath" has become a traditional part of the rite of graduation and, as such, plays a valuable role in the process, but the content is general enough to be subject to each individual's interpretations of current practices. The oath does not, however, obligate the individual in any way. Though fortunately most medical professionals hold themselves to a fairly high degree of ethics, there are no sanctions for those who do not adhere to the "oath."

Where a physician who participates in assisted suicide considers his actions moral and just, another might consider such activities contrary to the role of a physician. Doctors on both sides of the abortion issue believe their positions are founded in righteousness, and both might argue that they follow the tenets of the oath, but I assume few physicians go back to look up the oath when making decisions about practice and personal ethical standards.

Some interesting changes in the newer oaths accommodate recent changes in modern medical practice. The original addresses passing on what was known about the science to future generations of men, completely disregarding any consideration of training women as doctors. That certainly makes little sense today since over half of current medical students are female.

Another admonition is against using a knife, identifying a clear distinction between doctors in general and surgeons, who might make use of that type of invasive procedure. Today surgery has become a powerful part of the modern medical armamentarium, so no such distinctions are made in modern oaths. However, this distinction between "doctors" and "surgeons" persists well into the more modern era. In England in the early eighteenth century, doctors went to medical school and received the title "medical doctor," while surgeons were trained outside in apprenticeships. Most were barbers and were called simply "mister," and women doctors were not even given any real titles and were called, for example, "miss." By 1745 surgeons were more in line with mainstream medicine and formed the Royal Company of Surgeons, and the requirements included obtaining a medical degree from a university. However, upon graduation from medical school, surgeons usually reverted to being addressed as "mister" in a kind of reverse snobbishness, a practice that continues today.

The concept of training medical students without fee is certainly a bitter joke for any individual or parent who has footed the bill for medical school, particularly those who wind up with enormous financial obligations in the form of student loans.

Two other significant concepts, which are in successive sentences in the original oath but are eliminated in the new versions, involve terminating the life of an individual or a fetus. The quote is, "To please no one will I prescribe a deadly drug, nor give advice which may cause his death. Nor will I give a woman a pessary to procure abortion."

These two concepts have not been included in recent times because they do not apply to current practices of "doctor-assisted suicides" and the millions of abortions that have been performed.

Is it possible we can help avoid undue "pain and suffering" on the part of the condemned by applying techniques commonly used every day in operating rooms around the world? If relieving someone's suffering by helping terminate his or her life is generally regarded as a good and compassionate procedure, why do we not consider participation in a legal execution in the same light?

The answer is simple. The vast majority of Americans do not want to participate in any kind of execution, even though they might say they are pro–capital punishment. What that often means is that they are supportive of the death penalty as long as someone else is carrying it out and it is far from their personal experience. Reading in the paper about the legal execution of a convicted killer is fairly sterile, but getting down to actual hands-on participation is an entirely different matter.

Doctors are no different. Having spent a lifetime working with physicians, I can share that with the vast majority of practitioners (and I include other medical professionals, such as nurse anesthetists), no societal admonition or nonbinding "oath" would stop a doctor from doing what he thinks is the right thing to do, especially if there is consideration for promoting and publicizing a position or call to action. The point is that most medical people do not want to take part in executions, even though many in the profession might agree with capital punishment on a virtual level. The really striking point is that the anti-death-penalty sentiment among health-care professionals is so powerful, and permeates essentially everyone in the profession, that only rarely has anyone stepped forward to break ranks and participate. For the vast majority, the prohibition against taking part in legal executions does not come from any outside force but from the hearts and consciences of individual professionals.

The pharmaceutical companies are in the same camp, as is evidenced by the fact that their representatives refuse to make available the appropriate drugs to agencies that want to use them for executions.

Medical professionals and American pharmaceutical workers are among the many who really do not want the death penalty.

WHERE IS LETHAL INJECTION GOING?

Our nation has been using lethal injection for over three decades, and we still do not have it right. Every time there is a mishap, the outcry is so dramatic and vociferous that the media and death-penalty opponents depict the process as the worst form of torture imaginable, although it certainly is not even in its most botched examples. Opposition to the death penalty by any method and, in particular, roadblocks to lethal injection are squeezing the death penalty out of existence. We have arrived at such a bizarre level of the selection process that we now execute very few individuals out of the larger death-row population. Either we should execute murderers or not, but the selective approach we use makes little sense. Lethal injection is unquestionably the simplest method, and its demise will lead to either of two avenues: (1) complete elimination of the death penalty or (2) resorting to other methods of capital punishment. States that still have electrocution and hanging on the books might go back to those more barbaric methods, and novel conceptions such as the use of inert gases—nitrogen, for example—may evolve into common usage. Reason takes us to the first of these two options, eliminating capital punishment, but reason does not always win the day.

Lethal injection as a penal method is trying to die, and we should help it—and the death penalty in general—along toward its demise.

Chapter 4

COSTS

W hy are the costs so high in a death-penalty case?

The source of the problem for the high costs of the death penalty is the laudatory goal of trying to ensure that we do not execute an innocent person. In order to do that, however, we have established, by law and practice, so many safeguards that we have overloaded the death-penalty process to the point it cannot function efficiently in its present state. The requirements put in place have resulted in a ponderous capital-punishment system overwhelmed with costs in terms of money, personnel, and institutions. All of this amounts to extreme care in all aspects of a capital-punishment trial. Jury selection, witness testimony, expert opinions, attorney time and fees, and multiple other factors are all much more intense, time consuming, and expensive.

Most of this evolved naturally in our quest for justice and through motions from defense attorneys. The Supreme Court, by demanding more safeguards when it opened the door for capital punishment in the United States in its 1976 decision on *Gregg v. Georgia*, also contributed, imposing additional precautions before a state could proceed with execution, to ensure justice was carried out and to prevent putting an innocent man to death. To accommodate these precautions—such as dual-phased trials, which are broken into guilt and sentencing phases; increased qualifications for attorneys, judges, and juries; and the expansion of the appeals process—increased costs are tacked onto the capital-punishment system.

Prosecutors had to prepare additional aggravating evidence that was useful, especially in the sentencing phase, and also prepare to respond to mitigating arguments. They learned they had to deal with many more motions and spend a lot more time in court.

An example is that of the Scott Peterson trial, which consumed more than twenty thousand hours of prosecutor time and required the services of thirty-three people, including five attorneys and seven investigators.

The Supreme Court also established additional protection for the defense, requiring there be at least two attorneys and two investigators on a defense team, twice the requirements for a non-death-penalty murder case.

The sentencing phase brings on further costs for the defense team, as well, in that it must prepare mitigating evidence and also prepare for aggravating evidence prosecutors will present. During this phase more experts are required in the form of forensic scientists, psychologists, psychiatrists, and others.

As opposed to non-death-penalty murder cases, the process requires increased court time, sometimes in the range of many months. Jury selection takes much more time, and the need to exclude people who truly oppose the death penalty requires increased resources.

The appeals processes go on for years, and increased requirements for housing on death row obviously bring additional costs.

STATES ATTACKING COSTS

Every state that has eliminated the death penalty or established a moratorium has mentioned among its reasons for doing so the expenses involved in the system. The cost factor is gaining powerful significance on both sides of the debate. Even some who are pro—death penalty realize the heavy finances are of great significance, but many are willing to take on the costs and feel the institution of capital punishment is worth the added expenses. This is the position of Lubbock County Criminal District Attorney Matt Powell, who said, "I don't doubt that it's more expensive," but he also said he never took cost into account when deciding whether to seek the death penalty. If a jurisdiction feels the costs are justified, there is no debate. Still, a growing number of people question the financial value of maintaining a capital-punishment program.

The final report of the death-penalty subcommittee of the Committee on Public Defense, Washington State Bar Association, in December 2006 reported on the findings from several states that the death-penalty system was a huge financial drain and quite ineffective. One glaring example was New Jersey, where it was found that, since 1983, the system had cost taxpayers $253 million above and beyond the costs that would have been incurred had it used a LWOP system—and the state had only ten people on death row and had executed no one! Another example was Florida, which would save $51 million per year if the state were to sentence all first-degree murderers to LWOP. The analysis concluded that Florida had spent $24 million for *each* of forty-four executions carried out since 1976, the year capital punishment was reinstated. Even Texas, which carries out the most executions in the United States, found its death-penalty costs to be about three times what it would be to house someone in a single cell at the highest security level for forty years.

On October 20, 2009, an article that appeared in the *Lubbock Avalanche-Journal* discussed the cost issue in Texas and showed county estimates that the death penalty was significantly more expensive than life-imprisonment sentencing. The article related the case of Levi King, on whose prosecution Gray County spent almost a million dollars seeking the death penalty even though the defendant had already pleaded guilty to murder. The article points out that estimated expenses do not even take into consideration the costs of the appeals process or added costs when the death penalty is sought but not granted. By comparison, in Lubbock County, for example, a non-death-penalty case costs about $3,000. Estimates for just the legal costs for a death-penalty case from indictment to execution are about $1.2 million. Since it costs about $17,340 to house an inmate for a year, and therefore $693,600 for forty years, these numbers are far less than even *part* of the costs of a death-penalty case.

Since exact dollars are difficult to ascertain, people try to understand the issue through a variety of other approaches.

NEVADA

To gain an understanding of why different aspects of a capital case are so expensive, we can look at a very enlightening piece by Terance D. Miethe, PhD, from the Department of Criminal Justice at the University of Nevada, Las Vegas, in which he evaluates the time spent by Clark County defense attorneys in capital versus noncapital murder cases in a report dated February 21, 2012. Miethe surveyed twenty-two defense attorneys, asking them to break down the number of hours spent in the various phases of capital versus noncapital murder trials.

The combined time throughout all phases was 22.98 hours for a capital case versus 10.87 hours for a noncapital case, for a difference of 12.11 hours. He then used the hourly fees for both public defenders and private defense attorneys, calculating the differences between capital and noncapital murder cases. When the defense team was comprised of public defenders, the difference averaged out to $169,700 per case, and when private assigned counsel provided the manpower for the defense, it was $212,125 per case. Calculating this for the eighty cases that are still pending, this would come to a savings of $15,060,875 if all pending capital cases in Clark County were to be prosecuted as noncapital.

Of thirty-five cases in which notices of intent to seek the death penalty were filed in Clark County from 2009 to 2011, death sentences resulted in five cases (14.3 percent), and a life sentence without possibility of parole resulted in seventeen cases (48.6 percent). This means it cost Clark County over $1.3 million *extra* for defense attorney fees alone for each death sentence rendered.

On April 26, 2006, Nevada terminated convicted murderer Daryl Mack and has not executed anyone since, despite the fact that there are currently eighty people on the state's death row. It would seem, therefore, that the state of Nevada is spending a lot of money on a system that is essentially moribund.

COLORADO

In volume 3 of the *University of Denver Criminal Law Review*, Professors Justin Marceau and Hollis Whitson analyzed the cost of the death penalty in Colorado on the basis of court days, and they quoted Alternate Defense Counsel Lindy Froehlich's financial analysis before the Colorado House Judiciary Committee. Froehlich had stated that a regular first-degree murder case cost her agency about $16,000 per year per case, whereas a death-penalty case cost $400,000 per year per case.

The authors acknowledge that—while anyone who observes the process realizes it costs every agency more in high-level attorney, clerical, judicial, and investigative personnel, and more lawyers, more security, and more jurors—coming to exact dollar figures is extremely complex and cannot be done with any great precision. The report quotes the board of governors of the Washington State Bar Association, who acknowledge that the complexity of death-penalty cases—and the extra steps required by statute, case law, court rules, and the standard of practice—places extra burdens on courts, attorneys, and everyone else involved in the process.

The report also analyzes the time spent in death-prosecution/jury-trial cases versus LWOP cases, finding that death-penalty cases consume about 148 days in court versus twenty-five days in court for LWOP cases. The further breakdown for death-penalty cases indicates there were eighty-five court days of pretrial hearings, twenty-six days of jury questioning (*voir dire*) and selection, nineteen days for the presentation of evidence to determine guilt or innocence, and twenty-one days in court for jury sentencing procedures. In stark contrast LWOP cases required fewer than twenty-five days in court and were broken down into fourteen days of pretrial hearings, 1.5 court days of *voir dire*, eight days of trial, and less than a day before court sentencing proceedings. On average, therefore, a death-penalty trial requires more than six times the court days than does an LWOP case. The report also determines that the length of time per charge-to-sentence period in a death-penalty case was 1,902 days, whereas in an LWOP case, it was 526 days—a difference of 1,376 days, about four times that of an LWOP case.

* Since 1980 Colorado has gone through the exercise of over a 110 death prosecutions, resulting in the execution of only one man.
* Of the dozen death sentences imposed in Colorado since 1976, only three were not reversed on appeal.

The above statistics demonstrate that Colorado, much like California, really does not have a death penalty and is wasting resources of money, people, and time in *and* out of court.

The authors go even further, looking into whether the presence of a death penalty might allow more rapid results by the technique of the death-penalty defendant plea bargaining down to LWOP. They demonstrate that the average court days were about the same. LWOP prosecutions with jury trials lasted about twenty-five days in court, while death-prosecution and LWOP-plea-bargain cases lasted about twenty-four days. These numbers are essentially the same, but the difference comes when calculating the average length of time of filing a charge to the imposition of a sentence, where it shows death-prosecution and plea-bargain cases took 745 days and LWOP cases took 526 days, a difference of 219 more days for the plea-bargain group.

There are obviously aspects of cost other than the trials, and the existence of a death penalty contributes to the massive bureaucracy of the capital-punishment system and the costs within. The authors also discuss the cost-effectiveness of the death penalty as a deterrent, and they side with the majority of current scientists who feel there is little or no good argument for maintaining the system for its deterrent value—and this is particularly true in its current structure, which is a study of ineffectiveness.

CALIFORNIA

It would seem, then, that the vast majority of people who have looked into the issue should agree that the costs of the system are very onerous, but the big blockbuster comes from a study by US Ninth Circuit Court Judge Arthur L. Alarcon and Loyola Law School Professor Paula M. Mitchell. They are two massively dedicated people to whom we owe an enormous debt of gratitude for their work, not only for their time and expertise but also for their dogged determination to dig out the numbers, primarily through records from the California Department of Corrections and Rehabilitation.

The most striking single monetary number is one that punctuates the fact that California has spent over *$4 billion* on our capital-punishment system since it was reinstated in 1978. This amounts to about $308 million for each of the thirteen executions the state has carried out. The costs of the system, which include legal representation, enhanced security on death row, and the additional expenses of capital cases, add approximately $184 million a year to the state budget. Huge delays between conviction and execution are also cited, calculated to be about twenty-five years, but even that time estimate becomes meaningless since California is not executing anyone at all at this time. There always seems to be a reason for California's reluctance to resume executions, but at this time there is some confusion about implementing the one drug system, despite the fact that so many other states have moved to this method with minimal negative issues. When that is finally settled, there will likely be some other so-far-unforeseen, insurmountable barrier.

Death-penalty prosecution costs up to twenty times as much as a LWOP case, and the *least* expensive death-penalty trial costs $1.1 million more than the *most* expensive LWOP case. Jury selection alone in a death-penalty case costs $200,000 more than a LWOP case. Housing death-row prisoners costs $184 million more than housing those sentenced to life without the possibility of parole. Heightened security practices, which are mandated for death-row inmates, cost over $100,000 for each capital prisoner and multiplies to be $75 million per year.

The authors estimate that if this keeps going at the current rate, the overall costs will be over $9 billion by 2030. This is truly an astounding and irresponsible amount of money for a death-penalty system that does not execute anybody!

CANCELLATION OF THE NEW SAN QUENTIN DEATH ROW

The clash of the reality of the fiscal crisis in California and the surrealism of our dysfunctional capital-punishment system has resulted in a logical decision by Governor Jerry Brown—and kudos to him for doing so. There had been on the table a plan to build a new expanded death-row facility at San Quentin at a proposed cost of $356 million, in addition to which $28.5 million would come out of the general fund annually for debt service. According to Paul Verke, spokesman for the California

Department of Corrections, the new 541,000-square-foot facility would have housed 1,152 beds. Though the state still has to absorb the $20 million already spent on the planning phase, it is encouraging to note that a wave of reason and common sense has emerged, particularly pragmatic when the state needs the money for so many other things.

Arguments for the construction of the new facility partially revolved around the fact that the existing facility was designed to accommodate only 554 people, but it currently houses over 750. So the state of California has saved at least $336 million, possibly more, with the understanding that these construction costs are not warranted, hopefully with the realization that there will soon be no further need for a death row at all as Californians learn more about the realities of the flawed system.

SUMMARY OF COSTS

The expenses related to our capital-punishment system are enormous and certainly cannot be defended on the basis of the value received. This represents another benefit of eliminating the death penalty in that this wasted money can be used on much more constructive projects, such as embellishing projects for supporting prisoners toward rehabilitation when they are released and affording direction for identifiable at-risk young people. Any money that could go toward helping our beleaguered police departments would also be a much more reasonable use of assets.

Chapter 5

TIME

TIME AND ATTORNEY COMPENSATION

It took an average of almost eighteen years for the executions that were eventually carried out in 2014 to move from sentencing to execution. This is largely because of the complexity of the appeals process, which moves through a ponderous maze of an impacted legal system. There are other factors as well. In general attorneys do not want to take these cases because the pay is insufficient and they require far too many hours and years. The Sixth Amendment to the Constitution states that the accused is "to have the assistance of counsel for his defense." Even a loose interpretation of this amendment indicates a duty to provide attorneys for all defendants, but we, as a nation, fall short of complying with this obligation with anything that resembles efficiency and certainly not with any degree of enthusiasm. In a speech to the Minnesota Women Lawyers in 2001, Supreme Court Justice Sandra Day O'Connor expressed this problem as so severe that inadequate representation might contribute to the execution of innocent people. Elisabeth Semel, director of the American Bar Association's Death Penalty Representation Project called this issue "a crisis."

Government agencies do not pay sufficiently to supply court-appointed representation, and private firms cannot always afford to take on such cases. Prominent, highly respected law firms select who they think will be the best young lawyers they can find and offer them very good starting salaries, but they expect and demand production. Minimal compensation derived from death-penalty cases does not fit very well into that scenario, resulting in a situation in which only people who are very well-off can afford the best representation. The rest are left in the maze. This is not in any way intended to paint lawyers as uncaring but is simply an acknowledgment of the financial realities and competition for good lawyers. Numerous attorneys take on certain cases on a *pro bono* or limited-compensation basis, but there are not enough resources to handle the large numbers of people on death row.

The Pennsylvania Supreme Court recently dismissed litigation to reform Philadelphia's program to reimburse lawyers appointed to defend indigent clients facing the death penalty. Civil-rights attorney David Rudovsky, who joined the petition as cocounsel, declared that the decision ends the petition and that the indigent will continue to go through the appeals process with the burden that the compensation is inadequate to support an effective prolonged defense.

Financial realities thus blunt the Sixth Amendment and help create an inadequate defense system for those on death row. We do not provide enough compensation to supply adequate defense teams, and lawyers cannot afford to work for inadequate monetary return.

TYING UP THE COURTS

Capital cases take much longer than noncapital cases for several reasons. First, jury selection can go on for weeks because of the more intense questioning in various areas, including the prospective jurors' feelings about the death penalty. The guilt phase of the trial is more demanding and time consuming, but the biggest differences occur in the penalty phase, when the defendant's history comes into the picture. This can go on ad infinitum as all kinds of people, professional and otherwise, appear in court to attest to whether the individual is a good guy or bad guy and how his terrible upbringing affected his life choices and limited his opportunities.

Even though we go through so much time and effort in these cases to do it right, it is not uncommon for someone down the line in the reviewing process to find that every *t* was not properly crossed, so the case has to be retried as in the example of the Alcala case, which is detailed in the second chapter of this book. This is, of course, a misuse of our courts and the judges, lawyers, bailiffs, and others who comprise our professional jurisprudence system, but we overlook the jurors who actually make the decisions. They contribute weeks or months of time, pouring a lot of emotional energy into making very important and often gut-wrenching decisions, only to find out later that their efforts were essentially in vain and that the case is back to square one. This comes at an often-significant economic cost because jurors hear a case and deliberate for free, taking time away from work or home responsibilities. The court system does not pay for childcare. This cannot leave jurors with a feeling of satisfaction for a job well done, even though they might have done the job very well. Being a juror on a murder case is a huge commitment, and it is vexing to learn that, for example, if you served on a trial that resulted in a death sentence, the case may well have to be reviewed and retried. Even if the case is not retried, jurors face the frustration of their decisions and efforts being thwarted by the never ending appeals process.

DOWN THE TIMELINE

Another problem with the current death-penalty system is that the individual who is finally executed many years down the line is really not the same individual who committed the crime. We know most violent crimes are committed by younger people and that as they get older, there is much less tendency for such kinds of activities. What this comes down to is that when someone is executed so far down the timeline from when the crime was committed, we are executing a middle-age or older man, who, as we know from statistics, is much less likely to commit such a crime. It is very similar to a situation in which an individual commits a crime while high on a drug, but he is executed when he is clean and sober and, for the sake of argument, in a state of mind in which he might be incapable of committing such a crime.

The "change" argument should not for a moment suggest that criminals should be forgiven for their crimes because their personalities have evolved to a higher plane. All of us continuously change through time and experiences. The "change" argument does address, however, one of the many reasons we are reluctant to execute people.

Newer legislation from the US Supreme Court already recognizes current personality issues in the form of more leniency toward parole, more on the basis of a convict's behavior while incarcerated and less on the basis of the crime committed.

Criminals still must be held responsible for their actions because at some level they acted on free will. Our system of justice and respect for victims demand that those who perpetrate horrible crimes receive appropriate punishment. For those who feel capital punishment is the only answer for certain crimes regardless of changes in the condemned individual, this argument is meaningless. However, a strictly enforced sentence to LWOP seems more appropriate in that it conforms to our system of justice and respect for the victim. It also avoids the clash with American mores by which we are reluctant to execute someone who at the time might be totally helpless and defenseless and does not appear to be the same person who committed the crimes that brought him to this point.

TIME SUMMARY

If we want to maintain the current approach to the death penalty, with its structurally prolonged processes, we need to justify the use of that time, because as it now stands, the time factor negatively impacts other necessary functions of the judicial system. The corollary to the need for time is the huge cost involved in death-penalty cases, and our institutions, both private and governmental, are coming to understand these factors as onerous to the point of unacceptability.

The result is that our judicial system has largely joined the swelling ranks of individuals and institutions that effectively do not support the death penalty. If we really want it, we have to be willing to support its temporal and financial requirements. It is becoming increasingly apparent that we really do not want to do that, as evidenced by the inclusion of these factors in the reasons states are dropping the death penalty.

APPEALS

The following is a summary taken from "A Victim's Guide to the Capital Case Process" published by the Victims' Services Unit of the California Attorney General's office. This process varies from state to state, but California's approach is not atypical.

> After a defendant is found guilty and sentenced to death, the case is normally taken to both state and federal courts where it is reviewed. This is the beginning of the multiple steps of the appeals process. If the conviction or the sentence is reversed anywhere along the line of progressively higher court review, the state can take it to a higher court, but if the state is unsuccessful, the case may go to retrial or resentencing. Most cases take multiple appeals. Some take more than others, and the process can take

several years. This prolonged process only begins when the defendant finally gets an appeals attorney, and this process is also terribly lengthy. When the state of California sentenced Skylar Deleon to death in 2012, it was reported that it would take six years to find an attorney even to start the appeals process.

DIRECT APPEAL

After a death sentence, the defendant can have an automatic, direct appeal to the California Supreme Court, which assigns him a new attorney or two and reviews the entire record of the trial. The defense then argues for the reversal of the conviction or sentence, and the state presents its arguments, to which the defense may then respond. Subsequent to that, oral arguments before the Supreme Court are often heard. The Supreme Court then reviews all the data and affirms or reverses the decisions for conviction, sentence, or both. If the California Supreme Court affirms the sentence and conviction, the defendant may then appeal to the US Supreme Court, which can then decide if it should hear the case. Ordinarily, the court does not hear these cases, but that possibility does exist.

The defendant may also appeal to seek state *habeas corpus* review. *Habeas corpus* (Latin—you have the body) comes from old English law in which a superior court or legal body recognizes that a lesser court or entity has the individual in custody and seeks to review the case to assure justice for the defendant. This review is based on facts outside the trial and has to be filed while the direct appeal is still pending. If the California Supreme Court decides against the defendant, he may appeal to the US Supreme Court through what is called a writ of *certiorari* (roughly "to be certain"). The Supreme Court rarely reviews these cases, but it is possible. At this point the trial court sets the date for execution.

After exhaustion of the process through the state appeals route, the defense may appeal to the US district court on the basis of federal constitutional claims. Federal court will then review all the information and sometimes hold a hearing, but, if the US district court finally denies the defendant, he may then go to the US Court of Appeals for the Ninth Circuit.

At this point, on occasion, the defense can present new arguments to the California Supreme Court if they had not already brought those arguments to the court. If the defendant does go back to the California Supreme Court with the previously unheard claims, the federal proceedings can be delayed until the Supreme Court review is completed. If the Supreme Court decides against the defendant, the case goes back to the Ninth Circuit, which usually demands oral arguments. If, then, the Ninth Circuit decides against the defendant, he may then go to the US Supreme Court for review of the federal case and the Ninth Circuit hearing. Usually the US Supreme Court denies this petition, and it goes back to the trial court to set the execution date.

Typically, the defense files more than one *habeas corpus* petition in state and federal courts, but they usually limit the number of appeals that they will consider at this point.

After all these appeals processes have been completed, the defendant may appeal to the governor for clemency, in which the governor can grant pardons, reprieves of execution, and commutation of sentences. If the government decides not to honor the petition for clemency, we go back to the schedule for the execution date.

It is obvious that even if the individuals involved try to act expeditiously, the process takes forever, so to speak. But since prolonging these events is for the benefit of the defense, it is easy to see why it never seems to end.

NINTH CIRCUIT

The US Court of Appeals for the Ninth Circuit, which covers California, is thought to be one of the most liberal courts in the nation, particularly when contrasted with the Fifth Circuit that covers Texas. When evaluating writs of *habeas corpus* in California, the Ninth Circuit has found 70 percent of cases in which the sentence was capital punishment were somehow lacking and needed either reviews or retrials. So we go through the expensive and time-consuming process of the capital-punishment trial, find the defendant guilty, and apply the appropriate sentence only to find we did something wrong 70 percent of the time, wasting a lot of good people's time and money.

LAST-MINUTE APPEALS

The "last-minute appeal" is an extremely interesting ploy to stave off an execution at almost literally the very last minute. It is usually charged with emotional issues and garners support from various often well-known entities and individuals. By the time we finally get down to the rare scheduled execution, we have examined the case from so many different aspects, on so many different levels, and through so many different individuals that one would think there could not be any room for remaining dissent or argument, but it exists—at the emotional level. Because of extensive review processes, last-minute appeals have little chance of success, but they have the effect of causing angst, self-recrimination on a cultural level, and guilt. They play on our emotions, striking the raw nerve that screams, "We really do not want to carry out an execution!"

POLANSKI

In 1977 film director Roman Polanski pleaded guilty to the statutory rape of a thirteen-year-old girl. He served forty-two days in a mental-health facility and then fled to France. Legal maneuverings on his behalf prevent to this day the United States from having him extradited back to face trial and possible punishment. The interesting twist in this case is that the victim is now happily married, has three children, and has gotten over the crime to the point that she does not want to relive it in the courts. It appears she will get her wish and not be subjected to more unwanted emotional trauma.

By contrast, families of murdered victims cannot avoid reliving the horrors of the death of their loved ones, because the system insists on dragging them through the details every time there is another appeal.

There are far fewer appeals for criminals serving LWOP sentences, so families can move on with their lives with a feeling of confidence that the criminal will never be released and that they will not have to relive the horrible experiences of the past. In the vast majority of cases, these people suffer inordinately from the loss and need to move on. Every time the subject is brought up legally, old wounds are opened and salt freshly applied, so these procedures are certainly not in the best interests of victims' families.

The issue, therefore, is that, in addition to the enormous amount of time, judicial effort, and expense in the death-penalty appeals process, there is a very real personal suffering on the part of the families of the victims.

HOW IT SHOULD WORK

GARY TURNBEAU

Maybe the best observation of how the death penalty should really work was in a short letter to the editor that appeared in the *Orange County*

Register on December 2, 2009. It was written by an ex-marine named Gary Turnbeau in regard to the brutal murder of his comrade in 1983. The murderer was Randy Kraft, a serial killer who murdered several young men in California, often with torture and frequently in hideous ways. After a prolonged period, Kraft was finally sentenced to death, but at the time the letter appeared, he was still just getting into the earliest stages of the appeals process and was nowhere near execution. Turnbeau appears to have a very good understanding of what we call "capital punishment." I quote his final paragraph:

> **The answer is simple. Only one solitary inmate cell should exist on death row; when a new convict is sentenced to death, we just make room for him (or her) in that newly emptied cell.**

If it really were to work that way, it might be effective and could even impact others who might be considering a heinous crime, but as Turnbeau suggests, it does not happen.

Chapter 6

LOCATION, LOCATION, LOCATION: STATES AND CITIES

When repeated three times, "location" is most often used as advice for someone trying to start a successful restaurant business or buy prime real estate, but it also demonstrates a striking difference in how the death penalty is handled throughout the country. Table 1 (figures from the DPIC) shows a record of the numbers of executions, state by state, from 2011 through 2014.

The four-year data show a pattern of diminution in the numbers of executions and in the numbers of states taking part. Texas accounts for about a third of all executions, while its population represents only 8.25 percent of the American population, and we are down to only seven states that executed anyone in 2014. The one seeming anomaly in the data is the state of Missouri, which carried out ten executions in 2014 after only three in the past three years combined. This is attributed to a combination of factors, including conservative judicial appointments and getting to a backlog of cases as appeals were finally exhausted. In addition, Missouri was having the now-common difficulty of obtaining appropriate drugs until it started using single-dose pentobarbital, which was purchased from a compounding pharmacy for $11,000 in cash.

Table 1. Numbers of executions (2011–2014)

State	2011	2012	2013	2014
Texas	13	15	16	10
Florida	2	3	7	8
Oklahoma	2	6	6	3
Ohio	5	3	3	1
Arizona	4	6	2	1
Missouri	1	0	2	10
Alabama	6	0	1	0
Virginia	1	0	1	0
Georgia	4	0	1	2
Mississippi	2	6	0	0
South Carolina	1	0	0	0
South Dakota	0	2	0	0
Delaware	1	1	0	0
Idaho	1	1	0	0
Totals	**43**	**43**	**39**	**35**

Source: Death Penalty Information Center (www.deathpenaltyinfo.org).

The pattern of executions by state remains fairly consistent during the last several years, the majority occurring in the South and essentially none in the Northeast. Oregon still has the death penalty on its books, but in 2011, Governor John Kitzhaber granted a reprieve for double murderer Gary Haugen and effectively declared a moratorium on executions in the state while he is governor.

The Constitution leaves the issue of capital punishment up to individual states, resulting in the same crime being handled differently depending on where it is committed. We all understand life does not always seem fair, but this fact leads one to question whether or not the scales of justice are weighted properly. Since one admirable thing about America is that we go out of our way to see justice meted out as fairly as possible, it seems imbalanced that a murder carried out, for example, in Virginia could result in a murderer's execution but not if the very same crime were carried out one foot across the border in West Virginia. Table 2 lists nineteen states (plus District of Columbia) that do not have the death penalty.

Table 2. States that have abandoned the death penalty

Alaska (1957)	Michigan (1846)	Vermont (1964)
Connecticut (2012)	Minnesota (1911)	West Virginia (1965)
Hawaii (1957)	Nebraska (2015)	Wisconsin (1853)
Illinois (2011)	New Jersey (2007)	*Also* District of Columbia (1981)
Iowa (1965)	New Mexico (2009)	
Maine (1887)	New York (2007)	
Maryland (2013)	North Dakota (1973)	
Massachusetts (1984)	Rhode Island (1984)	

The US government and military, as well as the remaining thirty-one states, have not yet abandoned the death penalty, although twenty of those states have not executed anyone in several years.

JOHN ALLEN MUHAMMAD

The variability among states that have capital punishment has led to some interesting legal maneuvers to accomplish the goals of prosecutors and authorities. John Allen Muhammad and his junior accomplice, Lee Boyd Malvo, were involved in twenty-five sniper shootings, including sixteen murders, over a period of several weeks in 2002, primarily near Washington, DC, and surrounding areas, including Northern Virginia and Montgomery County, Maryland. Because of the reign of terror the so-called beltway sniper inflicted on the DC area, his defense attorneys felt he could not get a fair trial in that area and moved to change the venue. The US Department of Justice originally charged Muhammad and Malvo with federal violations, but they agreed to move the cases to state courts in Virginia, where the defendants would face "a wide range of possible penalties," an expression that indicated the availability of the death penalty. The prosecution felt they could get a fair jury in the areas where most of the crimes were committed, but they agreed to a venue change to Virginia Beach and focused on a murder near Manassas, Virginia, where Muhammad had used a Bushmaster XM-15 rifle to kill Dean Harold Meyers, who had been pumping gas at a gas station when he was shot.

There was sufficient concern about a fair trial on the part of the defense, but this change in venue proved to be a door opener for the prosecutors, who really wanted a death sentence because of the callousness and capriciousness of the crime spree. Muhammad and Malvo had carried out their grisly tasks without detection, understandably terrifying area residents. Malvo's subsequent revelation of their plan to kill six white people a day was so outrageous that authorities felt strongly about going after the death penalty. Descriptions of some of the homicides, such as the deadly shooting of a pregnant woman in the abdomen, further steeled the prosecution and led to the conviction and sentencing of John Muhammad.

Evaluations in regard to the possibility of the death penalty in various states led the prosecution to Virginia Beach, a community in a fairly aggressive capital-punishment state. That community accepted the responsibility, and Mayor Meyer Oberndorf, realizing the expense his city was facing, requested financial assistance from the federal government and the state.

These maneuvers led to a successful case for the prosecution, and the state executed John Allen Muhammad by lethal injection on November 10, 2009. His teenage accomplice, Lee Boyd Malvo, was sentenced to multiple life sentences without the possibility of parole.

The issue here is that this same horrible crime would have had different sentences depending on the venue. If tried in Maryland, the defendant would have faced a maximum of LWOP, whereas the Virginia court sentenced him to death—same crime, different punishment. Very few people have any semblance of a good feeling toward Muhammad or what he did, but still, this venue inconsistency seems to throw the scales of justice off kilter.

FEDERAL VERSUS STATE

An interesting venue issue arose in the murder case of Marvin Gabrion, who was convicted of the brutal kidnapping and drowning murder of nineteen-year-old Rachel Timmerman in 1997. The crime occurred in Manistee National Forest in Michigan, a state that does not have the death penalty. The question then arose as to whether the jurisdiction should be federal because the crime occurred in a national forest or state because it occurred in Michigan. In issues such as this, the federal jurisdiction almost always takes precedence as it did in the case of Gabrion, who received the death sentence. On May 28, 2013, the US Court of Appeals for the Sixth Circuit upheld the federal sentence.

NEW YORK'S MORATORIUM

New York reinstated the death penalty in 1995, but in June 2004, the Court of Appeals ruled that the death penalty was unconstitutional because of defective protocol. The following winter the state assembly conducted an exhaustive review of the issue and presented its report titled "The Death Penalty in New York." On the basis of its findings, the legislature opted not to try to reinstate the death penalty but instead to continue with the moratorium and thus end the ability of the state to perform executions.

The summary of the report elucidates major reasons to eliminate the death penalty, as well as other treatises on the subject. It concluded that the state of New York has sent many innocent people to prison on the basis of convictions for serious crimes. The New York State Bar Association found fifty-three wrongful convictions, and most involved human error. Multiple suggestions were examined of methods to eliminate wrongful convictions and executions of the innocent, but it was concluded that the problem could not be completely eliminated.

Murderers who killed white victims in New York were more than twice as likely to face the death penalty as those who murdered black victims, according to the Center for Law and Justice in Albany. A similar pattern involved Hispanic victims as the death penalty was also sought less frequently than in cases involving white victims.

There was also a geographic imbalance, with more than half the death sentences sought in the ten-year period of the report coming from just six counties.

The report also points out the expense and inefficiency of pursuing the death penalty. In 1995 New York spent over $200 million pursuing capital cases but performed no executions. The report concludes that housing the current death-row inhabitants in the general prison population is far less expensive than housing them on death row and exhausting the appeals processes.

There is no evidence for deterrence in that the crime rate in Manhattan was on a decline since 1981 and the death penalty was never sought there, whereas the crime rate increased in places where the death penalty was sought.

New York provided, through its Capital Defenders Office, well-respected, competent attorneys to defend capital suspects, but the budget was slashed, and the state was in the midst of attempts to completely defund the office. Since the recent moratorium decisions were made, the office is completely closed.

The report also points out the inability of severely mentally ill suspects to defend themselves adequately. In the case of mentally ill Stephen Lavalle, the Court of Appeals found the death-penalty statute unconstitutional.

Interviews with family members of murder victims resulted in mixed opinions, but there was the feeling that the drawn-out death-penalty process was very painful for the families.

This report summarizes succinctly the major negatives of the death penalty, leading the legislature to continue with the moratorium. The result in New York State is that it both does and does not have a death penalty. The state still has it on the books, but it cannot be enforced because of the moratorium. Although it is possible for the state to lift the moratorium at any time, for now the state has rid itself of all problems associated with the death penalty.

NEW JERSEY

On December 17, 2007, Governor Jon S. Corzine signed into law a measure that repealed the death sentence in New Jersey, making it the first state in over forty years to abolish capital punishment and the first since the Supreme Court of the United States lifted the ban in 1976.

New Jersey had not executed anyone since 1963, when the state electrocuted Ralph Hudson for the murder of his wife. In 1982 the state reestablished the death penalty, switched to lethal injection as its method of execution, and constructed a new execution chamber at the New Jersey State Prison, where death row is housed. Despite the fact that juries had sentenced more than four dozen people to death, most of those sentences were overturned during the appeals processes. In addition a state appeals court ruled in 2004 that the procedures for the death penalty were unconstitutional, resulting in New Jersey being unable to carry out an execution.

During the extensive process of studying the issues that led to the signing of the bill and thus to the removal of the death penalty, Kent Scheidigger, legal director for the Criminal Justice Legal Foundation, appeared before the New Jersey Death Penalty Study Commission on October 24, 2006, to present a scathing report on what he felt was dereliction in the way New Jersey handled murderers and the death penalty. He felt the swift and efficient application of capital punishment would have a significant deterrent effect and thus save lives, but this was certainly not the case in New Jersey, largely because of decision reversals after convictions and death sentences. Scheidigger was particularly critical of New Jersey's Supreme Court and of the way life tenure affected decision making within the state's legal system. He strongly suggested that the people of the state have a chance to vote for confirmation of the justices in order that those he felt were the most egregious abusers of judicial power could be eliminated.

The bill to ban the death penalty in New Jersey was introduced in November, after a state commission concluded that capital punishment did not prevent violent crime and might lead to the execution of innocent people.

Statements by the governor and legislators pointed out what they felt were moral and practical reasons for the law and that life sentencing was the best method to bring justice for murder. They also highlighted their pioneering role in serving as an example for other states.

NEW MEXICO

On March 18, 2009, Governor Bill Richardson repealed New Mexico's death penalty by signing a bill presented to him a week before by the legislature. This action affects all future cases but not the death-penalty sentences imposed on the two people already on death row. In what he called the most difficult decision in his political life, the governor cited imperfections of the system, and in expressing his concern over the possibility of executing an innocent person, he cited the 138 inmates who had been freed from death row in the United States since 1973. Since 1960 New Mexico has executed only one person, Terri Clark, a child killer, in 2001. The governor emphasized that his actions were in no way to be taken as lenience on murderers, but he felt the population would actually be safer and the process much more efficient using LWOP as a maximum sentence.

The governor was supported by officials of the Roman Catholic Church and the US Conference of Catholic Bishops. Lieutenant Governor Diane D. Denish delivered the governor a handwritten note indicating her support. On the other hand, the New Mexico Sheriffs and Police Association opposed the action on the grounds that capital punishment deterred violence against police officers, jailers, and prison guards. District attorneys oppose the legislation as well, indicating the death penalty is a useful prosecutorial tool.

Governor Richardson's moving statement succinctly describes the many frailties of the capital-punishment system, and it also poignantly expresses the evolution of his position on the matter. His decision came after much soul-searching and introspection, requiring a great deal of personal courage, particularly when so many people were opposed to his position. His comments really are an educational tool and in all likelihood reflect the positions of other governors who have taken this step and all those who oppose the death penalty. For that reason, Governor Richardson's statement follows here in its entirety.

Today marks the end of a long, personal journey for me and the issue of the death penalty.

Throughout my adult life, I have been a firm believer in the death penalty as a just punishment—in very rare instances, and only for the most heinous crimes. I still believe that.

But six years ago, when I took office as Governor of the State of New Mexico, I started to challenge my own thinking on the death penalty.

The issue became more real to me because I knew the day would come when one of two things might happen: I would either have to take action on legislation to repeal the death penalty, or more daunting, I might have to sign someone's death warrant.

I'll be honest. The prospect of either decision was extremely troubling. But I was elected by the people of New Mexico to make just this type of decision.

So, like many of the supporters who took the time to meet with me this week, I have believed the death penalty can serve as a deterrent to some who might consider murdering a law enforcement officer, a corrections officer, a witness to a crime or kidnapping and murdering a child. However, people continue to commit terrible crimes even in the face of the death penalty and responsible people on both sides of the debate disagree—strongly—on this issue.

But what we cannot disagree on is the finality of this ultimate punishment. Once a conclusive decision has been made and executed, it cannot be reversed. And it is in consideration of this, that I have made my decision.

I have decided to sign legislation that repeals the death penalty in the state of New Mexico.

Regardless of my personal opinion about the death penalty, I do not have confidence in the criminal justice system as it currently operates to be the final arbiter when it comes to who lives and who dies for their crime. If the State is going to undertake this awesome responsibility, the system to impose this ultimate penalty must be perfect and can never be wrong.

But the reality is the system is not perfect—far from it. The system is inherently defective.

DNA testing has proven that. Innocent people have been put on death row all across the country.

Even with advances in DNA and other forensic evidence technologies, we can't be 100 percent sure that only the truly guilty are convicted of capital crimes. Evidence, including DNA evidence, can be manipulated. Prosecutors can still abuse their powers. We cannot ensure competent defense counsel for all defendants. The sad truth is the wrong person can still be convicted in this day and age, and in cases where that conviction carries with it the ultimate sanction, we must have ultimate confidence—I would say certitude—that the system is without flaw or prejudice. Unfortunately, this is demonstrably not the case.

And it bothers me greatly that minorities are overrepresented in the prison population and on death row.

I have to say that all of the law enforcement officers, and especially the parents and spouses of murder victims, made compelling arguments to keep the death penalty. I respect their opinions and have taken their experiences to heart—which is why I struggled—even today—before making my final decision.

Yes, the death penalty is a tool for law enforcement. But it's not the only tool. For some would-be criminals, the death penalty may be a deterrent. But it's not, and never will be, for many, many others.

While today's focus will be on the repeal of the death penalty, I want to make clear that this bill I'm signing actually makes New Mexico safer. With my signature, we now have the option of sentencing the worst criminals to life in prison without the possibility of parole.

They will never get out of prison.

Faced with the reality that our system for imposing the death penalty can never be perfect, my conscience compels me to replace the death penalty with a solution that keeps society safe.

The bill I am signing today, which was courageously carried for so many years by Representative Gail Chasey, replaces the death penalty with true life without the possibility of parole—a sentence that ensures violent criminals are locked away from society forever, yet can be undone if an innocent person is wrongfully convicted. More than 130 death row inmates have been exonerated in the past ten years in this country, including four New Mexicans—a fact I cannot ignore.

From an international human rights perspective, there is no reason the United States should be behind the rest of the world on this issue. Many of the countries that continue to support and use the death penalty are also the most repressive nations in the world. That's not something to be proud of.

In a society which values individual life and liberty above all else, where justice and not vengeance is the singular guiding principle of our system of criminal law, the potential for wrongful conviction and, God forbid, execution of an innocent person stands as anathema to our very sensibilities as human beings. That is why I'm signing this bill into law.

The abolition movement is also gaining momentum in other states, and in general, these claim the same sentiments—both practical and philosophical. A growing number of governors are expressing their opposition to the death penalty, even though the majority of Americans still favor it for murderers. The issue here might well be the fact that governors still play a large role in the process of who is to be executed and who is not.

ARKANSAS

Arkansas Governor Mike Beebe, considered a conservative Democrat, declared that he would sign a bill eliminating the death penalty, even though the chances of the legislature of his conservative state sending him one were essentially nil. He declared that his role in deciding who was to be executed and who was not had proven to be an agonizing experience for him, and this factor might be the reason some governors leaned toward abolition. The governors who express opposition to the death penalty all echo the same thoughts and, in particular, the difficulty they have in deciding whether or not an individual should die by execution.

Once again an old problem is raising its head. People say they are in favor of the death penalty, but few are anxious to take active part in the actual process. It resurrects the protections that go into our system of actually performing the execution, which requires many steps and many participants so one individual is not the "executioner." In general, when people are polled, they say they are in favor of the death penalty, but they are not the ones to carry out what is truly a grisly task regardless of the horrible nature of the crime. Governors have to make these very difficult decisions, and when they get into all the aspects of these cases—including common arguments involving terrible histories of defendants' upbringings, mental status, and so forth—deciding who among them is to die is a monumental task. It is easy to see why many governors, like most everyone who has actively participated in the process, develop such negative attitudes.

ILLINOIS

On March 9, 2011, Governor Pat Quinn abolished the death penalty in the state of Illinois, largely out of concern for innocent people possibly being executed and his feelings that thirteen men had been wrongly condemned. He commuted the sentences of all remaining fifteen inmates on death row, converting them to sentences of LWOP. Illinois already had a moratorium on the death penalty when then-governor George Ryan suspended executions in the year 2000 and commuted the sentences of 167 men to LWOP.

In January 2011, state lawmakers voted to abandon capital punishment, and Governor Quinn went on to study every aspect of the state's death penalty and concluded it would be impossible to create a perfect system, "one that is free of all mistakes, free of all discrimination with respect to race or economic circumstance or geography."

CONNECTICUT

On April 25, 2012, in a private ceremony that included lawmakers, members of the clergy, and family members of victims, Connecticut Governor Daniel Malloy signed legislation that abolished the death penalty in that state for all future crimes. His action was not without controversy. It occurred on the same day that a new poll from Quinnipiac University showed 62 percent of Connecticut voters still supported the death penalty and 47 percent of them disapproved of the governor's handling of this issue, while only 33 percent approved of his actions. Of course Connecticut did not escape the political football show during this process. In a not-so-subtle undercurrent, the report emphasized that the Democratic governor signed the bill, whereas Malloy's Republican predecessor had refused to do so.

The status of the eleven people already on death row did not change immediately, and they—at least in theory—were subject to execution until the Connecticut Supreme Court ruled the death penalty unconstitutional and barred the execution of any inmate. At that time the sentences of those on death row were converted to LWOP.

The delay in eliminating the death penalty for those already on death row had to do mostly with Stephen Hayes and Joshua Komisarjevsky, the men convicted in the 2007 "Cheshire murders." They raped and sexually assaulted a mother and her two daughters, aged eleven and seventeen, before murdering them and setting the house on fire. This case still deeply permeates the minds and hearts of the people of Connecticut, and apparently a large part of the reasoning for maintaining the death penalty for those already on death row was the collective revulsion felt specifically toward these two murderers.

In some ways this action by the state of Connecticut is much more evolutionary than revolutionary, because there really has not been much of a death penalty in the state for many years. On April 21, 2012, *The Economist* reported the practical side of this story. The article cited the 2011 work by John Donohue of Stanford Law School in which he found that, of the 4,686 murders committed between 1973 and 2007, only sixty-six led to convictions of a capital felony and only nine defendants actually received the death sentence. This comes down to less than 0.2 percent of all murders resulting in death sentences. Of greater interest is the fact that there has only been one execution in Connecticut, and that was the case of serial killer Michael Ross, who died in 2005, but only after he waived all his future appeals. What Connecticut actually has done is put into law what was already reality for years—there really has not been an effective capital-punishment system in that state.

MARYLAND

On May 2, 2013, Maryland became the eighteenth state to abolish the death penalty when Governor Martin O'Malley signed the repeal bill.

In the official statement from the governor's office, the following comments were made: "Maryland has effectively eliminated a policy that is proven not to work. Evidence shows that the death penalty is not a deterrent, it cannot be administered without racial bias, and it costs three times as much as life in prison without parole. Furthermore, there is no way to reverse a mistake if an innocent person is put to death."

Unfortunately, there was a distinctly partisan nature to the voting in Maryland's House of Delegates, which voted for the legislation eighty-two to fifty-six. Only two of the eighty-two votes for the repeal were cast by Republicans, as the other thirty-eight voted against it. While he was still in office, Governor O'Malley had long sought to eliminate capital punishment and launched an abolitionist move subsequent to a narrow defeat in 2009. Governor O'Malley long considered the death penalty inconsistent with American values but primarily focused on the practical aspects of this issue in this battle for its abolition.

At the time of the signing, five men remained on death row, and the governor did not simultaneously commute their sentences to LWOP, but he did so on December 31, 2014.

NEBRASKA

On May 27, 2015, Nebraska became the nineteenth state to abolish the death penalty when the legislature voted thirty to nineteen to do so. This represented the end of a heated battle that pitted the unicameral legislature against the governor, requiring a veto-proof majority vote to override Governor Pete Ricketts, who supports the death penalty and joined in the debate over several months.

The anti-death-penalty arguments cited the inefficiency and cost, as well as moral and religious issues. The governor responded by declaring that he was appalled and that this vote represented the loss of a critical tool to protect law enforcement and Nebraska families.

Nebraska has not executed anyone since 1997. Though it formally considers itself nonpartisan, the Nebraskan legislature is dominated by Republicans. This vote also represented the first conservative state in over forty years to repeal the death sentence.

Passage of the anti-death-penalty bill in Nebraska added an element of drama not seen in the other five states that had recently overturned capital punishment. In this instance the governor did not sign the bill as the others had but instead fought the legislature vigorously and did not relent even after the bill was passed. One good sign in this vote was the break in stereotype that assumed all Republicans and conservatives were supposed to be pro–death penalty. In this case a conservative state and Republican legislature voted *against* the death penalty. That the system was ineffective as a deterrent and inefficient as a process—as reflected by the fact that it had not been used in almost two decades—seemed reasonable arguments in favor of the vote to abolish the death penalty. Abolition of the death penalty in Nebraska also applied to the ten prisoners on death row at the time.

TEXAS

Texas has long been regarded as the state that is most aggressive toward capital punishment and, in fact, has a reputation for having the most executions per year of all states. This is true for a variety of reasons. Texas has streamlined its appeals process, and their US Court of Appeals for the Fifth Circuit is more pro–death penalty than other appeals courts, like the more anti-death-penalty Ninth Circuit that handles California. According to the Texas Execution Information Center, other factors, such as the fact that Texas does not have a public-defender system from which to assign defense lawyers, also lead to more convictions. Texas also has a more layered system for the clemency process in that its Board of Pardons and Parole must first recommend commutation before the governor even has the opportunity to grant clemency.

However, there are signs of some changing public philosophies, and the same issues that affect the rest of the country are affecting Texas. The American Bar Association carried out a two-year study that found the Texas death-penalty system fell short of ensuring fairness, and the findings are documented in a five-hundred-page report. We also see grassroots movements, such as the Texas Coalition to Abolish the Death Penalty (TCADP), spring up in opposition. One important legal condition that has affected the capital-punishment sentencing rate is the introduction of a real LWOP sentence that allows jurors to offer justice in a more efficient manner. This allows the removal of an individual from society for life and, at the same time, avoids the death sentence and all its negativity. Following the national trend, only seven people where added to Texas's death row in 2012, nine in 2013, eleven in 2014, and three in 2015.

So even in the state with the most aggressive approach toward the death penalty, there is a significant decrease in its use.

RATIOS

When New Jersey, New Mexico, and Maryland abolished the death penalty, the ratios of men on death row versus the overall general population in those states were in the range of 1 to 1,000,000, while Connecticut was in the range of 1 to 350,000. In striking contrast, California's ratio has been, and still is, about 1 to 50,000. Illinois was in the range of 1 to 1,000,000 when Governor Quinn abolished the death penalty and commuted the capital-punishment sentences, but the ratio was about equal to California's when Illinois Governor Ryan commuted the sentences of the 167 men on death row in the year 2000.

These differences do not make a lot of sense, because they are based on inequalities rooted in geographic and legal peculiarities, and the trend is becoming more pronounced since California courts continue to sentence people to death but the state does not execute anyone.

STATES' DIFFERENCES

New York has opted to end the death penalty via moratorium, whereas the other six states that had recently eliminated capital punishment did so through changes in state law. Ah, finally, the sweet smell of equality! The latest states to join the non-death-penalty catalog have all done away with capital punishment and now treat all their prisoners with the same rules of justice from one state to another. But not so fast! This is not what is actually happening. Even though they all—to greater or lesser degrees—talk about the same issues, such as costs, inequalities, involvement of innocents, and other imperfections, they treat current death-row dwellers differently from state to state.

Illinois, Nebraska, and New Jersey reduced the sentences of their prisoners to LWOP, while New Mexico, Connecticut, and Maryland left current prisoners on death row and therefore subject to execution (although Connecticut and Maryland subsequently commuted those sentences). It seems the approach taken by New Jersey, Illinois, Connecticut, Nebraska, and Maryland has more of a thread of logic than that of New Mexico. It means that in the New Mexico program, sentencing can be treated differently, in that a murderer who committed his crime before the change in legislation had the possibility of facing the death penalty, whereas the identical crime committed after the legislation does not carry with it the same possibility. This creates a little confusion as to whether this is a non-death-penalty state or not. In New Mexico the answers to the questions "Are you a death-penalty state?" and "Are you a non-death-penalty state?" are the same: yes. For the other states, the answer to the first question is "no," and the answer to the second question is "yes." Logic seems to ride with New Jersey, Illinois, Connecticut, Nebraska, and Maryland.

CALIFORNIA

Many discussions throughout this book in regard to length of time on death row, financial costs, and misuse and overuse of our institutions and professionals already involve California, and I will not repeat these discussions at this time. However, there is probably no state in the union that demonstrates the folly of the death penalty more powerfully than California. First of all the state does not execute anybody even though there are over 750 inmates on death row. This represents a quarter of all people on death row nationally, even though California's population represents only one-tenth of the total US population. What this really amounts to is that California is not sentencing anyone to death row but is in fact sentencing them to life imprisonment. And in California, living on death row is a much better prospect than living in the general prison population. The advantages are many, but for one, safety is a prime consideration in that the chances of being assaulted are much less. Thus, California treats the criminals convicted of the worst crimes better than it treats its other prisoners.

Even though there have been no executions since 2006, the delusion continues by sentencing more people to death, even though using the term "death" is completely misleading.

JUDGE CARNEY

The latest assault on the death penalty came from Judge Cormac J. Carney of the US Central District of California in the case of Ernest Dewayne Jones, who was convicted in 1992 of the rape and murder of his girlfriend's mother and sentenced to death. In 2009 Jones's lawyers asked the court to review the sentence, arguing that the system was unconstitutional. On July 16, 2014, Judge Carney overturned Jones's death sentence, citing the dysfunctional administration of California's death-penalty system. Because of the length of time Jones would be subjected to the possibility of death via inordinate and unpredictable periods of delay, this constituted cruel and unusual punishment and thus violated the Eighth Amendment.

Judge Carney noted that while more than nine hundred people were sentenced to death in California since 1978, only thirteen have been executed and ninety died of natural causes. The rest sit for twenty-five years or more, waiting for an execution that never comes.

The judge's declaration that the death penalty is unconstitutional applies only to the Jones case, but it certainly has the possibility of causing wider implications and applications of this decision.

California Attorney General Kamala Harris appealed the case to the Ninth Circuit Court of Appeals, where a three-judge panel reviewed the ruling. Harris states that death-row inmates have a right to due process of law, which takes time (and thus the prolonged periods on death row). She also states, "I am appealing the court's decision because it is not supported by the law, and it undermines important protections that our courts provide to defendants." In November 2015 a three-judge panel overturned Judge Carney's decision on technical grounds but agreeing with him that the capital-punishment system is dysfunctional. This contention, that long delays provide a violation of the Eighth Amendment for the condemned on the basis of the interpretation of cruel and unusual punishment, is novel, but it is not without abolitionist supporters who can now add this approach to their arguments against capital punishment.

Both Judge Carney and Attorney General Harris acknowledge the prolonged period of time defendants spend on death row, but they have come up with different aspects of appreciation for the same issue. Judge Carney sees the time issue as only part of the death-penalty system's massive dysfunction, which leaves defendants in the confusing circumstance of waiting for the culmination of a sentence that never comes. Attorney General Harris meanwhile cites that the obligation for due process for defendants justifies the time issue.

Before the decision, Jones's attorney, Michael Laurence, executive director of the Habeas Corpus Resource Center, suggested, "We hope the court will recognize that a system that doesn't resolve the constitutionality of a person's death sentence within two generations is a broken system."

Support for Carney's decision came from various sources, including Stanford Law Professor John Donohue, who cited the $4 billion California had spent on the capital-punishment system since 1978, and State Senator Mark Leno of San Francisco.

BETHANY WEBB

Perhaps a more unexpected yet powerful voice of support has come from victims' families, including the family of Laura Webb Elody, who was one of eight people killed in a shooting rampage in a salon in Seal Beach, California, in October 2011.

Laura's sister, Bethany Webb, is an outspoken foe of the broken death-penalty system, citing how it repeatedly traumatizes victims' families. She has summed up her feelings this way: "These cases drag on for decades, and the reality is that [the convicted criminals are] never going to be executed. It's traumatizing for families." Her family asked the district attorney not to seek the death penalty for her sister's confessed killer, Scott Dekraai. Bethany has said her family lives in agony while the case drags on as the prosecution and defense battle over multiple issues such as the use of jailhouse informants.

Bethany said, "I don't want him to have the fame. If the death penalty is taken off the table, we'll never hear of him again and he can live the rest of his life without attention." Joining many others, the Webb family has submitted friend-of-the-court briefs urging the Ninth Circuit to uphold Judge Carney's ruling.

This ruling and its aftermath have brought support from legal and legislative professionals and, perhaps even more important, victims' family members, who live with the death-penalty system in a very personal, painful way.

IMPACT OF JUDGE CARNEY'S DECISION

This decision is extremely important because it documents that people in jurisprudence not only recognize the massive dysfunction in the California death penalty but are also willing to take significant legal steps to deny the death penalty because of its malfunction. At this time, we have no idea where this move will lead or what kind of momentum it might have, but even if nothing more comes of it, it is of extreme significance.

JUDGE FAYE D'OPAL

In 2012 Superior Court Judge Faye D'Opal of Marin County, home of San Quentin State Prison's death row, ordered a moratorium on lethal injection until the California Department of Corrections and Rehabilitation enacted new regulations in compliance with state rules, and a three-judge appeals court panel upheld this decision. This left state officials with the options of revising the rules in regard to lethal injection or appealing to the California Supreme Court. There will be no executions in the state until this issue is adequately addressed.

California's lethal injection protocol includes the original components of Chapman's Protocol, which are the anesthetic Sodium Pentothal, muscle paralyzer pancuronium bromide, and potassium chloride, whose function is to stop the heart. Judge D'Opal contended that the state failed to explore alternatives to this three-drug combination and questioned why a single drug could not be used effectively.

These arguments are really about the abolition of the death penalty in California, because if the state really wanted the death penalty, the issue could be solved instantly with conversion to the use of pentobarbital, the agent used almost exclusively by all other states at this time. It is evident, then, that California's legal system understands the dysfunction of the institution of capital punishment and will do whatever is possible to delay the use of legal execution and, ultimately, contribute to its abolition.

These legal maneuverings have resulted in, essentially, no effective death-penalty system in California. That does not mean, of course, that the state will stop delivering death sentences, discontinue the added expense of housing people on death row, or stop the malfunctioning appeals process.

One of many problems is that the state legislature and governor cannot simply eliminate the death penalty. It was voted in by the people, and the only way for the death penalty to disappear is for Californians to vote it away.

Nevertheless, it makes no difference how many people are sentenced to death row, because moratorium prevents the state from executing anyone. Still, the state continues down this meandering and endless path, which would be laughable if it were not so painfully serious.

Currently it is evident the tide of abolition of the death penalty in California is rising, but there are those who still feel it is an important and necessary part of our jurisprudence structure. In fact, people at this moment are planning to modify the current capital-punishment system to make it more efficient.

The battle to remove the death penalty is tougher in states like California and Oregon because it has to be done by a vote of the people and not by the legislature as in Connecticut and Illinois. The reason is that the people of California (1978) and Oregon (1981) voted to amend their states' constitutions to allow the death penalty, so the only way to change the law to eliminate capital punishment is by a vote, a more difficult pathway than via the legislature.

Anti-death-penalty supporters did go through the tedious process in California, presenting on the ballot in 2012 Proposition 34, which would have eliminated capital punishment in the state. It went down to defeat but by a very close margin in which 48 percent of the people voted for it—a result that is consistent with the rising tide of abolition across the United States.

On another front there is a pro-death-penalty movement to bolster and speed up the process toward execution and shorten the review process—by limiting appeals, easing qualification standards for defense lawyers, and eliminating public hearings on lethal injection procedures. Despite significant name recognition on the part of backers, such as former governors George Deukmejian, Pete Wilson, and Gray Davis, sponsors were able to obtain only a couple hundred thousand of the 807,605 signatures needed to qualify. Spokesman Chris Orrock said the first attempt was hampered by insufficient time to get the signatures and educate the public, but the movement is making preparations for the future, possibly as early as the 2016 elections.

INCORPORATION OF SPEED AND EFFICIENCY

Suppose, then, that the movement to speed up the process is victorious and voters adopt this kind of measure. To expedite this process, we cannot just execute one or two people, because that would certainly not be fair to those selected individuals since there are so many others on death row who would go on living, despite the fact that they also committed terrible crimes. We would need to go very quickly and eliminate as many death-row inmates as we can and as expeditiously as we can, and that, of course, especially in a liberal state like California, would require we enter the theater of the absurd.

Are we going to start executing large numbers of people? Will we even be able to keep up with the numbers added to the death-row population each year? How do we select which murderer is to be executed? Will it be those who finally run out of appeals or those whose lawyers run out of ideas first? Would that not mean defendants with the best lawyers will be way down the list? Would that not be discriminatory, since the wealthy can afford the best defenses? Or to avoid that accusation, maybe we should select those to be executed first according to how much money they have.

We could go strictly by cost. Find out which cases cost the most or even who has personally paid the defense team the most. That would eliminate the argument that we are selecting out the poor. It could be interpreted as being discriminatory against the rich, but no one really cares about that, and in fact it might help satisfy our communal jealousy of those who are better off.

Should we do it by the amount of time on death row so those waiting the longest go first? Should we do it by considering the level of cruelty of the murders? That of course would require appointed commissions to make those determinations. Which professionals should be selected as panel members?

Should we try to determine how sane the murderer is, or was at the time of the crime, and give the more severely mentally ill more breathing room because of their illnesses? We would have to establish another commission to determine those issues. Obviously that would have to include legal and psych professionals. But that would resurrect the old stumbling block that legal and psych experts speak such different languages that communication between them is extremely difficult. On the other hand, lack of communication is how the two professions currently function in the jurisprudence system. We are so used to that gap in logic that maybe we could transfer it to a new commission and continue on as though we were making sense.

Maybe we should go by age or degree of health and create a system in which we eliminate first the oldest and sickest. Starting with the sickest would save on medical bills, an approach that makes financial sense as well. Perhaps the other side of the coin makes more sense, to eliminate the youngest first to offset costs of extended years of incarceration.

Maybe we should go by race and each day select on that basis—one day white, the next day black, then Hispanic, and then other. That progression could be altered by the demographics of the death-row population or even of the population in general, but those details could be worked out later.

We should also not ignore the gender issue, since women comprise about 5 percent of the California death-row population. We somehow need to conquer our aversion to even considering executing women and make every twentieth execution that of a female. Even with our progressive attitude toward execution, we probably would not tolerate executing women because of the demographics of our population since that would mean every other execution would be that of a female.

To avoid any hint of ethnic, racial, or gender discrimination, the most expeditious approach might be to execute only white males at first and move on to other people only when all the whites are eliminated. This would make things a lot simpler for authorities because there would be less protest when the condemned person is white. This makes crowd control and media attention much less of an issue and, since crowds would be smaller, there would be much less cleanup after the event.

One more practical approach to selection might be by size, because in general smaller, thinner individuals are the easiest in whom to insert the intravenous catheter, and thus we avoid the fiasco of inability to insert the needle. In addition, since most protocols call for only one dosage level, we could be more confident in our ability to attain the goal of a rapid, painless death.

To accommodate sensitivities of other nations, many with no death penalties and vehemently opposed to it, we should strictly limit the execution process to American citizens at first. According to the DPIC, as of April 11, 2014, fifty-nine foreign nationals were on death row in California. These people would automatically go to the bottom of the execution selection list.

Other issues, such as IQ level, athletic ability, physical conditioning, and levels of baldness all could be incorporated in the future, but those considerations would be in the hands of one of the many commissions established to expedite these processes.

ALL THE KING'S MEN

Does anyone in his or her right mind think there can really be a reasonable approach to expediting the execution of 750 people living on death row in California, in 2016 and beyond? In 2014 there were thirty-five executions in the entire country! Can anyone imagine California even matching that number by itself? If we were to execute one man every workday, it would take over four years to clean out the house. Can anyone see California tolerating about two hundred executions per year? If we were to eliminate one person every week, it would still take over fifteen years to take care of the current death-row inmate population, to say nothing of the new people condemned every year.

Is there any real, practical chance to repair our system? Very unlikely!

It is time to realize our country's Humpty Dumpty of a system is so shattered that all the king's horses and all the king's men, no matter how well intentioned, cannot put it together again.

LWOP!

CHICAGO

Carnage in our major cities continues unabated, with heavy media attention on the mayhem in Chicago, which has the dubious distinction of having the most murders of any American city, including larger ones such as Los Angeles and New York. There is, however, a small ray of hope in that the murder rate is down to 456 murders in 2014, in contrast to 2001 during which there were 665, when considering statistics from the year 2000 to the present.

While violent crime has increased nationally, there are several other possible reasons for the improvement in Chicago. Some credit the inclement winter weather, which might have kept criminals at home, but more attention has been given to police efforts to combat the problem. Realizing conflict among gangs was a primary reason for high murder rates, police established databases on gang members to gather information about specific gangs, members, turf areas, and conflicts that existed or could potentially exist between gangs. This information was placed in the hands of beat officers, who hopefully could act on a preventive basis. They met with gangs to inform them that if any members committed murder, the police would track down *all* of that gang's members and cite them for any infraction whatsoever. They even set up meetings between gang members and parents of murder victims to help gangs understand more acutely the effects of violence. The police also created what they called "heat lists" comprised of people who were associates of murder victims and therefore more likely to be involved in murder in the future, either as killer or victim. They contacted these people and offered the police force's help to avoid further carnage, and this effort has met with significant success in avoiding loss of life.

There has also been a citywide summer jobs program that involved twenty thousand young people, and according to Evelyn Diaz, commissioner of Chicago's Department of Family and Support Services, there have been no shooting incidents in that group.

To accomplish these goals, the city of Chicago has paid out about $100 million in overtime to police, and many people fear this outlay is unsustainable and that, if the programs have to be cut back, the decrease in murders might reverse. On the bright side, the police academy recently graduated eight hundred new officers, and this is very hopeful to a large city that is among the many municipalities complaining that there are not enough police officers.

Mayor Rahm Emanuel has said he does not expect to spend nearly as much on police overtime in the future, because of new focus programs that have identified about one thousand people believed to be at the core of responsibility for much of the crime.

DEATH PENALTY AND CHICAGO MURDER RATES

From current statistics it appears the death penalty as a deterrent has little effect on Chicago's murder rate, especially since those rates have hit their lowest since the repeal of the death penalty. Certainly one cannot argue that the repeal contributed to the decrease in murders, but importantly, the numbers do not demonstrate any benefit from its presence. The previously mentioned measures all seem to play important roles in contributing to the decreases, but the sanction through the death penalty is not among them.

DEADLIEST CITIES

While the media have made all of America aware of the sickening and un-acceptable loss of young life in Chicago, some really bad news comes from statistics that show city murder rates per one hundred thousand. Chicago, at 18.5 per hundred thousand in 2012, did not even make to the top ten, as shown in table 3, which includes murder rates and the presence or absence of the death penalty.

Table 3. Top ten US cities as on the basis of murder rates

City	Murders per 100,000 population	Death penalty
Flint, Michigan	64.9	No
Detroit, Michigan	54.6	No
New Orleans, Louisiana	53.5	Yes
St. Louis, Missouri	35.5	Yes
Baltimore, Maryland	35.0	No
Birmingham, Alabama	33.7	Yes
Newark, New Jersey	33.1	No
Oakland, California	33.1	Yes
Baton Rouge, Louisiana	28.9	Yes
Memphis, Tennessee	24.1	Yes

These statistics seem to indicate that the presence or absence of the death penalty in a state has little effect on the murder rates in its large cities. There are several real reasons for these unacceptable statistics, and most are fairly obvious.

Poverty is a common factor in high-murder-rate areas with examples such as Flint, Michigan, where 38.2 percent of the city's population is below the poverty line, and Cleveland, Ohio, where 33 percent of the population is below that line. Reverend Jerome Warfield, chairman of the Detroit Board of Police Commissioners, addressed the needs for adequate employment and educational opportunities, both of which are sorely lacking. These issues obviously contribute to poverty and eventually crime, drug trafficking, and murder.

The battle for control of the drug trade is an extremely important part of this picture for many reasons. David Martin, program director for urban safety at the Center for Urban Studies at Wayne State University in Detroit, has said the homicide epidemic is tied to the illegal drug trade and that solving such problems is the equivalent of trying to solve the homicide problem.

Cities with high murder rates all struggle with similar issues, such as low levels of crimes that are solved, or "clearance rates." In Chicago in 2012, only 132 of its 507 murder cases were closed, a dismal rate of 26 percent. This is common in the vast majority of these cities, pointing to a shortage of police officers, urban culture's "no snitch" code, and problems with resistance to prosecution. These factors contribute to the sense that murderers can strike again with impunity.

Depopulation diminishes the presence of the middle class, leading to the loss of businesses with a resultant negative impact on the tax base. Places such as Detroit and Flint suffered from the automobile industry slowdown, and Chicago's population diminished by two hundred thousand people between 2000 and 2010.

There is considerable agreement that the breakdown of the family unit contributes to poverty, lack of education, loss of potential success in the legal business world, and in many cases descent into a life of crime.

The important point is that there are numerous reasons for violent crime and murder in our cities, and most are patently evident, but the presence or absence of the death penalty does not seem to be germane.

WHITEY

Now-retired detective Harold W. White wrote a fascinating book titled *Whitey's Career Case: The Insulin Murders*, in which he described his pioneering and tenacious pursuit of serial killer William Dale Archerd. Over a twenty-year period, Archerd used insulin overdoses to kill at least six people, three of whom were his wives. During his self-described bulldog approach to this case, White required the assistance of professionals from many different disciplines and traveled wherever necessary to pursue clues and factual materials. This included flights to Miami, Florida, as well as Medford, Oregon. The trial lasted eight months, and there were 5,476 pages of transcript and 134 prosecution witnesses, including twenty-one doctors, twenty-two registered nurses, seven lab technicians, two coroners, and one criminalist. The court found the defendant guilty, and Judge Adolph Alexander sentenced him to death. Archerd died of a stroke nine years later while on death row.

Detective White and his colleagues deserve all the credit and accolades they received for this groundbreaking Herculean effort, without which this case could never have been solved. A significant amount of resources was also critical in solving this case.

The book clearly demonstrates what is required to solve difficult cases, but it stands in stark contrast to what is available to inner-city police departments that cannot possibly offer any comparable focused effort to the murders they try to solve on a daily basis. There would be more death sentences and life imprisonment sentences if we were to pursue each murder case in major cities with the tenacity demonstrated by Detective

White, but of course this is not possible given the current availability of resources and the constraints of the "no snitch" code.

There are obvious racial overtones because the vast majority of murderers and the murdered in the statistics for the cities are young black men. Large inner-city ghettos are rife with illegal drugs, weapons, poverty, broken homes, and lack of education. There is enough blame to go around for these conditions, but the end result is that, for the most part, the death of a young black man in an urban environment far too often does not result in the punishment of his murderer.

SAFETY IN NEW YORK

As of 2013 New York City views itself as the safest large city in the United States, and its 2012 statistic of five murders per one hundred thousand people stands in stark contrast to the ten bloodiest cities in the country. Even the Bronx, the city's most dangerous borough, had a murder rate of only 8.1 per hundred thousand that year. In 1990 New York was regarded as the most dangerous city in the nation, because there were 2,245 murders in addition to other elevated crime statistics. The fact that there were only 417 murders in 2012 has caused considerable attention and investigation into what went right for New York City.

Gentrification of large parts of the city brings in improved real-estate values and tax bases. In contrast to the cities where murder rates are still far too high, improved economy drives poverty with all its social ills into the background.

Credit must go to former mayor Rudy Giuliani and Police Commissioner William Bratton for changes in policing techniques, which seem very effective. The first change was to take strong action against minor crimes, because of the concept that there is a continuum of criminality. This so-called "broken windows theory" led police to take strong action against offenses that were previously largely ignored, such as graffiti and fare-jumping in subways.

Former mayor Michael Bloomberg and Police Commissioner Ray Kelly Peart perpetuated these aggressive tactics, and the resulting statistics of 2012 are testaments to their efforts. Mayor Bloomberg credited the stop-and-frisk program, by which a police officer could stop and search an individual on the basis of a reasonable suspicion of criminal behavior. Many critics, however, felt the program led to human-rights violations as well as ineffectiveness since there were fewer arrests. However, this contributed to the philosophy that the city was not going to tolerate crime, and it effected the removal of a large number of weapons from the streets, including illegal handguns. In discussing the effectiveness of stop-and-frisk, Commissioner Kelly said, "We are taking eight thousand weapons annually out of the hands of people we stop, eight hundred of them illegal handguns. We're preventing crimes before someone is killed and before someone else has to go to prison for murder or other serious crimes. We're also forging new alliances with advocates for public safety in every corner of the city."

Other techniques, such as Operation Impact, increased the numbers of police on the beat in high-crime areas. And Operation Crew Cut focused attention on teens affiliated with gangs known to be responsible for high numbers of slayings. Police also focused more attention on social and family circles of known criminals, and they became more aggressive in incarcerating criminals.

Unquestionably the changing methods and concentrations of policing techniques made huge strides against crime. They are aided by a rising economy and national decrease in crime rates, but New York far outstrips other cities in this regard. The fact that the city did this without the assistance of a death penalty indicates it has very little influence on criminal behavior. Pro-death-penalty people might argue that things would be even better in New York with the hammer of the death penalty, but that is extremely difficult to document. We are left with the simple conclusion that New York accomplished its admirable goals without the death penalty.

CHANGING POLICE TACTICS

Despite the fact that aggressive policing seems to decrease violent crime, concerns that minorities are singled out for activities such as stop-and-frisk have led to the curtailing and moderation of some of these practices. On the other side of the coin, supporters of the tactics express concern that violence will increase since police are unable to take certain individuals off the streets before they commit crimes. Observation of the changes in criminal activities will undoubtedly lead to more debate and legislative changes on these issues.

Chapter 7

RACE

The perception of racial inequality in our justice system is much more sensitive than merely skin deep, as recent riots in Ferguson, Missouri, and in Baltimore, Maryland, so vividly demonstrate. Inequities in the history of the application of the death penalty undoubtedly contribute to these readily apparent feelings. Institutions like the Black Codes and lynching have left an indelible mark on our national consciousness with the result that such monumental inequalities can never occur again.

The Black Codes were a series of local ordinances in the early nineteenth century that put particular burdens on the black population in a variety of ways, and most unequal of these were the regulations in regard to capital punishment. During this period Virginia law authorized the death penalty for black slaves who committed any of about seventy crimes, while only five offenses warranted capital punishment for whites. Although the Civil War officially ended the Black Codes, their underlying philosophies did not come to such an abrupt end.

Even though this was an illegal form of execution not sanctioned by any official government agency, the history of the death penalty in the

United States is not complete without including a chapter on lynching. In the South, where the practice originated and was performed more frequently than elsewhere, lynching was a practice in which people ignored any official government agencies and took "matters" into their own hands, torturing and killing thousands of victims. The practice also became part of the fabric of life in other areas, particularly in the West, where official law enforcement was essentially nonexistent, and where it did exist, it might have actually contributed to that kind of "justice." In such an environment in California in the 1850s, vigilante groups—most notably, the San Francisco Vigilance Committee—formed to keep order where there was little else, and their activities had real support from the populace that recognized that it was probably the only means of control of a group of lawless individuals who came to the area during the gold rush. The problem, however, is that their unchallenged exploits encouraged other people to take the law into their own hands.

Figure 1 represents recorded lynchings in the United States according to the archives at the Tuskegee Institute.

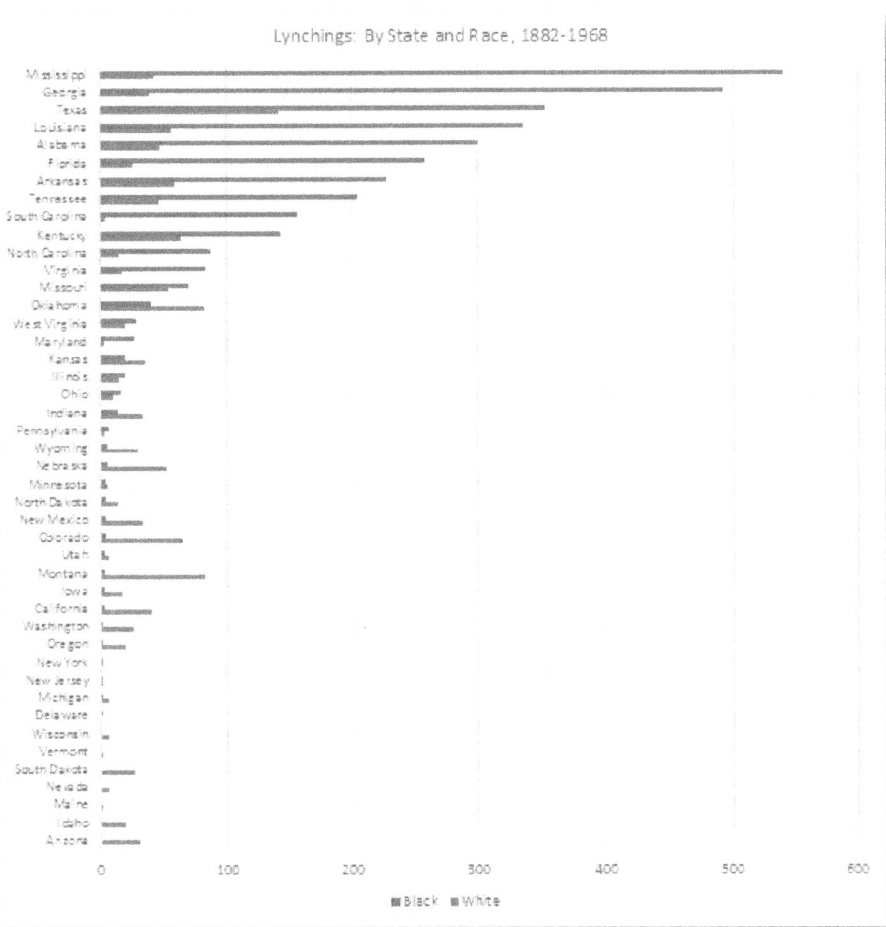

Figure 1. Lynchings in the United States between 1882 and 1968.

This compilation obviously does not include cases that did not make the books, but it shows a couple of interesting things. First, the ratio of black to white victims stands at about 3 to 1 overall, and the geographic component indicates the ratio was much higher in the South. There was an inverse ratio in the West, where victims were overwhelmingly white. Obviously these breakdowns also reflected the racial demographics of the time, when there were more blacks in the South and fewer in the West.

While we often hear complaints that we are too often overly concerned about the rights of criminals and suspects, it is certainly better than the vigilante and lynching mentalities that existed in the past, when rights to a legal defense as we understand it today were absent.

Phillip Dray, in his book *At the Hands of Persons Unknown: The Lynching of Black America*, identifies lynching as a method to "control" the black population. Mobs were known to act without much consideration for the guilt or innocence of the individual, and they sometimes proceeded with their grisly tasks for reasons hardly worthy of the torture and killings that occurred. The terror, pain, and humiliation victims suffered were bad enough for those who were guilty of crimes, but it is difficult to imagine the last moments of those who were innocent of any wrongdoing or guilty of a minor infringement.

DEATH ROW, EXECUTIONS, AND RACE

Several numbers in the pie charts shown in figure 2 are striking. Blacks compose 13 percent of the national population but 42 percent of the death-row inmate population. Conversely, whites compose 63 percent of the national population and 43 percent of those on death row, a number essentially equal to that of the black population on death row. The imbalance is remarkably clear. On the other hand, FBI statistics from 2011 show blacks responsible for 52 percent of murders and whites 45 percent. Data from 2013 indicate numbers of murderers are essentially equal for blacks and whites (figure 3).

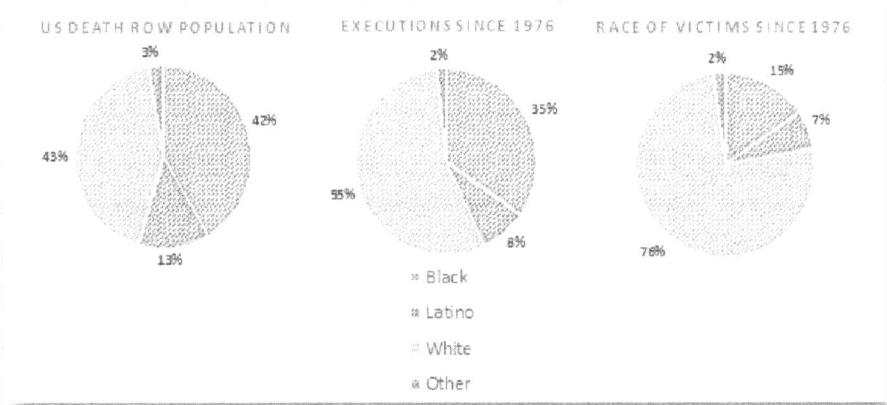

Figure 2. US death-row population—total executions and race of victims since 1976. (*Source:* Death Penalty Information Center—December 2015.)

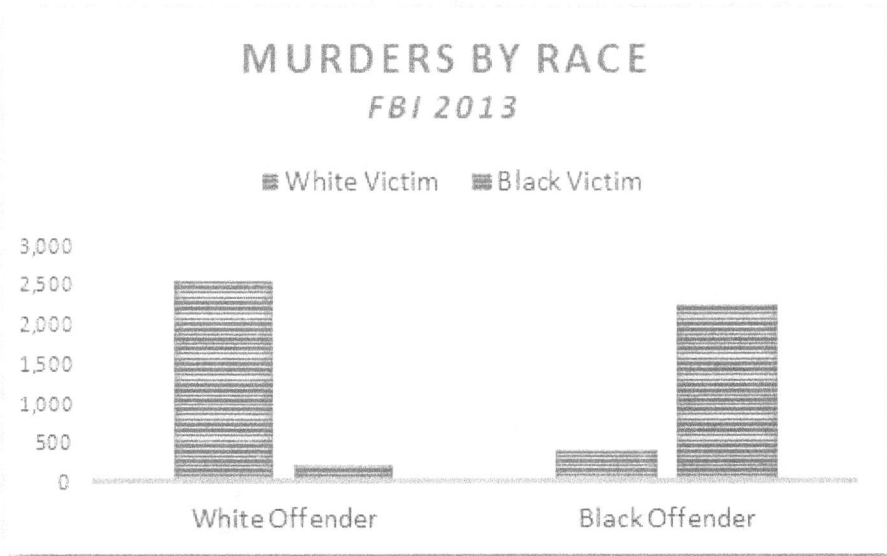

Figure 3. FBI data of 2013 indicating an equal number of white and black offenders. *Note:* single murderer/single victim.

These data indicate the death-row population by race is not far off from the demographics of the murderers, but there is an imbalance in racial composition of those executed—we execute eight whites for every five blacks. The explanation for the racial imbalance in those executed is in the area of victims, in which 76 percent were white and only 15 percent were black.

Since, as these data indicate, most murders stay within racial lines, and that executions are more frequent when the victim is white, we expect—and do find—that we terminate more whites on the basis of the race of the victims.

CRUEL AND UNUSUAL

The concept of cruel and unusual punishment has had a profound effect on recent American capital punishment. The origin of this term goes back to the English Bill of Rights of 1689, which was enacted to redress the wrongs attributed to the administration of King James II. King James was Roman Catholic and apparently accustomed to selecting Catholics for important positions at the expense of Protestants; many also thought he mistreated the populace, particularly the Protestant segment thereof. How extensive these practices were is debatable but moot at this point. The king's popularity waned, and he was succeeded by William and Mary in what was called the "Glorious Revolution." James fled, was captured, and eventually allowed to go to France.

In the English Bill of Rights of 1689 is a long catalog of transgressions that were to be corrected. Among them was referenced the fact that "illegal and cruel punishments" had been inflicted. The verbiage "cruel and unusual punishment," which is used in the Eighth Amendment, was apparently derived directly from the English Bill of Rights of 1689.

Virginia picked up the concept in 1776, and many other states followed. A close corollary to cruel and unusual punishment is the concept of proportionate punishment in the form of *lex talionis*, better known as "an eye for an eye," which goes back through the centuries. The laws of Hammurabi and the Mosaic laws are often cited, and it is emphasized in Leviticus. The British Magna Carta of 1215 was a monumental document drawn up by the archbishop of Canterbury and signed by King John and a group of rebellious barons for the purpose of outlining and protecting justice for all. Among its provisions was the concept that the punishment should fit the crime. Despite these strong historical mandates, in the 1670s and 1680s in England, several defendants received punishments disproportionate to their crimes.

In the United States in the late nineteenth and early twentieth centuries, the concept of cruel and unusual punishment was not used to debate capital punishment. During this time, however, a wave of abolition swept through Europe, Canada, Mexico, and South America. By the late 1960s, the United States was one of the only nations in all of Western Europe and North America still practicing capital punishment.

Then came a very significant pivotal event in Marion, Alabama, in the form of the 1957 Jimmy Wilson robbery case, which dramatically employed both concepts of proportionality and cruel and unusual punishment. Jimmy Wilson was a fifty-five-year-old black farmhand tried for robbing $1.95 from seventy-four-year-old Estelle Baker, who was white. Wilson had already served two sentences for grand larceny and was no stranger to Mrs. Baker, for whom he had worked. In the past he had gone to Mrs. Baker for money in the form of an advance on his salary, and in this instance, he went to her house in search of money on that basis. Mrs. Baker testified that after she told him she had no money, he left the house to go around to the back to obtain some water. He then reentered the house through the back door and demanded money, saying he did not believe she was out of cash. He opened her purse, threw a small amount of money on the bed, and removed about $1.95. Her further statements, which weighed heavily on his sentencing, indicated that Wilson then threw Mrs. Baker on the bed, threatened her life, and attempted to rape her, only to be dissuaded by outside noises, which caused him to flee the house. It should be noted that Wilson admitted he had been drinking and went to Mrs. Baker's home, but he denied any form of violence or threat. He did say she seemed frightened and poured out some money from her purse for him. His voice was largely ignored during the trial, which resulted in his death sentence.

Wilson was arrested on July 27, 1957, and put on trial facing an all-white jury in a very racially segregated community that still carried strong influences of Jim Crow laws, which were state and local laws that were enacted in the reconstruction period following the Civil War and whose purpose was to enforce racial segregation in public places. The underlying philosophy was that blacks were inferior and should be so treated. Southern Democratic politicians were the primary agents of enforcement of these rules and laws, which were gradually changed legislatively although some were not removed until the mid-1960s. The Voting Rights Act of 1965 was probably the pivotal piece of federal legislation that ended Jim Crow on the books, but its death was much more gradual in many areas and particularly in the rural South.

Despite the fact that the only crime for which Wilson was on trial was robbery, the jury found him guilty and sentenced him to death, primarily because of the testimony describing the violence associated with the crime. At that time, death was still an acceptable legal sentence for robbery in Alabama, but it had never been meted out for such a paltry sum. The inappropriate nature of a death sentence for robbery caused some consternation, which developed into a huge uproar nationally and, eventually, even internationally. The outcry resulted in Governor Jim Folsom commuting Wilson's sentence from death to life imprisonment. The sentence carried with it an obligation of fifteen years' imprisonment before parole could be considered, and Wilson did leave prison on October 1, 1973, after spending sixteen years in custody.

The outcome of this case stimulated a large wave of anti-death-penalty sentiment, support, and legislation. Typical of such reaction, after executing mass murderer Luis Monge via the gas chamber on January 2, 1967, Colorado suspended executions for a decade. Intense national reaction followed with the result that lower courts in all the states ruled to stay all pending executions, thus creating an unofficial de facto moratorium in the entire country for ten years.

There then developed the unusual situation in which people were still being sentenced to death but no executions were carried out. Commutations at that time accounted for about 15 percent of these sentences. The real delay in executions, however, came from the appeals process. Before the mid-twentieth century, appeals were very rare. By the 1960s, however, this process and attempts to oppose the death sentence increased significantly. Therefore, increased numbers of people remained on death row and did not move on to execution, and the numbers of appeals significantly increased as well.

In the 1950s the anti-capital-punishment movement was rejuvenated by civil-rights organizations like the NAACP's Legal Defense Fund (LDF). And the ACLU brought the battle to the level of litigation, focusing on many issues in regard to the death penalty, including that of racial disparity.

By the late 1960s, the multiple arguments against capital punishment slowed the process of the execution down. A logjam developed, and no one wanted to be the first to execute. Actually, there was a diminution in executions for years, but this momentum accentuated it even more.

Another victory for the abolitionist movement came from revisions to the Federal Kidnapping Act, which was enacted after the Lindbergh kidnapping case that involved the abduction and murder of Charles Lindbergh's young son. The purpose of the law, also known as the Lindbergh Law, was intended to let federal authorities pursue kidnappers once they crossed state lines with their victims. It was felt that because they had national enforcement authority, federal agents would be more effective in pursuing kidnappers countrywide. Several states implemented their own versions of the law, which were known as "Little Lindbergh" laws. These were to cover cases in which the kidnapping did not cross state lines. The point of interest in the development of the capital-punishment controversy is that several states enacted legislation that would allow for capital punishment only if the victim was harmed in any way. The US Supreme Court, in the 1970s, revised several aspects of the death-penalty laws and, in the course of doing so, established the fact that kidnapping alone was not a capital offense. These developments were drawn from the concept that seeking the death sentence for kidnapping alone represented cruel and unusual punishment and was therefore inappropriate.

Perhaps the most recent pivotal case was that of *Furman v. Georgia* in 1972, involving William Furman, who was burglarizing a home when the owner awakened. Furman shot and killed the homeowner. He made two contrary statements about how the gun went off. In his first statement, he told police he fired a shot blindly while trying to escape, but in his second statement, he said that in his haste he tripped and the gun went off. He was tried for murder and found guilty, largely from his own statements, and sentenced to death.

The Supreme Court considered this case in conjunction with two other death-sentence cases, one in Georgia and one in Texas. All three defendants were African Americans. One problem was that juries imposed the death penalty without being given any guidelines or discretionary limits.

The Supreme Court struck down the death penalty in these cases by a five-to-four margin. Three justices decided the jury's discretion represented a random pattern—and that this pattern was cruel and unusual. Two justices found the death penalty was a per se violation of the Constitution.

The Supreme Court's decision halted all executions in the thirty-nine states that still allowed for capital punishment. Resulting discussions, however, created three possible options that were acceptable under the

Eighth Amendment: (1) mandatory death sentences for crimes very carefully defined by statute, (2) the development of guidelines to standardize jury discretion, and (3) outright abolition.

Outright abolition gained essentially no significant momentum. Jury discretion on specific guidelines did gain momentum and was the factor that caused the court to accept the death penalty in the case of *Gregg v. Georgia* in 1976. The concept of juries considering aggravating and mitigating circumstances in the penalty phase of capital-punishment trials was intended to reduce the randomness of decision making on the part of those panels. These considerations eliminated the aspect of cruel and unusual punishment cited by the three justices who voted for the Furman case, and so the court lifted the four-year ban on legal executions. Capital punishment then officially resumed when a Utah firing squad executed Gary Gilmore on January 7, 1977.

MUMIA ABU JAMAL AND TROY DAVIS

In two famous cases involving black murderers, the issue of race became extremely important and far reaching.

The first case concerns Mumia Abu Jamal, who was convicted of murdering Philadelphia policeman Daniel Faulkner in 1981 and sentenced to death. He went through the usual prolonged system of the appeals process, on the basis of his claims of innocence, and in December 2011, prosecutors announced they were dropping the pursuit of the death penalty and settling for LWOP. Philadelphia District Attorney Seth Williams expressed his opinion at a news conference that Mumia was guilty and that the sentence was justified. He said the decision was difficult for him and that he consulted with Officer Faulkner's wife, Maureen, before making it. However, the Sisyphean nature of the process, in which the sentence was thwarted repeatedly by the appeals process and the fact that many witnesses were no longer available, made the pursuit no longer feasible.

A summary of the case as it first surfaced is as follows. At about 3:55 a.m. on December 9, 1981, Officer Daniel Faulkner stopped Mumia's brother, William Cook, on a Philadelphia street for a traffic violation. Officer Faulkner was in the process of handcuffing Cook when Mumia, who was behind the wheel of a taxi parked across the street, got out of his vehicle and shot Faulkner in the back. The officer was able to take out his pistol and fire back, shooting and wounding Mumia in the chest. Mumia then fired several shots into the officer, killing him with a bullet to the brain.

It seemed the evidence was fairly airtight, and there was even speculation that Mumia's presence in the area might have been a staged setup and murder. Three witnesses testified that Mumia was the killer. Two policemen and a security guard testified they heard Mumia shout repeatedly, "I shot the mother f— and I hope the mother f— dies." The jury sentenced him to death.

Later a second defense team took over the case to challenge the findings, facts, and trial. The case gained enormous international recognition and support, the city of Paris, France, even making Mumia an honorary citizen. Many famous celebrities joined the cause, and on and on it went.

The powerful undercurrent was, of course, race, and Mumia, his attorneys, and his support systems maximized the use of that issue, presenting him as a defender of the oppressed and downtrodden and—as a member of the Black Panthers—a victim of a racist political system. Mumia certainly gained a lot of support from the race issue, and it probably contributed to his avoiding execution.

Another famous case in which race played a role was that of Troy Davis, a black man convicted of shooting to death Savannah policeman Mark MacPhail, who was working as a security guard when killed on August 19, 1989.

On the evening of August 18, 1989, Davis was leaving a party when the occupants of a passing car shouted obscenities at him and his companion,

Darrell Collins. Davis responded by firing a shot into the car, wounding the face of Michael Cooper, who was a passenger. Davis and Collins then went on to meet another acquaintance, Sylvester "Redd" Coles, who was arguing about a beer with Larry Young, a homeless man. The confrontation, which occurred in a parking lot in Savannah, degenerated into a situation in which Davis was said to have pistol-whipped Young. Officer Mark MacPhail, who was working as a security guard at a nearby Burger King restaurant, came over to assist Young when Davis shot and wounded him. While MacPhail was lying on the ground, Davis fired more shots and killed him.

Davis was convicted of the murder of MacPhail and lesser charges, including the shooting of Michael Cooper, and sentenced to death in August 1991. The murder weapon was never found, but ballistic evidence linked the bullets found at the scenes of the two shootings. Seven witnesses testified that Davis was the killer, and two friends said Davis admitted the crime to them. Davis pleaded not guilty and maintained his innocence until his death.

Subsequent to the trial, numerous people and entities took up Davis's cause to protest the verdict and sentencing and demanded another trial. Amnesty International and the NAACP were prominent in their support, and many other individuals, including then-president Jimmy Carter, Reverend Al Sharpton, Pope Benedict XVI, and Archbishop Desmond Tutu, joined the cause.

Davis continued to maintain his innocence, and seven of the nine witnesses recanted their stories, claiming police coercion of various kinds and degrees. Nonetheless Davis was scheduled for execution on July 17, 2007, and this triggered reaction from many individuals and organizations that wanted a stay of execution and new trial. The tide of enthusiasm swept into Europe, and the Council of Europe and the European Parliament expressed opinions that the case needed review. In an article on September 14, 2011, in *Racism Review*, writer Jesse Daniels, in exhorting people to sign a petition to stop the execution, brought up the issue of the imbalance for execution when the victim is white. Because Officer MacPhail was white, Daniels argued that Davis was going to his death on the basis of a racially motivated unequal application of the death sentence.

Legal machinations to obtain a new trial met with failure, and execution was scheduled for September 21, 2011. On September 20, the Georgia Board of Pardons and Parole denied a request for clemency. White House press secretary Jay Carney announced that President Obama would not intervene, and the Supreme Court denied a petition to stay the execution. Davis died by lethal injection the night of September 21, 2011. The defendant's lawyer described the execution as a legal lynching and said that just because it was legal did not mean it was right. These comments demonstrate that, even though Troy Davis was dead, his battle was not over, for race continues to play a role in our decisions about who receives capital punishment.

These two famous cases shine a spotlight on the current status of race and the death penalty. The raw nerve both cases struck reached people of all races and many nations. The days of lynching, black laws, and Jim Crow are behind us, but their legacies live on, and it is close to the surface. Although some doubted these men's guilt, most people understood they were guilty and should have been punished. The objection was not to their punishment but to their executions, and the specter of inequity raised its head in several ways. Direct references were made to the concept that legal cards are stacked against blacks and death sentences are more likely when the victim is white.

In our quest to become a better society, fairness to all has to be a primary goal, and the issue of inequality in an institution as significant and profound as capital punishment needs to be addressed. Adding the inequities involving race to the abolitionist armamentarium provides another powerful weapon in the battle against the death penalty.

LWOP!

HATE CRIMES

Among the factors that have developed for aggravating circumstances is the concept of the so-called hate crime, which is when a person commits a crime on the basis of a victim's race, religion, ethnicity, or sexual orientation. These laws originated in the 1970s and 1980s when authorities noted an increase in such activities and wanted to bring this disturbing trend under control. Particularly troubling were crimes committed solely for the purpose of, for example, racial hatred. In most cases, the hate crime concept comes into play as a sentencing enhancement since it usually occurs during the commission of another crime.

There are those who feel there is an element of unfairness in hate crime legislation because it seems to diminish crimes that are not so designated. Is it really less evil to kill someone of the same race than if the murderer crosses racial lines?

One of the more enjoyable media commentaries on current issues involved phone calls radio host Larry Elder's mother made to his KABC 790 show in Los Angeles. She had a way of cutting through the smoke and getting down to the issues in a manner that was simple and profound at the same time. On one occasion, she addressed the issue of hate crimes, and her observation went something like this: "Now, let me get this straight. If a white man kills a black man or a black man kills a white man, that's a hate crime. OK, so when a black man kills a black man or a white man kills a white man, what do we call that—a love crime?" This amounted to a very clear enunciation of the opinions of people who feel any murder is heinous and must be so regarded. I have since heard several other similar interpretations of the same theme, and it remains a very powerful argument.

Still, a murder committed for no other reason than race, sexual orientation, or disability adds a level of senselessness to an already senseless act.

LAWRENCE BREWER

On the same day when Georgia executed Troy Davis, Texas executed Lawrence Russell Brewer, a white man convicted of murdering a black man, James Byrd Jr.

In the early morning hours of June 7,1998, three friends—Shawn Berry, Lawrence Brewer, and John King—were in a car and picked up Byrd, who was walking home from a friend's party, and offered to drive him. Instead of taking him home, however, they took him to a remote location where they beat him savagely and tied him to the back of their truck. They dragged him for about three miles until he was dead. Apparently totally unmoved by their participation in this ghastly crime, the three friends then went to a barbecue. The victim's remains were found in about seventy-five different locations along the dragging route. Since Brewer and King were well-known white supremacists, the FBI was called in within twenty-four hours. Brewer showed no remorse and stated that he would do it all over again.

All three were convicted in the case, and Brewer and King each received the death penalty, in part because they were white supremacists and this, therefore, was a hate crime. Actually, this case was the impetus for the passage of a Texas hate crime law, the James Byrd Jr. Hate Crimes Prevention Act, which established guidelines for strengthening punishments for those crimes.

In contrast to the Troy Davis case, there was less of an outpouring of support for Brewer, and most people were fully supportive of the decision for execution. However, support came from a variety of people, some quite influential, among them Martin Luther King III and Dick Gregory. Perhaps the most surprising was the victim's son, Ross Byrd, who, along with his mother and siblings, is an active anti-death-penalty voice. He said, "You can't fight murder with murder. Life in prison would have been fine. I know we can't hurt my daddy anymore. I wish the state would take in mind that this isn't what we want." He also quoted Gandhi, saying,

"An eye for an eye, and the whole world will go blind." Another powerful supporter for the family was Ross's friend, David Atwood, founder of the Texas Coalition to Abolish the Death Penalty.

This murder was indeed a horrible "hate crime," due to the fact that the victim was black, but a truly powerful message from this case is the fact that the people who came to support Brewer and oppose his execution were black.

Maybe there is hope.

Chapter 8

WOMEN

In the United States in 2013, there were 10,170 murders in which we knew the offender's gender. Of that number, 9,085 (89 percent) were male and 1,085 (11 percent) were female, and *none* of the thirty-nine people executed was female. In 2014, of the thirty-five people executed, two were women. This brought the total number of women executed since 1976 to sixteen, about 1 percent of the total. This discrepancy would indicate we are much less likely to pursue the death penalty when the defendant is a woman. Some investigators call this the chivalry effect—we are reluctant to punish women severely and certainly do not want to execute them. We already see that, through most of our history, we have been reluctant to execute *anyone*, even the vilest of people, as it goes against the grain of our national conscience. The thought of executing a woman simply accentuates that feeling to such a degree that, for the most part, we really do not want to do it at all.

While there is no doubt that in general we do not want to execute women, there are very likely other reasons for discrepancies in the figures in regard to the death penalty and gender. Men are simply more violent and commit the majority of violent crimes. Interpolating that into the statistics on murder, it is probable that men are much more likely to commit murders with the circumstances that contribute to a death sentence.

There are other factors as well, such as the consideration of "future dangerousness," in which we understand that, for the most part, women are inherently less violent than men and therefore less likely to repeat acts of violence in the future. Regardless of all the causes, there is a bias toward more lenient sentencing in the case of females, and this includes considerations of capital punishment.

Table 4 indicates that the percentage of white women on death row almost exactly mirrors the US population, but with the same comparison, black females are overrepresented, but not to the same extent as black men. Twelve white women and four black women have been executed, but this 3:1 ratio mirrors almost exactly the death-row population with a ratio of 2.9:1. It would seem, then, that once a female finds herself on death row, whites and blacks come to execution at the same rate. FBI figures from 2005 indicate that white females were murderers in 991 cases and black females in 800 cases. This is a ratio of five white female murderers for every four black female murderers, and this ratio does not correspond well with the race of women either on death row, which is 3:1 white to black, or those executed since 1976, which is also about 3:1 white to black. These numbers are fairly striking, indicating that a white female murderer is more likely to wind up on death row or be executed, and the reasons for this are not readily apparent until we look at the races of victims. Whites were victims in fifteen of the twenty cases in which female murderers were executed, and the murders were almost exclusively contained within racial boundaries. In fact, in only one case, that of Kimberly McCarthy, was there a cross-racial murder as she killed seventy-one-year-old Dorothy Booth, who was white. This is consistent with the fact that a death sentence is more likely if the victim is white, and since most murderers stay within racial boundaries, white female murderers are more likely to end up on death row and eventually be executed.

Table 4. Race and death-row females

US census by race 2014		Race of women on death row December 31, 2012			Race of women executed since 1976		
Race	*%*	*Race*	*n*	*%*	*Race*	*n*	*%*
White	62	White	37	61	White	12	75
Black	13	Black	13	21	Black	4	25
Latino	17	Latino	8	13			
Asian	5	Asian	2	3			
Native American	1	Native American	1	2			

Thus far, in our history, we have executed no Latina, Asian, or Native American women, even though they, as a group, currently represent 18 percent of the death-row population.

FEMALE VICTIMS

Researchers at Cornell Law School evaluated the gender of victims in the United States from 1976 to 2007 and found that when the victim was female, a death sentence was reached in 47.1 percent of the cases, whereas if the victim was male, 32.3 percent eventuated into a death sentence. It was conceded that there might be contributions from factors other than gender alone. Heinousness of the crime, sexual elements, and the nature of the relationships between victims and defendants all contribute to more stringent sentencing, and these factors are more often present when the victim is female.

FEMALE MURDERERS

The nagging question concerns the fact that if women commit almost two thousand murders a year, how is it that only sixty-one are on death row and only sixteen were executed since 1976? What happened to all the others? How did this group on death row and the smaller executed group get so unlucky? Murderers of either gender need to be treated appropriately, but might we not be able to interpret the six words of the Eighth Amendment in regard to cruel and unusual punishment to include the few women assigned to death? Were all the other murders that much less egregious, and were all the other victims that much less important for their murderers to be treated less aggressively?

Death sentencing on the male side is capricious enough, but the very few sentenced to death on the female side could be the subject of some clever satire on the subject of bad luck.

MATERNAL INFANTICIDE AND SANITY: CASE ONE

In 2014, an Orange County, California, judge sentenced a young woman (name withheld) to five years in prison for the drowning death of her newborn son. Apparently she gave birth directly into her toilet. She was single and claimed to feel terrible about the incident. Prosecutors agreed to drop the murder charge and allowed her to plead guilty to felony child abuse with a sentencing enhancement for inflicting great bodily harm— hence, the five-year sentence.

The question for the layman is how this comes about. She caused the death of the baby. So, why was this not pursued as such? The prosecution allowed her to plead to great bodily harm, but that really is not what happened. She killed the baby, and we are obligated to deal with that difficult issue. Yet we understand that she is emotionally unstable and needs help.

MATERNAL INFANTICIDE AND SANITY: CASE TWO

A jury sentenced a mother (name withheld) to twenty-five years to life for the murder of her baby. Forensic evidence indicated she shook the baby, strangled him, and threw him out the window. The interesting part of the decision is that the jury found her sane. On the basis of the concept of knowing right from wrong, this decision was probably correct in that, somewhere in her mind, she knew what she did was "wrong," as evidenced by the fact that she lied and said she accidentally dropped the baby out the window.

Let us look at this from the man-in-the-street definition of insanity of being so far out of the realm of normal as to do something this irrational. Obviously, this unfortunate woman was very distressed and out of control. How else could anyone do this to a baby, especially her own?

Yet the jury decided a mother could shake and strangle her baby and then toss him out the window in a state of sanity. *Really?*

SUMMATION OF MATERNAL INFANTICIDE

This issue creates a significant dilemma for the average person and also for professionals who deal with the sentencing. On the one hand, we find the crime to be abhorrent, but on the other, we understand the mother who could perform such an act cannot *really* be sane. The woman guilty of such a crime has acted in a way so far out of what we consider the norm of motherhood that we know she is not sane by any semblance of the layman's definition. The problem, then, is how to handle her disposition. Unquestionably she needs to be removed from society for a variety of reasons, the first of which is that someone who could commit such a crime might do something similar again. The second big reason is that someone who could commit such a crime might easily be a danger to herself.

In a more ideal world, we could institutionalize her and offer her the kind of psychiatric assistance she needs. We would then be taking someone's future—in regard to continued incarceration and the possibility of parole—out of the hands of legal professionals who do not necessarily understand psychiatric illness and instead placing it into the hands of those who do.

Fortunately, we almost never consider cases of these sorts for the death penalty because, essentially, we understand the complexity of the issues involved, particularly in regard to the mental stability of the mother.

We consider this form of killing to be in a different category than that of other murders, and one might ask, "Why is that the case?" Why can we sentence someone to death for murder when those of us who are laymen understand that *anyone* who could commit such a crime is psychiatrically imbalanced? There is, of course, a profound difference on the basis of the maternal relationship. Yes, these comparative considerations also make us question why we can execute anyone given the level of mental instability required to commit murder. The free-will argument justifies our putting murderers away, even for the rest of their lives, but the mental-aberration argument should prevent us from executing them.

MUSINGS ON SENTENCING

Since most mothers give 100% of themselves for their children, and that is what we expect and regard as normal, we consider someone who would kill her defenseless child as so deranged that we cannot and do not punish her severely.

The need for compromise in sentencing in some cases leads some to question the results. Pundits point out that, in the 2011 murder trial of Casey Anthony in regard to the death of her child, for instance, the jury did not find her "innocent," but also "not guilty," which some interpret as giving some level of satisfaction to the prosecution and to those who thought she was guilty, but it really seems to be two sides of the same coin. For those who have confidence in the jury system, since the jury did not convict her, Casey did not kill her little girl and should be free to live the rest of her life openly and certainly without the threats she has received. That is our system.

In the example of the young lady who killed her baby in Orange County, there was recognition that she was severely emotionally disturbed and that seeking a death penalty would be unreasonable, but how does one arrive at a sentence of five years? It seems an arbitrary number that does not make much sense. We take someone in need of psychiatric care and put her in jail for five years. How does that help anyone? It certainly does not bring back her baby, and it is difficult to see how it is going to help her. This result seems unsatisfactory to everyone, except that it wraps up the case and puts it away.

Still, why not nine years or two years? This is a very difficult problem. We are faced with a terrible event, and we do not have a good way to handle it. So we sent her away for five years and moved on. In a more perfect world context, the ideal approach might be to recognize her psychiatric pathology and sentence her to a state hospital for treatment until professionals decide her disposition. The issue is that people who are not competent to judge mental illness should not be the ones to make an arbitrary decision like "five years." Suppose, after five years in prison (or maybe sooner) and with minimal psychiatric treatment, she has satisfied her legal obligation and is released into society. If her pathology has not been adequately addressed, she possibly could be even more of a danger when her next stressful situation confronts her.

GERALDO RIVERA

TV reporter Geraldo Rivera, while investigating the Casey Anthony case for Fox News, brought up a disturbing possibility in that he felt strongly a part of the reason the prosecution sought the death penalty was because the defendant was white. On the May 20, 2011, segment on *The O'Reilly Factor*, Rivera suggested that the prosecutor, Jeff Ashton, wanted to run for the office of state's attorney and that his winning a death-penalty case with a white woman defendant would bring him positive notoriety and assist his quest for the position. Geraldo said there were about two hundred cases a year (later revised to a thousand cases a year) in which mothers killed their children, and essentially none are prosecuted with the intention of the death sentence. Geraldo further reported that there were really only two death-penalty cases for this crime and that in both the murderers were serial killers. He felt if the defendant had been black or Puerto Rican, the prosecution would never have sought the death penalty in the first place. On a later *O'Reilly* show, political journalist Bernie Goldberg agreed with Geraldo that there would be no attempt at a death-penalty conviction or the overwhelming media coverage if Casey had not been white. Both TV personalities expressed a fairly strong sentiment that the defendant's being white weighed heavily in the prosecution's decision-making process as to the death penalty.

JEFF ASHTON

Jeff Ashton is a seasoned and accomplished prosecuting attorney, whose history includes being the first to introduce DNA evidence in a case to obtain a conviction. He felt strongly that Casey was guilty and that she would have and should have been sentenced. In his book *Imperfect Justice: Prosecuting Casey Anthony*, he explains that at first he did not want to introduce a first-degree murder charge because he felt the jury would not go for it. His boss, Lawson Lamar, suggested it, and he decided to introduce it only after he saw pictures of Caylee's remains and felt it should be introduced to the jury to aid in their decision-making process.

Ashton offered Casey and her defense team a plea-bargain opportunity in which she would plead guilty to a second-degree murder charge in exchange for a thirty-year sentence and avoidance of the death penalty. She refused that possibility and eventually went on to freedom.

Jeff Ashton won an election against his former boss, Lawson Lamar, and became the state attorney for the Florida counties of Orange and Osceola. His reluctance to pursue a first-degree murder conviction speaks against the possibility that he put that issue on the table to win an election. That explanation contends that he did not seek the death penalty for his own political purposes, and hopefully that is the truth, because it is abhorrent to think someone would put considerations for the betterment of his own career at the expense of a death sentence for another individual.

SPECULATION OF RACIAL IMPROPRIETY

So why was the Anthony case so big? Since no one in the media was without an opinion, the public could not avoid this case. Was her race that important to make this such a continuous public spectacle? The case brings up, however, the possibility of factors other than the merits of a case that might influence prosecution decisions—and how that affects the capriciousness of the system and contributes to a lack of balance in the scales of justice.

GOING FOR DEATH

The decision to go for the death penalty propelled the Casey Anthony case into national headlines. Successfully going for a prison sentence would, of course, also have an enormous impact, but pursuing the death penalty was far more dramatic even though, even in the state of Florida, it would be a long time before she actually came to execution, if ever.

Going for the death penalty does not mean the jury is limited only to that conviction, because it always has the option of lesser possibilities, which in legal jargon are called "necessary and lesser included offenses." These include the following:

* **Second-degree murder** is ordinarily defined as an unintentional killing that is not premeditated or planned, nor committed in a reasonable "heat of passion," or a killing caused by dangerous conduct and the offender's lack of concern for human life.
* **Voluntary manslaughter** classically involves a killing done "in the heat of passion," such as the husband who, upon finding his wife in bed with another man, becomes enraged and kills her paramour.
* **Involuntary manslaughter** is a killing done totally unintentionally. An example of this level of conviction is an automobile accident in which the driver kills a pedestrian. This level, of course, could be elevated if, for instance, the driver is grossly negligent.
* **Justifiable homicide** is primarily a killing done in self-defense.
* **Excusable homicide** is a killing done, for example, in war.

At the outset, every homicide case is presumed to be second-degree murder. This charge can be lowered if attorneys, usually the defense, successfully convince the judge and other attorneys that it is an appropriate move.

In a similar way, attorneys, usually the prosecutors, can seek to move to first-degree murder, but to do so, the prosecution usually must set out to prove what is described as "premeditation, lying in wait felony murder." This includes murders committed during certain felonies, including robbery, burglary, lewd acts with a child, rape, and kidnapping. Moving to a first-degree murder charge carries great significance because the sentence can include death or LWOP.

The Casey Anthony case probably would have, of its own accord, garnered a sufficient amount of media attention, but propelling it to the possibility of a first-degree murder conviction sent it to the viral stage nationally. The other usual significant effect of such a move is to increase the cost of the case from the hundreds of thousands into the millions of dollars range.

Enhanced legal safeguards in first-degree murder cases require, of course, more time, more professional demands, increased use of witnesses and other professionals, such as those in mental health care, and other components—all of which add up to more money. All of these elements afford the case added exposure, which provides the media with expanded time for coverage, opinions, and speculation, and this is exactly what happened in the Anthony case.

The other very significant thing that promotion to a first-degree murder case changes is the complexion of the jury because now we demand that the panel is what is call "death qualified." This means that, during jury selection, or *voir dire*, the attorneys must select only jurors willing to sentence the defendant to death. This, then, at pretrial level, skews the jury away from what is supposed to be a jury of peers by eliminating the approximately 40 percent of the American public who would not or could not participate in sentencing someone to death. So the jury is comprised of pro-death-penalty individuals who are classically more law-and-order oriented and inclined to punish more severely, even to the point of a death sentence. It is, therefore, of some interest that even such a jury did not find Casey guilty.

Chapter 9

LEX TALIONIS AND PROPORTIONALITY

*L*ex talionis is closely related to the concept of proportionality, a concept used in many disciplines, but in the case of international law and criminal law, it essentially means reactions must be appropriate to the initial action. Thus, it is unacceptable to send in bombers and destroy cities of an adjacent country for a relatively minor offense. In criminal law, there is a similar concept that the punishment must be proportional to the crime. For example, a death sentence for a minor theft unaccompanied by physical injury to any individual is completely unacceptable. The European Union uses this term more frequently than Americans do, but we discuss the same concepts and understand the punishment must fit the crime when we discuss the appropriateness of the Eighth Amendment and that the punishment must not be cruel and unusual, and these ideas take us back to the older concepts of *lex talionis*. All of these are expressions of the same legal philosophy, the need for the level of sentencing to be appropriately proportionate to the level of the offense.

EIGHTH AMENDMENT

People who argue on behalf of criminals when discussing lethal injection, for example, will almost always refer to the Eighth Amendment and the concept of cruel and unusual punishment. The defendant might wake up during the lethal injection process and therefore be subject to cruel and unusual punishment, or the multiple attempts at starting an IV might cause such discomfort to be called cruel and unusual punishment. In fact, such arguments refer to "cruel and unusual" and the Eighth Amendment more frequently than any other constitutional source. The layman, therefore, might think this amendment would be replete with guidelines and directions so our jurisprudence people could refer to it on a sound basis, but that is hardly the case. The entire Eighth Amendment reads as follows: "Excessive bail shall not be required, nor excessive fines imposed, nor cruel and unusual punishments inflicted." That is it. The last six words of this amendment are the basis for innumerable arguments against perceived unfair and excessive punishments.

The interpretation of this amendment therefore is wide open and limited only by the imagination of lawyers, justices, and anyone else who might want to voice an opinion. What does cruel mean? Should we consider any discomfort cruel, or should we discern what is cruel on a relative basis, perhaps in comparison to the suffering of the victim and his family? How should we interpret "unusual?" What does that really mean? Does it mean unusually severe punishment or perhaps a different new punishment? It really does not seem to matter, because simple reference to the Eighth Amendment carries a powerful tool in any argument, especially since we have such a national reluctance to execute. We want to do everything in our power to make sure it is done correctly and justly.

The Eighth Amendment remains an extremely powerful tool even though it carries with it no instructional guidelines and is really only the heading of a topic that is wide open to interpretation.

Chapter 10

THE DEATH PENALTY AS A SERVICE TO THE MURDERER

Nidal Hasan is the army major who carried out the infamous mass shootings at Fort Hood in Texas. On August 28, 2013, a military court sentenced him to death, making him the first soldier in over fifty years to be sentenced as such. Are we really punishing him, or are we leading him to martyrdom, a state he probably desires as the method for his obtaining a preferred status in the afterlife?

The military has not executed anyone for so long that you can be assured the wheels of justice will move extremely slow so that, by the time Hasan comes to his fate of being executed—if that should ever happen—many years will have passed and the effectiveness of this sentence will be blunted in a very significant manner by the hands of time alone. By the same token, we very likely will contribute to his terrorist brethren by prolonged martyrdom, and this probably will become a major issue no matter how far down the time line it occurs. Hasan wants martyrdom as the culmination of his life, and we played into his hands by sentencing him to death, thereby helping establish him as a hero in the radical Islamic culture.

We missed the opportunity to sentence him to life imprisonment and take him out of the public consciousness as quickly as possible. Certainly, we consider Hasan's deeds incredibly evil, but to radical elements, they are acts of great devotion and heroism. We now place him on the slow train of the death-penalty system, which travels seemingly forever with its incredible tortoise-level velocity, all serving as a source of inspiration for radicals everywhere. So not only do we give a killer what he wants but we also give massive psychological and spiritual support to those who revel in being our sworn enemies.

MARILYN EDGE

Marilyn Edge was a terribly distraught forty-two-year-old mother when she drowned her two children, aged nine and thirteen. She then put two cans of propane gas in her car and drove it into a pole in a Home Depot parking lot in an apparent attempt to blow up the car. When police arrived on the scene and requested she leave the vehicle, she attempted to strangle herself with an electrical cord, whereupon police forcibly broke into a car window to prevent her suicide. She told police of the murders and the location of her children's bodies. She was arrested, and during her first appearance before Judge Craig Robison, she requested the death penalty.

Fortunately, Mrs. Edge did not get her wish. In December 2015, she pleaded guilty to the murders, and although she was eligible for a death sentence, the Orange County District Attorney's Office opted to seek a life sentence, and in January of 2016, Edge was sentenced to LWOP.

THE DEATH PENALTY AS ASSISTED SUICIDE

We are programmed to assume capital punishment is our way of imposing the maximal punishment on an individual; however, in some cases, we are not punishing but aiding and abetting murderers who for one reason or another wish to die. Is this capital punishment or assisted suicide? How should the defendant's needs and desire to die play a role in how we decide these issues?

For obvious reasons, a death sentence makes very little sense for either of the people mentioned prior. If we execute Hasan, we are complicit in his plan that began with a murderous rampage and would end in "glorious" martyrdom. Meting out justice entails more than the immediate collective desire for revenge on Hasan, and thus his execution. Circumspection of the broader scenario demands a different solution.

Mrs. Edge presents a contrasting problem. On the one hand, her actions are horrible enough to demand a significant sentence, but on the other, it is evident that she is terribly troubled. We did not acquiesce to her wish for death, and we cannot and do not execute people who are this sick, but at the same time, she needs to be removed from society. The decision for LWOP satisfies both ends of this dilemma.

BILLY JOE JOHNSON

Billy Joe Johnson, forty-six, was convicted of murder for slaying a former gang colleague, Scott Miller, thirty-eight. Special circumstances of murder by lying in wait plus murder for the benefit of his gang, Public Enemy Number One, in addition to the special circumstance that he had another murder conviction on his record, qualified Johnson for the death penalty. He was already serving forty-five years for the previous murder.

Theoretically, one would think an individual would make every effort to avoid a conviction of death. Instead, in this case, Johnson and his attorney, Michael Molfetta, *requested* the death penalty. Their contention was that life is much better on death row and that, by the time the sentence could even be carried out, Johnson would be an old man. In addition they understood that, especially since he is incarcerated in California, the chances of Johnson ever being executed are minimal.

The defense tried to convince the jury that a life sentence would be the harsher of the two possible punishments—that is, LWOP or a death sentence. Molfetta told the jury, "If you really want to stick it to Billy Joe, you'll give him life." However, Deputy District Attorney Ebrahim Baytieh told the jury the only appropriate penalty would be death.

This was an unusual circumstance in which both the prosecuting attorney and defense attorney recommended the death sentence, but for seemingly diametrically opposite reasons. The prosecution wanted it as the ultimate punishment, and the defense wanted it because they viewed it as more lenient than a life sentence.

On November 23, 2009, the jury sentenced Billy Joe Johnson to death. The expected scenario of being sentenced to death would typically be one of disappointment, sadness, and even tears, but that is not reality, particularly with the understanding of what a death sentence really means to the prisoner. He feels his life will be much better on death row because of the better conditions experienced as a member of that inmate population. He can expect a larger cell, no cellmate, more frequent visitations, more time out of his cell, and other amenities. He knows that if he is ever put to death, it will be many years down the line after many appeals. The likelihood is, however, that he will probably die of old age or some other natural cause. Day by day, he is safer, because he does not have to mingle with the general prison population and face the more serious possibility of violence.

So now we have come full circle, to the point where the death penalty, instead of being the ultimate punishment, is now viewed as an easier way to serve time for those facing lifelong incarceration.

DIFFERENT NEEDS FOR DEATH

The previously mentioned cases represent three requests for the death sentence for three very different reasons. Major Hasan has not requested death by his words but by his actions, which are the culmination, by *our* understanding, of the goals of the Jihadist and, by *his* understanding, of what "martyrdom" means to him—the enhancement of his position among his colleagues and in the afterlife. The other two made the request verbally in court.

One of the requests for the death sentence was based on a religious cause, one grew out of mental illness, and one arose from the perception of a more lenient sentence with its resultant improved lifestyle.

If we were to execute Marilyn Edge and Nidal Hasan, we would be participating in assisted suicides rather than imposing terrible sentences.

When the American man in the street learns what is really going on in these cases, his solutions might be entirely different.

To many Americans the desired approach would be to take Hasan out and execute him immediately. Granted there are those who would like to see a prolonged and dramatic conclusion to Hasan's life because he has enjoyed the American lifestyle and had all the privileges of US citizenship yet still found a way to slaughter innocent people. The point is that his rapid disappearance from the public eye into life imprisonment would be a better approach than prolonged adulation he will receive from fellow radicals. After all, rapid jurisprudence often decides the way of life for those of his persuasion. By contrast we do not execute "immediately" because of our concern for every individual's rights, despite the fact he may have forfeited them by his actions. This prolonged death without dying (at least for many years) actually contributes to the cause of our enemies.

Understanding the misdirection of the effectiveness of the death sentence on the basis of these unusual defendant-oriented requests and needs adds to the acknowledgment of another weakness in our capital-punishment system and yet another argument for its elimination.

Chapter 11

"I CONFESS"

During the process of trying to decide if a defendant is guilty of murder, his confession to the crime, if it could be obtained, would seem to be the most important element. Multiple television crime-drama shows educate the public on the importance of such things as forensic evidence, but other kinds of information, such as direct and circumstantial evidence, are also vitally important. The problem with a lot of evidence, however, is that it involves testimonies from witnesses, and that factor can cause doubts on the basis of the frailty of the human condition in a variety of ways. Memories of events can be clouded, particularly when they involve an emotionally laden situation such as a crime. A witness might even question his own recollections when faced with bits of information from other witnesses and from the results of criminal investigations.

Ulterior motives can come in to play, including selfish motives in which a coconspirator might be willing to place blame on someone else to obtain his own freedom, or at least a lesser sentence, and thus contribute to the conviction and sentencing of the defendant. The witness could have a personal vendetta against the defendant or simply be unreliable. The jailhouse snitch is a classic example of someone who might witness to a defendant's admission of guilt, but because such an individual could be offering information in return for his own benefit, there is room for doubt in his veracity. It is also possible someone might try to protect himself or someone else and offer false testimony to shift the blame.

It is, well, evident that evidence and witnesses can be less than reliable, so we depend on attorneys to seek and sort out truth, often a tall order. It would seem, then, that a confession by the defendant is a definitive solution to the question of guilt. The problem is that a defendant's confession is by no means a 100-percent solution.

The Innocence Project, affiliated with the Benjamin N. Cardozo School of Law at Yeshiva University in New York, has made use of DNA evidence to obtain exoneration for 271 people wrongly convicted of crimes, and many of those had served years in prison. The most unusual finding, however, is that, in about a quarter of cases, the incarcerated individuals had confessed or pleaded guilty to the crimes. This number is shocking and somewhat inexplicable, but there might be some common threads for at least some of these individuals.

PSYCHOLOGICAL ISSUES

It is obvious that a person with psychological issues, some of which might cause him to confuse issues of reality, could admit to a crime he did not commit, leading to serious conviction decisions, particularly if his mental illness goes undetected.

Jerry Frank Townsend was almost twenty-two years into a life sentence for six murders and one rape in the state of Florida when DNA testing proved his innocence and led to his release from prison. Townsend suffers from severe mental disabilities and has the intellectual capacity of an eight year old. He was arrested for the rape of a pregnant woman and confessed not only to that crime but also volunteered confessions to six murders. DNA evidence helped to prove his innocence in the rape case and further investigations relieved him from guilt in all the other cases.

Apparently, all of his fabricated confessions were the result of his desire to please authority figures, which is a common adaptive practice in people of his limited mental capacity.

COERCED CONFESSION

Forced confessions because of aggressive interrogations are, thankfully, extremely uncommon today in the United States, but there are some cases in which individuals under this kind of pressure admit to crimes they did not commit.

Jon Burge was a Chicago police officer, who from 1972 to 1991 tortured over a hundred African American prisoners from the South Side of Chicago. He and colleagues forced confessions through beatings, suffocation with plastic bags, and electric shock. Many of these cases are still being reviewed, and several men have been released from prison. In these cases, the men confessed as a survival mechanism and to terminate the interrogations. Burge's outrageous techniques have so far cost the city of Chicago over $100 million.

Because the statute of limitations had run out, prosecutors were unable to convict Burge for his interrogation techniques, but they did convict him of perjury since he denied his activities under oath. He was sentenced to four and a half years in prison. After serving two, he was sent to a halfway house in Florida.

Governor George Ryan's indignation about the abuse after reviewing case reports was a primary factor that led him to suspend executions in Illinois and commute 167 death sentences to LWOP.

In an unrelated case, Harold Hall is thankful his first jury sentenced him to life imprisonment instead of death. Hall was eighteen years old when South Los Angeles police arrested him for double murder and rape. He was interrogated for seventeen hours while handcuffed to a chair, deprived of food and water. He was told there was evidence he was the guilty party, and he was terrified. The interrogation eventually wore him down to the point of confessing to the crimes, and he was sentenced to LWOP. During his time in prison, Hall repeatedly requested DNA testing, but the courts refused every time. Eventually, in 2003, his second trial documented he was innocent because of DNA evidence and the re-evaluation of the jailhouse informant's shaky testimony.

TENDENCY TO CONFESS

Scientists have identified a strange tendency for people to confess to things they have not done. Although most of the studies have been done in a laboratory-type environment, there is some consideration that the more intense setting of a questioning session in a jail might intensify this tendency, even when the accused is not necessarily being coerced and even though the stakes are extremely high.

REACTION-TIME TEST

Researchers Saul Kassin and Jennifer Carrillo of the John Jay College of Criminal Justice in New York published a report of a test given to university students who were supposedly taking a test of their reaction times. Although they were told the Alt key on a keyboard was faulty and that pressing it would cause a computer to crash and lose all its data, the reality was that the computer was set up to crash about a minute after the test began. When the expected crash occurred, the experimenter asked the individuals if they had pressed the key and, if they had, to sign a confession. The shock of this accusation was such that a quarter of the innocent participants were led to confess to something they had not done. Similar tests have had similar results.

This inexplicable need to confess, especially under some form of duress, whether under coercion or not, might contribute to the tendency for people who are being interrogated to cooperate and confess even though they are innocent. Understanding this phenomenon is not easy, but it does exist and has been documented.

ILL-ADVISED ADVICE

Brian Banks went to prison for six years for a crime he did not commit. Banks was an outstanding high-school linebacker, planned to go to University of Southern California on a football scholarship, and dreamed of a professional football career. Unfortunately, his plans came to a screeching halt when a classmate, Wanetta Gibson, accused Banks of rape. Although he was steadfast in proclaiming his innocence and there was no DNA evidence to support her claim, he pleaded no contest and went to prison.

Why would someone make such a plea when he is innocent? Someone evaluating this case from the outside might conclude that because he did not plead "not guilty," he really was guilty and got off with a lighter sentence by avoiding a jury trial. Banks took this course of action at the advice of his lawyer, who told him that if he were to go to trial, there was a very good chance he would be found guilty and looking at forty-one years to life. Banks thought he could avoid the jury trial and accept the lesser of two evils because his understanding was that he would be sentenced to eighteen months for his plea of no contest. Unfortunately, the judge sentenced him to six years. Banks served five.

Since his release, Banks's accuser contacted him on Facebook and indicated she would like to help clear his name. She admitted to him in the presence of a third party that she had not been raped, but she was reluctant to go too far with that information because she did not want to return $1.5 million the Long Beach Unified School District had awarded her in a settlement on the basis of her claim that the school was unsafe. The day after she made this statement, however, a reporter contacted her and she claimed Banks offered her $10,000 to say the rape never happened.

The California Innocence Project has taken this case and filed a petition to exonerate Brian Banks. He is suing the state for $100 for each day spent in prison. This comes to about $200,000, which really is not a lot of money when measured against what he lost.

The travesty of this case becomes all the more real when imagining a frightened sixteen-year-old forced to admit to a crime he did not commit because he had to select the lesser of two evils. Even so, he realized the "lesser" sentence would destroy the life he had planned and deserved.

DEAL FOR A LESSER SENTENCE

On the basis of a confession by the real killer and supported by DNA evidence, Kenneth Kagonyera and Robert Wilcoxson walked free after serving eleven years for a crime they did not commit, despite the fact they each pleaded guilty to second-degree murder. The case involved the shooting death of Walter Bowman during a home invasion by several black men and the arrest of Kagonyera and Wilcoxson for the crimes. At first blush, pleading guilty to a crime they did not commit seemed quite illogical, but the two men felt pressured at the time and were concerned they would face a death sentence or life imprisonment if brought to trial for the greater charges. To avoid the possibility of facing a first-degree murder conviction, which could have led to a death sentence, they pleaded guilty to the second-degree murder charge since they figured this would be the best chance of seeing the light of day somewhere down the line.

North Carolina has the country's only state-run agency dedicated to investigating claims of innocence; through that body's intervention, these men were given their freedom.

These cases bring up a very interesting dilemma. If the practice of pleading to a lesser charge is carried out to avoid harsher punishments for crimes people did not commit, we potentially have a way out for real killers to avoid punishment. Death is the biggest hammer the prosecution has to intimidate people, and that threat can—and did in these cases—lead to admissions of guilt because of the perception by defendants that confessions to lesser crimes allows them the possibility of ever seeing freedom again.

TAKING THE BLAME

Although fairly remote, the possibility exists that someone might admit to a crime to protect someone else. It is entirely possible that this could happen to protect a loved one or for the benefit of others, such as gang members. A judge in Milwaukee, Wisconsin, vacated the sentence of a man who spent one year of a five-year sentence in prison. He had falsely taken the blame for a fatal hit-and-run to protect his son, who later admitted he was actually the driver that night. Prosecutors have stated they will not pursue forty-five-year-old Juan Silva Sr. for his faulty admission of guilt, but they have charged his son, Juan Silva Jr., for the crime, and he faces three felony counts, including hit-and-run involving death. This ruse went on undetected until Juan's wife revealed it to a coworker, who informed authorities, who then proceeded to correct the situation, with the result that the senior Juan Silva admitted the truth and police took his son into custody. On September 18, 2015, a judge sentenced Juan Silva Jr. to ten years in prison and another five years of extended supervision.

This is a situation in which someone confessed to a crime, which he did not commit, out of love for his son, representing one of several reasons we cannot trust an admission of guilt without other evidence.

CONCLUSION FOR CONFESSION

Logic suggests that a confession should be almost infallibly reliable in the consideration of guilt or innocence, but the tendency of people in a variety of circumstances to confess despite their innocence puts even this powerful dynamic into doubt. In the cases cited, the individuals were exonerated, and even though their innocence represents a tremendous miscarriage of justice, they walked free. Of course since it is too late to exonerate an individual who's already executed, even confession becomes a questionable factor in the support of the death penalty.

Chapter 12

INSANITY

INSANITY DEFINITIONS HISTORICALLY

To grasp our current legal concept of insanity, one must go back to 1843 England to the case of Daniel McNaughton, who suffered from paranoid delusion in which he thought he was the victim of a conspiracy perpetrated by Catholic priests and the Tories, who were a powerful political party in England for several hundred years. He claimed people harassed and persecuted him, following him everywhere, falsely accusing him of crimes, and wishing to kill him. McNaughton appealed to the commissioner of police to put a stop to this perceived persecution, and two years later, he planned to kill Tory Prime Minister Sir Robert Peel, because he deemed the Tories largely responsible for his personal problems.

On June 20, 1843, McNaughton set out to kill the prime minister but, in a case of mistaken identity, fatally shot Sir Peel's private secretary, Edward Drummond. During the trial medical experts established McNaughton as truly delusional, claiming he had acted under the influence of those delusions. They concluded he was insane. The jury agreed, acquitting him of murder and forcibly institutionalizing him for the rest of his life under the Criminal Lunatics Act of 1800. The outcome of this trial caused a huge uproar, and Queen Victoria herself intervened and ordered the court to develop stricter tests for insanity. This resulted in the McNaughton Rule, establishing that the jury would function under a presumption of sanity unless the defense could prove "at the time of committing the act, the accused was laboring under such a defect of reason, from disease of the mind, as not to know the nature and quality of the act he was doing or, if he did know it, that he did not know what he was doing was wrong." The simplification of this interpretation is that the definition and proof of insanity involve the concept that the perpetrator did not know his actions were wrong. This rule eventually became the standard for insanity in the United Kingdom and United States, and it is essentially still the standard.

In 1929 the District of Columbia supplemented this rule with an "irresistible impulse test," which allows inquiry into whether the accused suffers from a "diseased mental condition" that prevents him from resisting an "insane impulse."

Advancements in psychiatry and psychology, and the growing appreciation for and acceptance of them, partially led to the next step in the evolution of the legal understanding of insanity. By the mid-1950s, there was a growing dissatisfaction with the McNaughton Rule, because many people felt it was outdated and did not take into account the understanding of the mental aberration modern science had defined. In 1954, Judge David Bazelon of the United States Court of Appeals for the District of Columbia, created the Durham Rule, which states that "an accused is not criminally responsible if his unlawful act was the product of mental disease."

The purpose was to interject into the courtroom the current scientific concepts of mental illness and apply them to our jurisprudence system in open discussions for juries. The implementation of this concept did not go as well as planned, and the dueling between prosecutors and psychiatric experts took the place of well-thought-out scientific discussion. It came down to this simple question that sought a definitive "yes" or "no" answer: "Was the defendant's act a product of mental disease?" So instead of stimulating an open discussion for the jury's education and allowing them to make an intelligent, scientifically sound decision on the sanity issue, it came down to relying on expert testimony by psychiatric professionals. In addition, defense teams used a wide variety of issues, such as alcoholism, compulsive gambling, and drug addiction, to argue for leniency and were sometimes successful.

The Durham Rule eventually fell into disfavor, and in 1972, the District of Columbia Circuit Court unanimously rejected it and replaced it with the standard developed by the American Law Institute (ALI). This states that "a person is not responsible for criminal conduct if at the time of such conduct as a result of mental illness or defect he lacks substantial capacity to appreciate the wrongfulness of his conduct or to conform his conduct to the requirements of the law." The spirit of the law indicates the jury should make the decisions about insanity and that experts should explain the rationale for their opinions and not merely give "yes" or "no" answers. This standard was part of the Model Penal Code, which the ALI framed in 1962, and it is still the major philosophy on insanity in twenty states and the District of Columbia.

The next significant event in the history of "insanity" was John Hinckley Jr.'s attempted assassination of President Ronald Reagan in 1981 and his successful insanity defense, which launched protests across the country. It resulted in Congress's passage of the Insanity Defense Reform Act, which eliminated the irresistible impulse test from federal courts. Reagan had lobbied for the complete abolition of the insanity defense, but intense lobbying by professional organizations prevented that from becoming law.

The end result is that the states have differences in regard to guidelines for the insanity plea, but in general, there are two basic constants: (1) all states rely largely on the concept that to be deemed insane, particularly at the time of the crime, the defendant has to prove he didn't know that what he was doing was wrong and (2) the insanity plea rarely works.

PSYCHIATRIC DEFINITIONS

PSYCHOSIS

The term "psychosis" refers to any of a heterogeneous and complex category of mental illnesses in which there is a loss of or impaired contact with reality. These illnesses can manifest in numerous ways, but common definitions include *hallucinations*, in which the individual sees or hears things that don't exist outside of his own mind, and *delusions*, in which the individual holds unusual or strange but unshakable beliefs about things that are untrue.

Psychiatrists and psychologists differ from legal professionals in some of the terminology used in regard to mental aberration. Psychiatrists and psychologists do not use the term "insanity," but they deal in concepts such as psychosis and personality disorders. Their most significant issue is the diagnosis of psychosis, which indicates the individual cannot distinguish what is real from what is not. The classic example of a simpatico relationship between the psychiatric and legal concerns is the case of the paranoid schizophrenic who strolls down the street and detects someone is walking behind him. The individual who happens to be walking behind the paranoid schizophrenic has no concern for our paranoid person at all, but the delusion is such that the schizophrenic truly thinks the individual is going to kill him, so he turns and murders the unsuspecting victim. In this scenario, there is satisfaction for both the legal definition of insanity and the psychiatric definition of psychosis. He really did not think what he was doing was wrong, having lost touch with reality in that he mistook a totally innocent individual for an attacker, and so what he did was purely an act of self-defense. The problem is that things are rarely that straightforward.

A confirmed diagnosis of a psychiatric illness is not in itself enough to warrant a successful defense on the basis of insanity because people with mental illnesses of this type, even if fairly severe, often function normally in most circumstances. So the debate develops as to how much the mental disease contributed to the defendant's inability to realize what he did was wrong during the commission of the crime. A large area for subjectivity develops, with the result that insanity becomes very difficult to prove most of the time.

TRANSLATION OF PSYCHOSIS

One problem with the translation of psychosis into a legal framework is the misunderstanding about people who are delusional and their ability to plan and act normally in a variety of circumstances. An individual who plans a mass murder, for instance, can act in an absolutely normal manner in every other aspect of his life and still plot his horrible deed on the basis of delusional concepts. He may even act reasonably in the planning of his crime, but his delusion and the crimes to which it drives him are out of contact with reality. Unfortunately, legal arguments to demonstrate that such an individual is sane revolve around the fact that because he functions normally in so many areas of his life and is able to plan his deeds effectively, he is assumed to be sane. Within the framework of delusion, a perpetrator can even understand his crime is against the law and try to hide his misdeeds, resulting in further satisfaction of the legal definition of sanity. The argument, then, that he could act normally and reasonably in so many areas of his life and is therefore rational is a persuasive one, but it misses the point that there still can be a psychotic delusion that, by definition, renders one out of reach of his understanding of what is real and not real in that pathologic portion of his mind.

ANTISOCIAL PERSONALITY DISORDERS

Personality disorder is an area of immense interest because most criminals fall in that category. Psychopaths and sociopaths constitute a large number of criminals in prison. These two terms are often used interchangeably, but some mental-health professionals make distinctions between them in terms of impulsivity, tendencies toward violence, genetic versus environmental etiologies, and multiple other issues. Dr. Robert Hare, probably the foremost expert in the field of psychopathy today, makes a distinction between the two on the basis of multiple issues, but the most striking is his holding that the psychopath has no empathy or sense of morality, whereas the sociopath possesses a sense of conscience and a sense of what is right and wrong, but these concepts are not the same as those of the parent culture. Dr. Hare's experience with understanding these entities led him to develop the acclaimed Psychopathy Checklist, which is a widely used testing method to determine whether someone is truly psychopathic. Though individual practitioners continue to treat people on the basis of their own concepts of the difference between psychopathy and sociopathy, the *Diagnostic and Statistical Manual of Mental Disorders V*, which is the 2013 version of the American Psychiatric Association's "bible" for diagnoses, settles the issue to some extent in that it eliminates the subjectivity that might be involved in assigning a patient to one of those two categories by lumping together psychopathy and sociopathy in section 301.7 under the heading "Antisocial Personality Disorder." The diagnostic criteria for this category include the following:

    A. A pervasive pattern of disregard and violation of the rights of others, occurring since age fifteen years, as indicated by three (or more) of the following:
        1. Failure to conform to social norms with respect to lawful behaviors, as indicated by repeatedly performing acts that are grounds for arrest.

2. Deceitfulness, as indicated by repeated lying, use of aliases, or conning others for personal profit or pleasure.
3. Impulsivity or failure to plan ahead.
4. Irritability and aggressiveness, as indicated by repeated physical fights or assaults.
5. Reckless disregard for safety of self or others.
6. Consistent irresponsibility, as indicated by repeated failure to sustain consistent work behavior or honor financial obligations.
7. Lack of remorse, as indicated by being indifferent to or rationalizing having hurt, mistreated, or stolen from another.

B. The individual is at least age eighteen years.
C. There is evidence of conduct disorder with onset before age fifteen years.
D. The occurrence of antisocial behavior is not exclusively during the course of schizophrenia or bipolar disorder.

For many practitioners, the discussion of the differences is still important for proper diagnosis and treatment of the individual patient, but the salient issue for nonprofessionals is that these individuals are truly different from the rest of us. Their pathology is such that they might understand our sense of right from wrong on an intellectual level but not on a visceral one, and they really do not care at all if they hurt others or even themselves. In extreme cases, they do not even care if they kill. "Right" to them is if they get away with it, and "wrong" is if they get caught. To the victim it does not matter, and it also does not matter to the courts. Neither diagnosis has gained any traction as a defense ploy.

Closely related is narcissism, a condition in which an individual has concerns only for himself to the exclusion of any real interest in other people, has a massively inflated sense of self-importance, and is exploitative. We should understand it because, as a dual diagnosis, it can be associated with other personality disorders, including the category of antisocial disorders. It is easy to understand how this personality defect could easily blend in with the antisocial personality and contribute to the excesses of both. Granted, individuals are not cursed with these "antisocial" conditions to the same degree, so many function at a more reasonable level, and in some cases, the "get ahead at all costs" approach can even be helpful in certain lines of endeavor.

That these conditions are real is demonstrated in many ways, but most dramatically by brain scan during which scientists present various stimuli and then observe brain activity responses that are different from the norm and point to the pathology. This "diagnostic" maneuver is still at this time experimental and is in no way definitive and thus useful in a court of law. Other methods of detection correlate significant aberrant responses that point to lack of emotion and feeling in the psychopath.

The old question in regard to these conditions is this: "Are they sick or bad?" The problem is that the insanity diagnosis cannot be used with individuals with antisocial personality disorders because they know what is right and wrong and they know when they do something wrong, but they don't care. In our current definition, they are sane. They have a choice as do the rest of us, and if they decide to do the wrong thing, they made that decision. Even though they have a defect, they are held accountable.

EVERYMAN'S DEFINITION OF INSANITY

Because professionals have somewhat varying languages in regard to mental illness and instability, there are communication issues. There is, however, another way to look at and diagnose insanity, and that is with the method of the man in the street. The everyman's definition of insanity involves the understanding that *anyone* who commits a horrible crime is "insane." This is heard every time a truly terrible crime is committed and reported to the media, and the man in the street acknowledges this understanding of insanity and freely offers a method of punishment often very graphic and usually not publishable.

Jeffry Dahmer is an excellent case in point. Here is a man who killed people, butchered them, refrigerated body parts, and later ate some of them. He tried to make some of his victims into living "zombies" so he could have totally submissive sexual partners on a perpetual basis. He did this by drilling holes into their skulls and pouring in acid to throw their brains into neutral forever. The jury did not find him insane, and part of their conclusion came from the prosecution's argument that he "engineered" his gruesome activities and was therefore in control of his decision-making processes. Support for the concept that he was sane came from many experts in the field.

In an article by Anastasia Toufexis in the May/June 1999 issue of *Psychology Today*, noted forensic psychiatrist Park Dietz claims Jeffrey Dahmer was sane because he knew right from wrong. He based this conclusion on the fact that Dahmer had tried to conceal the bodies of his victims and therefore knew what he was doing was wrong, and in our current legal definition of sanity, Dietz is correct, but that certainly doesn't fit with what the rest of us call "sane." By our definition, we nonprofessionals know he was insane, because most of us believe anyone who could commit such atrocities has to be insane. We, also appreciate that insane people can plan and make preparations for their actions, good, bad, or neutral. Legal folks can argue about whether he knew right from wrong, and the psych people can talk about his grasp on reality and whether he had a personality disorder, but we know by the enormity of his transgressions that he was insane. If the courts couldn't figure that out, we can understand why the psychiatric defense is so rarely successful and that the concept of an insanity defense is as seriously broken as is the whole death-penalty system. Diagnosing sanity or insanity solely on the basis of the McNaughton Rule or concepts of purposeful engineering or planning highlights discrepancies in our definitions. Activities so out of synch with what we know are the boundaries of the norm constitute another meaningful contribution to the definition of insanity, especially for nonprofessionals.

There is nothing immutable about any of our definitions and concepts. Queen Victoria successfully stepped in when she thought the McNaughton decision was wrong, and the outcry over the Hinckley decision caused big changes in our legal concepts of insanity. So maybe there is room for more significant changes now, since we realize the inadequacies of how we tackle the insanity issue. This brings up the argument that coming to a definition of what is normal might be an even more difficult one, a good point of discussion for armchair philosophers. Even though we may all have different limits for what we consider "normal," the majority understand when something is so far out of the boundaries as to be "abnormal." Still, the man-in the-street definition cannot gain any traction in the legal pursuit of justice because there are no guidelines to determine the boundary line to ascertain what is abnormal enough to be considered "insane."

BAD OR INSANE?

The man-in-the-street's understanding of who is bad is not always much different from his understanding of who is insane. We know the psychopath who commits an atrocious crime has a serious defect and that he has no interest in what we think of as right or wrong. We learn from professionals that he has no moral compass but understands that getting caught is "wrong." We already knew that, and we understand he really has no interest in changing because he feels that what he is doing is "right." We understand that people who commit atrocious crimes are bad people, and we categorize them as insane because their actions are so far out of the norm, but we also understand converting such an individual to a normal lifestyle is essentially impossible. Attempts to modify and lessen levels of conviction and sentences on the basis of the diagnosis of psychopathy have almost uniformly met with failure, largely because, despite mental aberrations, such individuals still have free will and make use of that faculty in the decision-making that goes into the commission of their crimes. The man-in-the-street view agrees with that approach and really does not want them "off the hook."

SKYLAR DELEON

The Skylar Deleon case is an excellent example of an individual whose moral compass was without direction and who functioned without the benefit of a conscience. Thomas and Jackie Hawks advertised for sale their fifty-five-foot boat named *Well Deserved* and intended to move to Arizona to spend more time with their new grandchild. On November 9, 2004, Skylar Deleon and his pregnant wife, Jennifer, came to the boat with their nine-month-old baby. The presentation of this cute little family completely disarmed the Hawks, and they arranged for Skylar to come back on November 15 for a test run with the hope of a sale. Deleon returned with three hired thugs, and they all set out on the trial sail. Once out to sea, the group overpowered Mr. and Mrs. Hawks, forcing them to sign the transfer of title documents. They handcuffed them, tied them to the anchor, and cast them overboard. Deleon then removed money from the Hawkses' bank account in Arizona and deposited it into an account in Mexico.

All the perpetrators were arrested, and during the investigation, detectives found clues that led them to realize Deleon had also killed John Jarvi in Mexico in 2003 by slashing his throat before dumping his body in the desert. Jarvi had withdrawn money and gone to Mexico with Deleon to help him start a business. While in jail Deleon also tried to solicit the murders of his father and cousin because of possible detrimental testimonies they might give during the trial. The jury found all those involved guilty, sentencing Jennifer Deleon to two life terms and Skylar Deleon to death.

In 2009, when *ABC News* interviewed him about his crimes, Deleon discussed his feelings about what he had done and said, "I've never really felt evil. I felt more of, 'I don't care. I don't care about my life. I don't care about what happens to you.'"

That apologia really sums up the mind-set of someone who is either a psychopath or sociopath. He does not care at all about who gets hurt, including himself. In addition, he does not think there is anything wrong with him, and this latter concept contributes to the difficulty in treatment. For the individual to start on the path to cure or correction, he needs to first recognize the problem to move on to the therapeutic phase. But psychopaths and sociopaths don't recognize there is anything wrong with them. How can one progress to treatment when he doesn't think he has a problem?

GENESIS OF THE ANTISOCIAL PERSONALITY DISORDER

There are three basic concepts of why an individual might have an antisocial personality disorder: (1) genetic, (2) environmental, and (3) developmental. We can understand the genetic origin, in which a person simply has a genetic defect, and we can understand the person who is brought up in a totally antisocial environment, but the developmental origin is more poorly understood. It postulates that the brain does not develop in a normal fashion, arresting the progress of its development at certain points and resulting in an incomplete and undesirable endpoint for the brain and consequent behavioral abnormalities.

The Skylar Deleon case is a good example of the difficulty in assigning a cause to his disability. Apparently his father treated him poorly during his upbringing, but the question has to do with whether he is a product of a genetic defect obtained from his father or of poor treatment received during his development, and whether either factor contributed to developmental changes in his brain. From a very practical standpoint, it really does not matter. Perhaps someday the ability to differentiate these origins and identify their roles in a particular patient might offer therapeutic benefit, particularly if identified before the individual has gone over the top morally and legally.

Although there might well be practitioners to whom these different causative agents are important, when an affected individual commits a serious crime, our system will not excuse it. However, juries can be swayed to render less onerous verdicts.

COMPETENCE TO STAND TRIAL

Before going to trial, where the question of insanity can arise, there is the issue of competence, which refers to the defendant's ability to understand legal proceedings and effectively participate in his defense. He must be able to recall the events of the crime, discuss them, and if necessary testify on his own behalf. The issue of competence refers to the mental status of the defendant at the time of the *trial*, not at the time of the *crime*. It is most often addressed prior to trial, but it may come up at any time before, during, or even after. If the defendant is unable to understand and participate, the defense may request from the judge a competency evaluation. In some states it is obligatory for the defense to make such a request if they suspect their client is incompetent. Others, such as prosecutors or the judge may make such a request, but that is quite rare. The procedure, as outlined in California Penal Code 1368, often involves the selection of two psychiatrists or licensed psychologists, one by the defense and one by the prosecution. The two mental-health professionals evaluate the defendant and present opinions to the judge, who makes the decision on competence.

If the defendant is declared competent, the trial proceeds. If declared incompetent, he is sent to a facility, usually a state mental hospital, where he receives treatment until deemed competent and able to stand trial. The length of time for this varies, and it is conceivable that he might never gain a sufficient level of competence to come back to the courtroom. Regardless of the crime, we do not prosecute individuals with this level of incapacity.

INSANITY PLEA

INSANITY DEFENSE

Kansas, Montana, Idaho, and Utah do not allow the insanity defense. Twenty-five states use the McNaughton Rule or some variant thereof, twenty states and the District of Columbia use the Model Penal Code, and New Hampshire alone uses the Durham Rule. In addition, some states also accept the Irresistible Impulse Rule, which indicates the defendant should not be held liable, even though his crime was against the law, because he was not able to control his actions. In states that apply the McNaughton Rule, there are basically two elements: (1) the defendant did not know the nature or quality of the act, and (2) if he did, he did not know that what he was doing was wrong. For the plea to be successful in the Model Penal Code system, the defendant must be diagnosed with severe mental retardation or schizophrenia at the time of the crime, unable to appreciate that his actions were wrong or criminal, or could not control his conduct to the requirements of law. The Durham Rule is much broader and simpler, asking the question of whether the defendant's actions were the result of a mental disorder.

The elements of a lack of control or mental illness also play into the interpretation in some states. These elements all play in various degrees in different states, but there is a certain amount of continuity regardless.

THE PROCESS

The defense may enter a plea of not guilty by reason of insanity (NGI or NGRI) by itself or, more commonly, with another plea. The jury must decide on the two issues of guilt and sanity in what is called a "bifurcated trial." The prosecution presents its best case, demonstrating a crime was committed and that the defendant is guilty. The defense argues first that the defendant is not guilty, and if they are unsuccessful and the defendant is found guilty of the crime, they can then argue in a following second trial that he is innocent by virtue of insanity. If the second phase is necessary, the judge offers the jury a second and different set of instructions. Although it makes the most sense to retain the same jury, which has heard all the evidence, it is also possible for the judge to impanel a second jury. In certain cases, usually upon recommendations from either the prosecution and defense or both, the judge may waive the jury entirely and hear the case himself, but this usually occurs only in obvious cases.

If the defendant is found to be insane, he is sent to a state hospital, where treatment is carried out and further disposition decided. If he is found to be sane, he is sentenced according to the parameters of his conviction.

COURTROOM CONFUSION

Picture the courtroom scene dealing with a heinous murderer who has tortured people to death in unspeakable ways. Because of the nature of the crime, the defense questions the man's sanity. So, logically, to address the issue of insanity, experts in the field are brought in—psychiatrists and psychologists, who are really the only ones who should be able to settle this question, as it is their area of expertise.

The psychiatrist or psychologist comes in as the expert who presents his or her opinions on the basis of available information so the jury can decide whether or not the defendant is insane. The bizarre twist is that our expert cannot or at least should not use the word "insane" when discussing the individual's pathology from a psychiatric standpoint. We already see the disassociation between the science of psychosis and the legal definition of insanity, but suppose the psychiatrist brings in the topic of a certain personality disorder and then goes on to describe it in scientific terms. The jurors have heard graphic, horrible descriptions of murder and then take the psychologist's testimony, which of necessity is scientific and devoid of emotion, and look at one another as if to say, "No shit—he's got a personality disorder." They were supposed to get answers to the question of whether or not the man is insane, but instead, they hear about a personality disorder. They then tend to discount what the psychiatric professional says because his or her definitions seem so bland when compared with the horror of the crime, even though to psychiatric and psychological scientists these definitions might be quite powerful and very significant. Scientific comments do not translate well into the language used by juries.

The aforementioned is exactly what happened on the final day of the Rodney Alcala trial, when the prosecution went into descriptions of the gruesome murders and made a massive impression on the jury and everyone in the courtroom. Prosecutor Matthew Murphy referred to the report of the psychologist who discussed the defendant's personality disorders and how inconsequential those reports and opinions seemed, resulting in the psychologist's presentation essentially being dismissed by the jury—and with good reason—in large part because of the contrast between the enormity of the crimes and the *perceived* blandness of the psychologist's testimony.

DUELING PSYCHIATRISTS

The extent to which a psychiatric illness is the causative factor for the commission of a crime is often difficult to determine, sometimes even for different psychiatrists. There are occasions when two psychiatrists come to different conclusions for and against insanity, and they then present information that defends each side of the insanity question. The jury, faced with two experts who have come to opposite conclusions, must decide which of the two they should essentially ratify. This, of course, leaves the jurors somewhat confused, but they tend to side with the argument for sanity because since the experts could not prove beyond a reasonable doubt that the defendant was insane, they are instructed to find the defendant sane. In addition, they are uncomfortable with the enormity of the crime and desire to see a "just" outcome.

Renowned criminologist and Harvard professor Sheldon Glueck (1896 - 1980), in rejecting the simple criteria established by the McNaughton Rule, stated about its deficiencies, "The various versions of the McNaughton knowledge tests' scientifically abstract out of the total personality but one of its elements, the cognitive capacity which in this age of dynamic psychiatry in recognition of the influence of unconscious motivation, has been found to be not the most significant mental influence on conduct and its disorder." This challenges the courtroom finding that if at some level the defendant knew right from wrong, he is therefore sane. Solely on that basis, such findings should not be translated into the legal definition of insanity. Still, jury instructions are such that they obscure this psychiatric opinion and conform to its narrow legal definition.

There is also the element of some confusion on the part of jurors as to what would happen if the defendant were found insane. Often they are not told, so they have the feeling the defendant might be in some way "off the hook." That is not the case, however, because in the vast majority of cases, people declared insane spend at least as much time (and often more) in confinement as if they had been found sane and sentenced appropriately.

Unfortunately, psychiatric illness cannot be diagnosed by something very concrete, such as an x-ray or lab value. If it could, jury panels would understand a diagnosis of mental illness much more definitively, but listening to two opposing experts contributes to a gray area and the difficulty in convincing themselves of the presence or absence of sanity.

Again, the insanity defense, if decided by a jury, is rarely successful.

QUESTIONS ON THE DEFINITION OF INSANITY

"Insanity" rests on the notion that a mental illness is responsible for the inability to recognize that the crime is wrong. This is to be distinguished from other situations in which there is a lack of appreciation for the wrongfulness of the act, but not due to what we recognize as some form of mental illness.

Honor killing is the murder of a female relative or relatives committed by a male who feels that she or they brought the family dishonor, usually through what is considered in forbidden sexual activity. This is almost always someone from a different culture who feels killing for this type of transgression is the right thing to do. Recently a father killed his wife and three daughters in a case described as an honor killing. Obviously, killing your family for an "honorable" reason is for us—with our Western Judeo-Christian tradition—abhorrent, but for someone from another culture, this can be the "right" thing to do. We do not know how this man felt about this act. Let us suppose, for argument's sake, this was extremely painful for him but that he went through with it because, for him, it felt right. He did not think what he was doing was wrong, but because it was not due to what we define as mental illness, he was not legally insane.

The terrorist who comes to our country and kills Americans has no idea that what he is doing is wrong and indeed feels he is doing the right thing. The man in the street knows this is an act of war or treason and should be so treated, but suppose this is treated as an act of murder. How, for instance, do we treat the Fort Hood murderer, since there are those who argue his was not an act of war? If we do not treat this as an act of war or terrorism (which, of course, it was) and if he truly thinks that what he did was not wrong, he, too, is not insane.

Take the situation of the individual who refuses to pay taxes because he truly thinks the law is wrong. By definition, he does not agree with our concept of right from wrong, but he is not "insane."

Another example is the extreme antiabortion activist, who not only believes but is also consumed by the concept that abortions are murder. With his overwhelming concern for murder of the innocents, he breaks into an abortion clinic, beats up the doctor he considers a murderer, and destroys the clinic. He knows he broke the law but feels he has done what's right. Though he did not believe his actions were wrong, he, too, is not "insane."

Even in cases of people who choose to function under a different culture's set of rules, there is a strong element of culpability, because they know our laws and choose to ignore them. An individual's conception that he does not like a law and wants to function outside of it does not grant him immunity to ignore it, and the man who does so provides us with the definition of "criminal." If we allowed each individual to function under his own set of rules, chaos would ensue, and there is also the corollary concept that just punishment begets an ordered society. In all these examples, there is sufficient misuse of free will to permit our demands for responsibility and appropriate disposition.

INSANITY CONCLUSIONS

From the discussion above, we can draw the following conclusions:

* The insanity plea rarely works.
* The man-in-the-street concept of insanity relates to the enormity of the crime.

* The "dueling psychiatrists" battle usually means that the defendant will be declared sane, even though he may not be.

* Probably most who commit horrendous crimes are mentally ill. This conflicts with the desires of those who feel that the "worst" should receive the "worst" punishment (death), because the "worst" are mentally ill and need to be so treated.

* The definitions of psychiatric mental illness (psychosis) and legal mental illness (insanity) are not always in sync. The issue is not of significance in the obvious or extreme cases, but there are a large number of cases that fall into the gray area of subjectivity and individual interpretation.

* The insanity issue is an attempt to determine if the defendant's mental illness was the reason he committed this crime. The basic question all of our methods (the McNaughton Rule, Model Penal Code, or Durham Rule) is this: "Was the mental illness the reason the defendant was unable to know that his actions were wrong?" This is the correct question, but the interpretations and implementations have caused some divide between the psychiatric and legal definitions of mental illness. Psychiatrists hold that a delusional (therefore psychotic) person can plan and hide his misdeeds, but on the legal side, those activities have been used to show that the individual knew right from wrong and is therefore "sane," as in the case of Jeffry Dahmer. The result of these areas of confusion for the jurors is that the insanity defense is rarely successful and lends credence to the argument that insanity is often underdiagnosed in the courtroom.

Chapter 13

JURIES

DEATH QUALIFICATION

One of the biggest inequalities in death-penalty cases in the United States comes from the issue of death qualification of the jury. Such a jury is one in which all members who categorically object to capital punishment are removed from the panel. The jury that remains is one skewed toward convictions that lead to death sentences, since the process removes the 40 percent of Americans who are opposed to capital punishment. Jury panelists who are pro–death penalty are shown to be more likely to convict more harshly, and in murder cases, this leads to more death-penalty sentences. A capital murder case does not have a real jury of one's peers since it is hardly a cross section of America. The defendant goes into a trial situation that is stacked against him and toward the prosecution.

JURY SELECTION

The process of jury selection, or *voir dire*, becomes critical and, in some eyes, the most important step in a capital-punishment trial. In most cases attorneys for the prosecution and defense carry out their own processes of jury selection. From these issues, however, a subset of legal specialists, known as "jury consultants," has evolved, and many specialize in this area of trial exclusively.

In addition to attorneys Robert Shapiro and Johnnie Cochran, the highly respected Jo-Ellan Demitrius performed this function in the O. J. Simpson trial, and it is generally agreed her efforts were critical to the success of Simpson's defense. The biggest break the defense received early on was the decision by the prosecution to file the case in downtown Los Angeles rather than in the district where the crime occurred, which was Santa Monica. This changed the potential racial profile of the jury because Santa Monica is mostly white, while Los Angeles had more of a chance of winding up with black jurors. This is important because polling at that time showed most whites already thought O. J. Simpson was guilty and most blacks thought he was innocent. There was also a greater chance a white juror would be pro—death penalty, since blacks generally are more opposed to it. Women, too, are more often opposed to the death penalty and are more likely to be prodefense.

Largely due to the expertise of Demitrius and the efforts of Cochran, who approached the bench every time the prosecution challenged a potential black juror, suggesting the possibility of racial motivation for that maneuver, the defense obtained the jury makeup it wanted. There were ten women and two men, and the racial breakdown was nine blacks, one Hispanic, and two whites. Demographically this panel was more likely to be opposed to the death penalty, and in this particular case, the group might have sympathies for a local, famous, and charismatic athlete. There is no question the makeup of this jury and the expert way the defense undertook its selection were critical factors in the acquittal that resulted.

JUDGE GREGORY WEEKS

The issue of race and the death sentence came into the national spotlight in Fayetteville, North Carolina, on December 13, 2012, when a judge

commuted the death sentences of three separate and unrelated convicted killers to life without the possibility of parole because of evidence of
race-related jury-selection improprieties. Cumberland County Superior
Court Judge Gregory Weeks, who is African American, based his ruling
partially on the state's Racial Justice Act and relied on handwritten notes
as evidence that prosecutors made special efforts to keep blacks off the
jury pool. A slain highway patrolman's brother, Al Lowry, was outraged
at the ruling, shouted an expletive at the judge, and threatened defendant
Tilmon Golphin before deputies removed Lowry from the courtroom.

Defendants Golphin and Quintel Augustine are black, and Christina
"Queen" Walters is a Lumbee Indian. Walters was the leader of a
Fayetteville street gang convicted of killing two women and shooting
another during a misguided initiation ritual in 1998. Augustine killed
Fayetteville policeman Roy Turner Jr. in 2001, and Golphin killed North
Carolina highway patrolman Ed Lowry and Cumberland County Sheriff's
Deputy David Hathcock during a traffic stop in 1997.

In all three cases, prosecutors were trying to keep black people off
the panel, in all likelihood because they felt such jurors might be more
sympathetic toward black defendants on a racial basis and possibly, once
again, because black people are not as prone to condone a death sentence
as are whites. This ploy was the exact opposite of the one successfully
used in the O. J. Simpson case, but in all of these cases, the judge found
this impropriety significant enough to lessen the sentence from death to
LWOP. It appears to an outsider that Judge Weeks used a large modicum
of common sense when he found these irregularities for not demanding
retrials. Realizing that, despite jury-selection issues, the defendants were
guilty, he changed their sentences to more appropriate ones, ending the
cases efficiently and quickly.

This element of jury selection is another factor that can affect sentencing, not so much on the basis of the intrinsic nature of the case but on the
basis of the ploys used by attorneys on both sides of the case.

JUROR RULINGS MAKE A DIFFERENCE

In 1984 the Supreme Court ruled that the death penalty had to be reversed automatically if a potential juror was dismissed because of his written views about capital punishment. This means that if a juror makes confusing statements about his views on capital punishment, the decision for death automatically has to be reversed, regardless of whether that juror's opinions and decisions in any way led to an unfair outcome. This of course has nothing to do with the crime and its sentencing, but only with the process by which we select jurors, some of whom are confused about their opinions on capital punishment.

The use of the word "automatic" in this consideration seems to the layman to be inappropriate because it takes the work of so many people who have come to the decision for death and throws it under the bus because of contradictory and possibly confused statements of one individual. If courts think such statements are important enough to throw out a sentence arrived at by so many others, then a reconsideration is in order, to address the issue with the defense to see if they feel a retrial makes sense. If attorneys conclude that a retrial is necessary, then it will happen, despite the costs and effort. One would think they would decide against it since there was a unanimous decision by the original panel, but regardless, it appears reconsideration, rather than the more ponderous "automatic" reversal, offers a better chance for a more just outcome. When we finally eliminate the death penalty, this consideration, among others, will thankfully become moot.

This issue took on great significance in the case of John Riccardi, who killed Connie Navarro, forty-one, and her friend Susan Jory, forty-two. As an aside, Dave Navarro, Connie Navarro's son, who became a famous guitarist with Jane's Addiction and Red Hot Chili Peppers, stated that a week before his mother's death, Riccardi broke into the home, handcuffed him, and pointed a gun at him. This harrowing experience, as one might expect, caused a huge amount of emotional distress and psychological damage.

Riccardi escaped to Houston and had plastic surgery to avoid detection, and he was successful for eight years until a neighbor identified him in 1991 from a special on television's *America's Most Wanted*. Authorities promptly arrested him and sent him back to California for trial, where in 1994, a jury found him guilty and sentenced him to death. However, on July 12, 2012, courts reversed that sentence because of a juror-selection consideration. In her pretrial questionnaire, a potential juror suggested she supported capital punishment and believed it should be used more often but later answered in the affirmative to a question that she would refuse to convict Riccardi of murder because of her opposition to the death penalty.

Riccardi's death penalty was reversed because of this seemingly questionable Supreme Court decision owing to the confusion of a potential juror. Once again, this decision had nothing to do with the actual crime.

What does this mean practically? At the time of the new ruling, John Riccardi was seventy-six years old and had already spent eighteen years in prison. He will die in jail of natural causes, regardless of the sentence given to him. There is no way California will execute him, because the state does not execute anybody, and that remote possibility is even further removed from consideration because of his age. Had his sentence stood, he would have been in a private cell, had access to attorneys, and spent time on his appeals. His life in the general population will not be as comfortable, but the probability he will die of natural causes is about the same.

This is another area of capriciousness in our system of capital-punishment sentencing. Two duplicate crimes can eventuate in two different sentences on the basis of not justification but a Supreme Court ruling designed to protect a defendant from being put on death row unfairly. Such a ruling creates one more example of the unequal application of justice owing to the issues divorced from the intrinsic nature of the crime.

In two exactly duplicated crimes, Defendant A goes through the process, the system sentences him to death, and he proceeds to death row, while Defendant B goes through the same process and receives the same sentence but winds up on a different path because a juror made contradictory statements about his or her belief in capital punishment. The death sentence is reversed, and the defendant instead goes to life imprisonment. This might be an example of the naturally capricious nature of Lady Luck, ostensibly good for Defendant B and bad for Defendant A. It could also be Defendant B had better, or more thorough, attorneys. A cynic might suggest it a ploy on the part of attorneys to retain from the beginning a juror they knew could be so used or manipulated. Abolitionists might suggest this is simply another tool to fend off the death penalty.

JURORS' "DEFINITIVE" DECISIONS OFTEN NOT SO DEFINITIVE

Jurors do not take sentencing someone to death lightly. The trial is long and arduous, and members of the panel take the issue of sentencing someone to death very seriously, often to the point of severe emotional consideration. Sometimes our system rejects their decision and lets the panel know its efforts were, to a large extent, wasted. What jurors considered a death sentence is only the first of many in a long line of steps. Among many injustices and frustrations of the process, it renders meaningless what they had considered a definitive decision, one they struggled to obtain fairly. If we really have confidence in our jury system, we should trust the decisions a jury makes. Their considerations are theoretically the method by which a jury of peers decides on the fate of a defendant, but it does not always happen that way. This ruling about the confused juror is only one of many. Delays alone frustrate the theoretical power of a jury ruling, as does the appeals process, especially in places such as California, where fully 70 percent of death sentences have to be "reconsidered" in one way or another.

Eliminating the death sentence and relying on life imprisonment is not a total panacea, but it would be a giant step toward correcting a broken system—like opening a huge window and allowing a gust of fresh air to clean out a terribly stodgy and cobwebbed inefficient institution.

Chapter 14

NO ENTHUSIASM

There is a contrast in that when Americans are asked in questionnaires or in the ballot box if they are in favor of the death penalty, most answer in the affirmative, but when it comes down to taking part in any way, including even handing down the sentence, we find ourselves reluctant to proceed with great enthusiasm. This really speaks to our national ethos and for a people who have such a great respect for life.

EINSATZGRUPPEN

We are not unique in this tendency to avoid the actual performance of an execution as evidenced by a television piece National Geographic did on the German Einsatzgruppen of World War II. These were four task forces that followed the German Army in its invasion of the Soviet Union countries, such as Lithuania, Ukraine, and others. The assignment of this task force was to "purify" the populace of these newly conquered areas. This essentially came down to the job of killing those perceived to be social or political enemies found behind the lines in the Soviet Union. The hit lists for these murder squads consisted of Jews, Gypsies, the mentally challenged, and officials of the Soviet state and Communist Party. These killers were very effective in their task, killing over one million Jews and many other people.

Nazi commander Heinrich Himmler went to Minsk to observe his minions carrying out his orders, but when he got to observe the actual executions, he reportedly became fairly hysterical and shouted, "Kill them quickly! Kill them quickly!" Apparently this architect of mass killings had no real desire to participate in the actual events he had orchestrated. So this man we associate with utmost cruelty in ordering the horrible deaths of so many people did *not* want to observe the killings much less do the killing himself.

Leaders of these groups recognized another unexpected development in that the men who did carry out the Holocaust killings had very serious psychological issues themselves as a result of their gruesome activities. So here we have men whose job it was to kill, and even they did not want to participate. Narrators of the National Geographic special pointed out that in many cases the executioners grouped up in order that they might dissipate the guilt and even consider the notion that you as an individual did not really kill an innocent person or persons and that maybe the bullets of your confrères actually hit their totally defenseless marks.

Partially because of the adverse effect this method of mass murder had on the executioners and partially because the powers that be were looking for a more efficient and less costly manner of carrying out the task, they adopted the use of carbon monoxide gas chambers, which were brought to local areas by truck. Nazis were able to kill large numbers of people more expeditiously. This development heralded the more permanent, larger chambers used in concentration camps.

It appears to be a very strong human trait that we really do not want to execute anyone who is not threatening to us, even in a case of genocide, because at the time of the execution, the victims pose no threat, and most of us have a difficult time participating in such an event. Given that mass murderers of World War II found they really did not want to participate, we can understand why those to whom we assign the tasks of carrying out capital punishments do not wish to do so.

ISIS TERRORISTS AND THE UNITED STATES

Recent developments in the Middle East highlight very significant contrasts in the cultural mores of the United States and ISIS and their terrorist brethren. We have shown that we as a society do not want to execute anyone, the reason being we cannot tolerate killing a completely helpless individual even though he might have committed some hideous crimes. Members of ISIS, on the other hand, seem to relish in it, producing videos of torture and executions.

They capture an enemy pilot and set him on fire. We detain prisoners at Guantánamo Bay and flagellate ourselves because we waterboarded three to obtain valuable information. Gaining information was certainly not the purpose of those who immolated the Jordanian pilot who was shot down and captured in Syria. ISIS members have executed people for the "crimes" of being Jewish, Christian, or the all-encompassing "infidel" label. In general our country lives with acceptance of every religion, cult, and sect. ISIS members slit the throat of American journalist Daniel Pearl, who wanted to obtain an honest interview, but unfortunately for him, he came with the baggage of being Jewish as well as American.

On September 27, 2014, ISIS terrorists publicly executed a human-rights lawyer on the basis of apostasy. Her work involved seeking justice for fellow citizens in Mosul, and in her Facebook comments, she objected to the destruction of certain mosques and shrines. ISIS terrorists seized Samira Salih al-Nuaimi in her home, tried and convicted her in a Sharia court, tortured her for five days, and then killed her. I wonder how many of her captors were concerned about Samira's rights or discomfort. Obviously, they do not have much of an appeals process.

Members of ISIS crucify, bury alive, torture, behead, shoot, immolate, and drown with the goal of subjecting the victim to pain and humiliation and with an attempt to terrify the rest of the world, and their victims are guilty of no crime with the exception of their not being "them," or even of not conforming to ISIS tenets.

As a nation we are becoming more liberal toward the concept of gay marriage, and there is a level of guilt in legislation that opposes it, while ISIS handles homosexuality by tossing gay men off the roofs of tall buildings. They stone women adulterers, but in our country those stories sell magazines.

The postscript to all of this is that when we examine the various approaches to capital punishment, we come to understand and appreciate our national ethos.

THE LAST MEAL

There probably are more Americans who would rather participate in giving a condemned man his last meal than participate in his execution. It really does not resonate in a lot of ways because we usually think of a meal as a time for celebration and fellowship, and in this situation, the last meal is part of the ritual of death. Deborah Denno, a professor at Fordham University School of Law in New York, commented on this unusual sequence for prisoners as "a humane, warm gesture before we execute them—I see it as just another ambivalence we have about the death penalty." That is probably true, and it emphasizes the issue of our guilt for the negative feelings we have about taking a man's life, regardless of his crimes. Is it possible we are in some way recognizing that what we are doing is wrong and at the same time assuaging our consciences even though this meal is only a small act of kindness?

Lawrence Brewer, who was convicted in the horrendous dragging death of James Byrd Jr., ordered an enormous last meal that would have served a large number of people. As expected of a person about to die, Brewer's appetite was not up to it. He ate none of it. Senator John Whitmore, who was the chair of the Senate Criminal Justice Committee, suggested by letter to Brad Livingston, executive director of the Texas Department of Criminal Justice, that this practice is inappropriate and should be abandoned. Livingstone agreed and stated that the practice of allowing a death-row inmate the right to choose his last meal was over. Henceforth, in Texas the condemned is served the same meal as the rest of the prisoners on death row on the day of execution.

Apparently, according to William Hayes, a death-penalty historian, there are references to the condemned selecting their own last meals as far back as the ancient Greeks, Romans, and Chinese. The practice apparently has at least part of its roots in the superstition that the last meal, as selected by the condemned, contributes to warding off haunting by the executed prisoner's spirit or ghost. One wonders, however, about the effectiveness of this benevolent act when it is juxtaposed to the realities of events that could be summarized in a statement by an ancient jailer, which would go something like this: "Enjoy this, your favorite meal, but remember tomorrow we are going to torture you to death in as horrible a way as possible. Bon appétit!" Since our form of execution is so much more benign today, our current jailer's comments would be a little gentler and essentially would be like this: "Enjoy this steak, because we know it is your favorite meal, but, don't forget you are on the schedule for ten in the morning when we are going to kill you in as painless a method as possible."

It is hard to disagree that serving a giant meal to a condemned person who probably will not eat it anyway makes little sense on a practical level. Many might agree that the historical basis for this practice—that is, to avoid future haunting by the condemned person's ghost—does not have any basis in reality and certainly does not argue for us to continue this last-meal request. Still, the issue stands out as a great oxymoron as we extend a very small act of benevolence before the enormously significant act of termination.

Chapter 15

FORGIVENESS AND RECONCILIATION

One of the more powerful behind-the-scenes factors in a prosecution's attempt to seek the death penalty is the pressure applied by family and friends of the victim. This, of course, is more significant and can be a more powerful influence if the family and friends are powerful in any of a number of ways. Probably in the majority of cases, family members wish to do whatever they can to obtain a maximal punishment for their loved one's murderer, and one of the arguments death-penalty supporters use against abolitionists is to suggest they would not be opposed to sentencing a murderer to death if the victim were a member of *their* family. This probably is a very valid point, and you would think it applies essentially to everyone and that most would be in favor of the death penalty under those conditions. This argument is not new and was used against Founding Father Benjamin Rush in the late eighteenth century, when he became one of the first outspoken abolitionists at a time when that viewpoint was, at best, rare.

The desire for vengeance by family members, however, is not universal. Rachel King, in her very well-documented book *Don't Kill in Our*

Names, describes several people opposed to capital punishment for the murderers of their loved ones. Some family members even developed close relationships with and affection for the murderers, and in these cases family members were usually quite religious and applied the religious tenets of forgiveness.

KARLA FAYE TUCKER

Author King included in her book the famous case of Karla Tucker, who was sentenced to death for killing two people with a pickax. Her history indicated she had a very terrible upbringing and became involved in drugs and prostitution at a very young age. During her time in jail, she apparently gained rehabilitation, came clean, and found religion. The brother of one of her murder victims befriended her, and he even tried to have her execution stayed and her sentence converted to LWOP. His efforts met with failure, and Tucker was executed by lethal injection.

There is a very interesting quote from Joe Magliolo, the prosecutor who tried Tucker. He stated that he thought the jury's verdict of death was appropriate at the time and should be respected. But he also said, "If she is executed, I'll be a little sad but really sad for society almost more than for Karla. We allowed Karla to get into the predicament that she was in. She was a child when she started going down the wrong path and someone should've noticed that and cared enough about her to help her."

Magliolo very succinctly articulated one of the anti-death-penalty arguments that make us probe our social conscience. While some feel the perpetrator is completely and solely responsible for all of his activities, there is a strong opinion that most people who commit crimes are the product of society's unfairness and hence we hold some blame. The vast majority of people who commit heinous acts did not have warm and fuzzy relationships as they grew up, and by and large, a childhood of abuse is typical. Prosecutor Magliolo defined a large part of the problem because he realized someone should have helped at a time when it might have made a difference, and that is the case with so many people whose lives lead them in the direction Karla Faye Tucker's did.

The penalty phases of capital murder trials usually document that people like her have been dealt a very unfair hand, and defending attorneys argue that these factors should influence our decision on whether or not to impose the death sentence. The majority of us agree that people who commit murder should not be free, but the death sentence is inappropriate and beneath us as the benevolent nation we are.

COLLECTIVE GUILT

The concept of collective guilt places universal blame for an individual's criminal activity because of the bad hand he was given. Largely because we as individuals do not feel any personal responsibility since we had no direct contact with or even knowledge of the individual and his negative experiences, trying to blame a criminal's activities on "us" or on "society" does not fly well with the vast majority of the American population. People who commit heinous crimes, despite all their negative baggage, still have free will and are, therefore, responsible for their own actions. Yet, the national recognition that there are inequities for opportunity for certain people and that we have not been able to correct these imbalances gives us pause and some compassion for these defendants. Short of "everyone" taking blame for an individual's criminal behavior, we still consider, when sentencing, the inequities of opportunity.

CLARENCE DARROW

In the famous 1924 "Trial of the Century," attorney Clarence Darrow finished with a twelve-hour summary that was essentially a speech against the death penalty. He already had Nathan Leopold and Richard Loeb plead guilty for the murder of fourteen-year-old Bobby Franks and so was not trying to proclaim their innocence but to argue against sentencing them to death. He tried to shift the blame from the killers onto factors over which they had no control, such as their genetics, upbringings, and childhood experiences. Darrow expressed it like this: "Nature is strong and pitiless, and we are her victims. Your Honor, how can anyone seriously say that for what nature has done, for what life has done, and for training as done to them, you should hang these boys?" He thus concluded that Leopold and Loeb were driven to their actions by other factors, and in this argument, he turned at least some of the blame for the crime away from them personally. Meyer Levin's novel *Compulsion* echoes these sentiments in regard to a murderer's personal guilt.

Darrow achieved his goal as both men were sentenced to life plus ninety-nine years. A fellow prisoner killed Loeb in 1936, and Leopold was paroled in 1958 and died in freedom in 1971.

BETTY WARREN

On Veterans Day 2003, Curtis James Hill and his accomplice, John McKinney, savagely assaulted ex–World War II paratrooper Cecil Warren, seventy-seven, during the course of a robbery of some garden tools. Mr. Warren lapsed into a coma from which he never recovered and died four years later. Hill was still serving time for the beating when Warren passed away. Orange County, California, prosecutors filed murder charges against Hill, and Huntington Beach Superior Court Judge Thomas Goethals sentenced him to the maximum punishment of life without possibility of parole.

At the time of sentencing, Betty Warren, Cecil's wife of sixty years, wept for the defendant. She told reporters, "It may sound crazy to cry for him, but I feel sorry daily that he ruined his life just because he was drinking and it is such a stupid waste."

Here we have another case of a victim's family member showing genuine sympathy for the criminal and reacting in a way many probably would not have. It is obvious Mrs. Warren did not want to see Hill sentenced to death, and judging from her reaction, she probably has hopes for his repentance and some form of conversion and rehabilitation while he is incarcerated.

MARK COSMAN

On June 1, 1991, Paul Crowder shot Berlyn Cosman to death as she lay sleeping in her hotel bed on her prom night. He had attended the prom, even though he was not a student at the school and had no date. He arrived at the dance with alcohol and two guns, threatening several people during the night. He wanted to spend the night in Berlyn's room, but she refused and went to bed. Crowder came back in the early morning and shot her to death as she slept. He was tried, convicted, and sentenced to fifteen years to life in prison.

In 2010, a parole board found Crowder suitable for release and recommended it, but then-governor Arnold Schwarzenegger overruled the decision. A superior court judge countermanded the reversal and recommended the case be sent back to the governor's office for further review. This time Governor Brown agreed with Schwarzenegger and also revoked the 2010 parole grant. In 2011 a different parole board also found Crowder suitable for release, but Governor Brown again denied parole. In a very unusual turn of events, Crowder now enjoys support for his release from what most would consider an unexpected source—Berlyn's father, Mark Cosman. To get some understanding of why his daughter had to die, Cosman corresponded with her killer. Over the years, Cosman developed a changing opinion of Crowder as a person who was no longer the wild young man who had taken Berlyn's life years before. Though Cosman had opposed Crowder's release in the past, on the latest occasion, he wrote a letter in support of release, and apparently this had a significant influence on the board's decision to recommend release. Cosman made this statement: "I found no refuge in maintaining hatred or seeking his continuous suffering."

This case has many interesting aspects that teach many lessons. There are two opposing positions on the release. On the one hand, the parole board and the victim's father feel he should be released. On the other hand, the victim's sister and mother continue to oppose it, as does the Orange County district attorney. Two governors, as mentioned, opposed his release as well. The question that remains is this: Is Crowder the same man who committed the murder, or has he matured or rehabilitated enough that he should be released from prison?

First, most might think we would never, under any circumstances, come to the aid of someone who killed a daughter, but here we have a case in which a father did exactly that.

QISAS

The act of forgiving a loved one's murderer is not limited to examples in the United States, as it is a growing trend in Iran. On April 15, 2014, Samereh Alinejad spared the life of her son's killer moments before his hanging was to take place. There is a tradition in many Muslim countries for "an eye for an eye" provision called *qisas*, wherein families of murder victims are the final arbiters over whether killers live or die. The murderer was standing on a chair with a noose around his neck, and Mrs. Alinejad had the opportunity to kick the chair out from under him in revenge for the death of her son. Instead she slapped him in the face and removed the rope from his neck. Some in the crowd applauded, and others were stunned. The result for this mother was relief and peace. Her statement was this: "I became peaceful. I do not think about revenge anymore."

This act of mercy is often accompanied by blood-money payments to victims' families of at least $35,000 to spare the life of the killer. In this case, money had been raised for the killer, but the family refused to take it and instead contributed it to local charities.

Mrs. Alinejad's statement emphasizes the relief she felt from the burden of revenge she had carried with her. Instead of death, the killer faces the rest of his twelve-year sentence in prison. It is of interest that foreign cultures are trending toward punishment other than execution, on the basis of the magnanimous acts of forgiveness by the victims' families.

BOSTONIANS' DESIRES FOR THE BOMBER

A recent poll conducted by Boston's NPR news station WBUR indicates that 62 percent of Boston voters would prefer Dzhokhar Tsarnaev, who is the surviving Boston Marathon bomber, receive a sentence of LWOP, while only 27 percent feel he should receive the death sentence. Massachusetts outlawed the death penalty in 1984, but this case is exclusively under federal jurisdiction due to the nature of the crimes. The two elements that place him in federal court involve the use of a weapon of mass destruction resulting in death and conspiracy to bomb a public place resulting in death. The state still has the authority to try Tsarnaev in state court after the federal court completes its trial.

While it is clear federal prosecutors are simply following the law and seeking the death penalty because it is one of the possible sentences in cases such as this, it is of interest that the people most involved in this case—victims' families and the people of Boston—do not want the death penalty for Tsarnaev.

TSARNAEV

We have decided to deal with the Boston mass murderer with the ultimate punishment, death, because we feel his actions were so egregious that only this maximal solution is sufficient to equate to the horror of the crime—and so we obtain some semblance of *lex talionis*, "an eye for an eye." The problem is that this "solution" misses the mark in so many ways. First of all Tsarnaev's execution might never happen, and if it does, it will be so far down the timeline from when the crime was committed that whatever effectiveness it might have will be, for the most part, lost. He will be an old, or at least older, man—no longer the brash young terrorist who has been presented as misguided and under the influence of his dominating older brother.

Finally, we should consider the wishes of the victims and their families, and we have not heard an overwhelming desire for the death penalty from them. In fact we have heard exactly the opposite from the Richard family, who suffered as much as anyone at the hands of the murderous brothers during the Boston Marathon mayhem. Their eight-year-old son died, and their daughter lost a leg. Mrs. Richard lost an eye, and Mr. Richard suffered burns to his legs and a ruptured eardrum, which left him with significant hearing loss and tinnitus. They report that their intense emotional suffering continues unabated. However, they understand how the death penalty works and does not work, and how much better it would be to remove Tsarnaev from society quickly and permanently into a maximum security cell where he should remain for the rest of his life, whereas a death sentence "could bring years of appeals and prolong reliving the most painful day of our lives."

"We are in favor of and would support the department of justice in taking the death penalty off the table in exchange for the defendant spending the rest of his life in prison without any possibility of release and waving all rights to appeal," they added. In another statement, they commented, "As long as the defendant is in the spotlight, we have no choice but to live a story told on his terms, not ours."

It remains something of a mystery that our jurisprudence system that is supposed to work for us ignores the desires of those who are most affected and the voice of common sense, instead plodding along a well-worn path that goes on pointlessly without end.

These opposing approaches to sentencing bring up an interesting issue in that it appears the people want one thing, but "government" wants something else. Who or what *is* the government? Aren't "We the People" the government? Shouldn't the agencies that work *for* us reflect our wishes, or are we dealing with a set of rules and regulations overseen by some faceless monolith that rules *over* us rather than the other way around?

LAURA WEBB

On October 12, 2011, a man walked into a Seal Beach, California, beauty salon and shot eight people to death in an act of senseless violence, and Bethany Webb's sister, Laura, was among those who lost their lives that day. Less than a year later, on September 25, 2012, Bethany had already been through enough with our capital-punishment system to become a supporter of Prop 34, which aimed to eliminate the death sentence in California. She succinctly described so many of the major weaknesses of the system that she has recently discovered the "obscene amount of money" it costs, rarity of actual execution, prolonged appeals process, improved lifestyle on death row, possibility of executing the innocent, and terrible burden imposed on families of victims.

She described the understandable pain she and her family have suffered because of their loss, and she knew the decision to seek the death penalty would only make it worse. The family has had to go to court several times to see Laura's killer, and Bethany knows this will go on for decades during the appeals processes and that their wounds will be continually reopened. She voices her support for LWOP, because it would save her and her family years of pain, and they would have the satisfaction of knowing the killer was in custody for the rest of his life, and they would not have continual reminders of the tragedy.

AZIM KHAMISA

Tariq Khamisa was doing all the right things. He was twenty years old, a journalism major at San Diego State University, engaged to be married, and was self-reliant enough to take on a job delivering pizza twice a week to cover some of his own expenses. He loved travel and photography, and his goal was to work for National Geographic.

Tony Hicks's mother was fifteen when she gave birth to him, and his father, who was a gang member, had never been in the boy's life. He grew up in South Central Los Angeles and watched as another gang member shot his favorite cousin to death. A family member's girlfriend sexually abused him when he was nine. His grandfather, Ples Felix, a city employee and former military man, took him in when he was a teenager. Hicks rebelled against his grandfather's rules and curfew requirements and ran away from home, taking up with three other gang members.

The paths of these two individuals, Khamisa and Hicks, crossed just three days after Hicks left home. He and his friends partied, got high on marijuana, and hatched a plan that would settle both their gastronomic and economic needs for the moment. They called for a pizza with the intent of robbing the delivery man. When Tariq Khamisa showed up at the bogus address with the delivery, Hicks brandished a 9-mm handgun and demanded both money and pizza. Tariq refused and Hicks, egged on by his companions, shot him to death.

When the news of his son's death reached Tariq's father, Azim, his initial reaction was disbelief until reality set in. He said, "And then it felt like an atom bomb went off in my heart." His next reaction was not one of hatred and revenge but what he described as an out-of-body experience and the "loving embrace of God." A Sufi Muslim, Azim Khamisa believes he woke up with the following words in his head: "There were victims at both ends of the gun." At that point he had already forgiven Tony Hicks and had no hatred or bitterness in his heart.

Within nine months of his son's death, Azim started the Tariq Khamisa Foundation, and his project partner was Tony Hicks's grandfather, Felix. The foundation provides mentorship and other resources for at-risk children. The two men travel, giving talks about nonviolence, forgiveness, and restorative justice. Azim gave up his career as a successful investment banker the same year his son died and devoted himself to his foundation and giving talks worldwide.

Hicks pleaded guilty, the first one to be tried as an adult under state law that lowered the age at which one can be so considered from sixteen to fourteen. On June 19, 1996, at age fifteen, Hicks was sentenced to twenty-five years to life. Khamisa did not attend the hearing, but delivered a message through the prosecutor that his fondest wish was for Tony to be transformed into a productive man and work for the foundation.

Hicks did not have a smooth ride in prison, earning an additional ten years to his sentence for plotting to attack a jailer. He was transferred to Pelican Bay State Prison, where he spent most of his time in solitary confinement. That move proved to be transformative in that he studied there and earned his high-school degree and took college courses with the goal of becoming a child psychologist.

Four years after the sentencing, Khamisa and Felix went to Folsom State Prison and met with Tony. Azim surprised his son's killer with a bear hug and did not perceive him as a killer. Khamisa has written four books, and Tony Hicks wrote the foreword for his second book, titled *From Forgiveness to Fulfillment*. Khamisa has received numerous awards for his work and has drawn praise from world leaders, including former US president Bill Clinton and the Dalai Lama. Renate Johnson, director of the nonprofit Community Service Program's victim assistance services, looks to Khamisa's message as a source of empowerment for everyone and as a positive method for reconstructing victims' lives.

Tony Hicks is due for parole in 2016, and Azim Khamisa will be there to support his release.

PATRICIA WENSKUNAS

Patricia Wenskunas is a woman who grew from a position of fear and frailty to one of power, owing, to a large extent, to how she handled her feelings of hatred toward a trusted individual who sexually assaulted her, tried to smother her with Saran wrap, and threatened the life of her twelve-year-old son. The additional insult came when he was sentenced to a mere 120 days in jail for the crimes of assault with a deadly weapon and making criminal threats. Other charges, such as attempted murder, were thrown out.

The slap-on-the-wrist conviction and sentencing of her attacker was really a second assault, and it drove Wenskunas deeper into emotional nadir. The scene raises the hair on the back of your neck. Here is a woman who was savagely attacked and who's being was massively affronted, and "We the People," through our judicial system, are supposed to set things right and mete out justice for the criminal, and in so doing, validate for the victim her value as an individual. Instead, a sentence akin to what one would get for a DUI (driving under the influence) was handed down, and in the course of these actions, the message to the victim was essentially, "You are not very important, even though this crime was so devastating to you."

Subsequent to the attack, Wenskunas was, as one would expect, devastated and barely functional. She then heard her son express the need to have his mother back to take care of him, and that snapped her out of her doldrums and into action. In 2003 she founded Crime Survivors, an organization that offers support services for crime victims. In 2011 she founded OC Crime Stoppers, a nonprofit tip line that works with countywide law-enforcement agencies to get leads and information from the public.

These programs helped her heal and begin to forgive her attacker. Immediately after her attack, she hated her attacker, wished him ill, and fantasized about punching him. She came to realize, however, that those feelings dominated her life, thoughts, and actions, and so still controlled her. She knew she had to get over those dominant thoughts and somehow find forgiveness for her attacker and secondarily for the justice system that was less than, well, just. Devoting herself to the community was a massive help, and it took several years for her to finally get to the point where she no longer hated. The intense feeling she had toward her attacker has diminished, as he is nothing to her and therefore has no control over her whatsoever. She said, "I was a shell of the person before, but today he's a shell of a person to me, and to me, this is forgiveness."

This is one woman's story of her journey, but it is a powerful one that requires the strength and understanding that comes from meaningful introspection. Through community activities and organizations, Patricia helps many others through the same steps toward an unencumbered life.

FORGIVENESS THROUGH MITIGATION

When, in the penalty phase of a murder case, we consider mitigating circumstances such as a flawed upbringing, we introduce an element through which we feel justified in minimizing sentences. This factor, which has nothing to do with the victim or circumstances of the murder, is a form of forgiveness by our system in which we are, in essence, saying to the perpetrator, "We are sorry you have had such a bad experience, and we understand that because of it you are damaged and not as responsible as someone who has not undergone what you have. Therefore, we will lessen your sentence and not send you to death row but give you a diminished sentence." This form of forgiveness comes down to a reality in which we actually absolve the defendant from *some* guilt for the crime.

This "social injustice" leads us to acknowledge that any of us might have gone down the same path had we been faced with the same obstacles. Is this another example of "there but for the grace of God"?

The problem here is that essentially everyone who could commit a heinous murder has had bad experiences leading to a flawed condition that made it possible for him to commit an act a "normal" individual could not. The continuous problem for our jurisprudence professionals is to decide where to draw a line between the goals of punishment for crime, requirements based on personal responsibility and free will, and sympathy for the pathology of a criminal.

There are people on both sides of this discussion, but it is essential to understand or at least admit that this form of "forgiveness" exists.

FORGIVENESS AND RECONCILIATION

There are different instances in which people have been able to forgive or at least come to some form of reconciliation within their own minds and, in so doing, minimize the importance of the criminal and the criminal act to the point that they can get on with their lives. Here is a quick review of some of the moving acts of forgiveness featured in this chapter.

The brother of one of Karla Faye Tucker's victims befriended her as he admired her efforts to become a better person, and this was all the more impressive in the context of her scarred upbringing and early life. Prosecutor Joe Magliolo later found sympathy for her because of the terrible obstacles placed in her path and the fact that no part of society reached out to help.

Clarence Darrow argued for leniency for Leopold and Loeb because he felt their DNA and life experiences drove them to the crime.

Betty Warren forgave her husband's killer because of his circumstance of being under the influence of alcohol at the time of the crime, a factor that contributed to the waste of his life.

Mark Cosman forgave his daughter's killer because he realized he found no solace in continued hatred.

In sparing her son's killer, Mrs. Alinejad found relief from the burden of revenge.

Patricia Wenskunas found her form of forgiveness for her attacker, and secondarily to the system that failed her, by overcoming those emotions to emancipate herself.

Bethany Webb talked about how our death-penalty system contributed to the fame of the murderer, as well as the pain of the families, and that the better approach was to remove the murderer quickly and efficiently out of the limelight and into life imprisonment, allowing families to attain some form of reconciliation.

The Richards family wants their son's killer to avoid the death sentence because they understand years of appeals would cause them to relive repeatedly the most painful days of their lives, a condition that would be alleviated by a life sentence without the possibility of parole or appeal.

Looking through and beyond his own pain, Azim Khamisa immediately understood that, to commit such an act, the shooter had to be flawed and also a victim. This recognition led him to forgive Tony Hicks and become a significant source of support for him.

Chapter 16

DETERRENCE

M ost experts agree that the current death penalty has essentially no effect on deterring other crimes, and there are some who feel it might actually *increase* the murder rate because of what some people describe as the brutalizing effect of execution. Even many who believe in the potential for a deterrent effect hold that the malfunction of our current system makes it ineffective on a practical level.

During his statement to the New Jersey Death Penalty Study Commission on October 24, 2006, practicing attorney Kent Scheidegger expressed this very opinion. He stated that most of the studies in peer-reviewed journals indicate the death penalty has a deterrent effect and saves innocent lives if it is actually enforced. He cited as an example the state of Delaware, which in 2004 had the greatest drop in homicides since the moratorium was lifted, but it also had the most effective capital-punishment system of any state by a wide margin. He indicated, however, that New Jersey did not have an effective death penalty, largely because the court of last resort was determined to block it and even go to some lengths to twist the law to accomplish that goal.

It appears that even those who see the potential for a deterrent effect realize the flawed manner in which capital punishment is used today destroys that possibility.

NATIONAL RESEARCH COUNCIL

In the early days of the death penalty in the United States, a good part of the lengthy ceremony was to instill in the minds of the many attendees that they should be turned away from similar crimes, stimulating a sense of personal morality or fear. The condemned was supposed to go on about his repentance and the errors of his ways, and the preacher was supposed to do the "fire and brimstone" approach, all of those efforts designed to influence the assemblage.

Early on, very few challenged the concept that the death penalty and execution were deterrents, and protagonists still believe it is effective. Some even calculated the numbers of lives saved by each execution, and of course, abolitionist thinkers have challenged these figures. Furthermore, there are those who hold that the death penalty and execution *increase* chances of future murders through the "brutalization" effect on society.

The debate has become somewhat confused because of this diversity of opinion, and in many cases, its intensity. To make some sense of this complexity of data, the National Research Council's Committee on Deterrence and the Death Penalty, chaired by Daniel S. Nagin of Carnegie Mellon University, focuses on, among other things, the deterrent effects of diverse penalties and criminal behavior, through the development of statistical methods for analysis of these issues. The committee is comprised of scientists and professionals of various disciplines, and their report is generally considered the definitive work on the subject. Since this analysis is of such importance, I quote these conclusions:

> CONCLUSION AND RECOMMENDATION: The committee concludes that research to date on the effect of capital punishment on homicide is not informative about whether capital punishment decreases, increases, or has no effect on homicide rates. Therefore, the committee recommends that the studies not be used to inform deliberations requiring judgments about the effect of the death penalty on homicide. Consequently, claims that research demonstrates

that capital punishment decreases or increases the homicide rate by a specified amount or has no effect on the homicide rate should not influence policy judgments about capital punishment.

The committee reviewed essentially all the significant studies on the deterrence issue and concluded that the available body of information provided no evidence that the death penalty affected homicide rates. Out of challenges to the current body of information, they brought up two issues that seemed most significant. If a study is to show the death penalty was a deterrent, we would have to hear from people who are actually deterred from committing a crime because of the death penalty and the possibility of their being sentenced to it. Obtaining such information is, of course, not possible. The studies we have rely on statistics and are often accompanied by opinions of the authors, when really the only meaningful opinions would be from those who turned away from crime because of the death penalty. If it were possible to obtain numbers of the people who were dissuaded from crime, we could know the answer to the question of how many lives would have been saved. Failing that, we have to rely on statistics and opinions of professionals in the area.

The other significant factor the council considered is the effect noncapital sentences and punishments have on deterrence. There are scenarios in which capital and noncapital approaches interact. At one extreme, the jurisdiction spends so much of its energies on capital cases that it has little left for noncapital cases. At the other extreme is the jurisdiction that concentrates heavily on noncapital cases and as a result has minimal resources for capital cases. Obviously there can be many variations of these themes, including possibilities that a jurisdiction can be heavy or weak on both. The problem comes down to the fact that there is little information about the interaction of capital versus noncapital approaches, and this deficiency detracts from information we have about the effectiveness of deterrence.

The study also took a hard look at the infrequency with which cases actually moved on to capital convictions, finding the rate of capital convictions extremely low. When evaluating cases that could be charged as capital offenses, they found the numbers that were actually so charged were also extremely low. Furthermore, the numbers of cases that eventually move on to a sentence of death, to say nothing of the numbers that move on to execution, are minute when compared with the homicide rate.

As an example, the study cites P. J. Cook who, in 2009, reporting on the North Carolina figures for the years 2005 and 2006, found 26.5 percent of murder arraignments—which numbered 1,034—were charged as capital offenses, and of that number so prosecuted, only four eventuated in death sentences. His point is that capital cases very rarely result in a death sentence.

The reasons are many. A few cases are dismissed or found not guilty at trial. Plea bargaining to a noncapital sentence accounts for more, and others are found guilty of lesser offenses, such as manslaughter or second-degree murder. Finally, jurors often do not recommend death even for those found guilty of first-degree murder.

Most inferences regarding deterrence come from data involving numbers of homicides versus numbers of death sentences or executions, and these ratios are very small even in high-use states. The problem is studies that compare high- and low-use states base conclusions on numbers so small relative to the total number of homicides that there is limited conclusive evidence in either direction.

HOMICIDE RATES

The chart in figure 4, taken from statistics from DPIC, shows comparisons among states with and without the death penalty in regard to homicide rates per one hundred thousand.

Murder Rates: Death Penalty vs Non-Death Penalty States

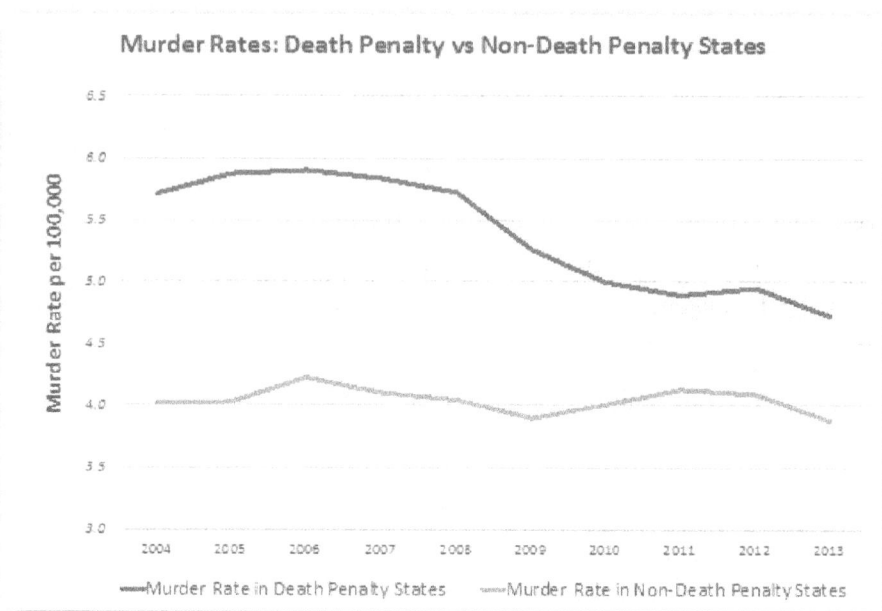

Figure 4. Comparisons of murder rates among states with and without the death penalty.

These numbers would indicate that non-death-penalty states have lower homicide rates than death-penalty states, and while these figures alone do not prove it to be ineffective, they certainly do not show anything that could support the deterrent effect of the death penalty.

RADELET AND LACOCK

In a pivotal article in the *Journal of Criminal Law and Criminology* in spring 2009, Michael L. Radelet and Tracy L. Lacock present information on the trends of thinking in the United States, showing that both experts and laypeople are coming to the conclusion that the death penalty is not a deterrent. The article cites a 1985 Gallup poll that shows 62 percent of members of the general public believed the death penalty was a deterrent to murder and that, in a repeat poll in 2006, that number fell to 34 percent. On the other side of the coin, 31 percent felt the death penalty was not a deterrent in 1985, and that number doubled to 62 percent in 2004. In addition, it cited a 1995 survey that showed two-thirds of four hundred police chiefs and county sheriffs did not believe the death penalty significantly lowered numbers of murders.

The article's authors also reported on a panel set up by the National Academy of Sciences and chaired by Nobel Laureate Lawrence R. Klein. The panel's charge was to evaluate studies that pointed to the deterrent effect of the death penalty. The conclusion was that "the available studies provide no useful evidence on the deterrent effect of capital punishment" and "research on the deterrent effects of capital sanctions is not likely to provide results that will or should have much influence on policy makers."

NULL HYPOTHESIS

In discussing the frailties of many of the studies evaluated, the article addresses scientific methods and issues such as the null hypothesis, which is the classic starting point of one common method of proof. With a null hypothesis, we start out with the theory that there is no relationship between two phenomena, in this case the death penalty and the deterrence of homicides.

Suppose a scientist for a pharmaceutical company is trying to determine if a certain drug has a beneficial effect on, say, lowering blood pressure. He starts with the hypothesis that there is no relationship between the drug and the lowering of blood pressure. To defend the product, the company scientist must disprove the null hypothesis and demonstrate that the drug is effective in lowering blood pressure.

This scientific method demands we start with the null hypothesis that there is no relationship between the death penalty and deterrence. To establish that the death penalty is a deterrent, we have to show the relationship and refute the null hypothesis. The burden of proof is on the shoulders of those who proclaim the death penalty is a deterrent, and thus far that has not been done with any conviction. We cannot conclude that there is a deterrent effect, at least by this method, which is one of the bulwarks of scientific investigation.

MYRON LOVE

Myron Love, a judge in Harris County, Texas, which at that time was responsible for about 10 percent of all the nation's executions, admitted, back in 1976, that "[w]e are not getting what I think we should be wanting and that is to deter crime...In fact, the result is the opposite. We're having more violence, more crime." It is of interest that, even at a time when there was little counterbalance to the concept of the deterrent value of the death penalty, a respected judge expressed his opinion that the aggressive use of execution did not affect the violent crime rate.

DETERRENCE CONCLUSIONS

What can we conclude about the effectiveness of the death penalty as a deterrent?

There are two similar trends in regard to the use of the death penalty and the murder rate, in that both are decreasing. There are, of course, multiple reasons for these statistics, but they certainly do not support the argument for the effectiveness of the death penalty.

Can there be an argument for a positive relationship in defense of the concept of "brutalization," which holds that capital punishment causes an increase in violent crime and murder rates? Many great thinkers, including early abolitionist Cesare Beccaria, felt capital punishment had a negative effect on the mores of the society. Do these trends support that argument for the United States in the same way people argue about the negative effect on society of violence in the media and video games? The argument is that the more commonplace the presence of violence and its representations is, the less repulsed by it the people are. Although this makes an interesting arrow in the abolitionist quiver, it is extremely difficult to prove and, at this point, must remain on the level of philosophical discussion.

Two studies from the National Academy of Sciences and the National Research Council failed to show any causal relationship between the death penalty and murder rate in the studies reviewed. They indicated that, lacking such proof, no recommendations for using the death penalty could be made.

Polls indicate that Americans, both professional and laical, are coming to understand the foibles of the system and conclude that there is no deterrent effect. The most important trend is the thinking of some death-penalty supporters who offer very powerful arguments but realize the system is so broken and deficient that it must go.

Professional evaluation of the mind-set of the murderer at the time of the crime indicates there is essentially no thought to apprehension and punishment and that the argument for the deterrent effect of the death penalty on the murderer at the time of the commission of the crime is without merit.

Dr. Nagin's committee pointed out that the most meaningful study that could defend the death penalty would be one that showed a large number of people were dissuaded from committing murder by their consideration of the death penalty. If we could document such a group, an argument for maintaining the system could exist, but the statistics thus far do not support such a concept, and the possibility of producing such a study is fairly nonexistent.

DETERRENCE SUMMARY

Let us summarize some facts about deterrence:

1. National think tanks do not support it.
2. Professionals do not believe in it.
3. Laypeople do not believe in it.
4. Statistics do not support its deterrent effects.
5. Consideration of the mind-set of the murderer at the time of the crime leads to a conclusion that he is far from thinking about consequences.
6. Support for the concept that the death penalty increases the murder rate, possibly through a brutalization effect on society, is intriguing and debatable but not provable at this juncture.

Chapter 17

EXTRADITION

EXTRADITION AND INDIVIDUAL RIGHTS

Prior to the relatively recent treaties on extradition, two significant elements were in play. One was the fact that an individual who could escape a state or nation in which he had committed his crimes had an excellent chance of not being caught because there was no obligation by the nation he had moved to return him to the country where the offense was committed. The other factor is that a more powerful state could overwhelm a weaker one and do whatever it wanted to return an offender.

Part of the purpose of the United Nations Charter was to assure sovereign equality of states and to renounce the use of force in international relationships so stronger nations could not simply use their power over a weaker one. This promulgated the concept of equality for all involved nations whether they are weak or strong. Extradition agreements were constructed under the concepts of sovereignty and equality so no sovereign nation could exercise its power in another nation unless permitted to do so by the second state.

The nature of the crimes for which a nation requests extradition from another country varies depending on how important the issue is to the requesting nation. Petty criminals usually escape extradition because the efforts for the process are quite great and too impractical for the minimal beneficial result. There is some variation for type of crimes a nation might request extradition, on the basis of the degree of seriousness attached to the crime. A theistic state might consider a certain religious affront a very serious matter, while a secular one might not.

The hallowed documents that arose from the French and American Revolutions established the concept that power resided in the individual and that this emanated from the Creator, and extradition treaties were established to provide protection for individuals. The result is that countries, even with extradition treaties, are not absolutely obligated to extradite an individual due to a variety of issues.

If there is the feeling the requesting country violates suspected norms of human-rights obligations, the requested country may refuse to extradite to protect the fugitive's rights. The requested country may also refuse to extradite if it does not hold as criminal the act for which the extradition is requested.

The United States has entered into multilateral and bilateral treaties with over a hundred countries, and these agreements cover a wide variety of international issues, including extradition. Many of these countries do not practice capital punishment and can refuse to extradite a murderer if there is a chance we will execute him. The extradition process is complex enough, and adding the issue of capital punishment makes it that much more difficult. Adamant stands from many of these nations force us into sentences for perpetrators of less than death. The problem is two murderers can commit the same type of crime and face different punishments on the basis of not the crime but their actions after it, specifically whether they travel to and are apprehended in a country that will not extradite them if there is the possibility of their receiving the death penalty. Our maintenance of the death penalty leads us to mollify sentences on the basis of not our parameters and prerogatives but the principles of another nation.

The perfect example is Mexico, which does not have capital punishment, and even though it has an extradition treaty with the United States, it will not cooperate if there is a possibility we would seek a death penalty. So an individual who commits a murder in the United States and is apprehended in Mexico by Mexican authorities will not face the death sentence, while the same man, if caught in the United States, might have that possibility. This is another factor that can produce a different sentence for the same crime, on the basis of not the act itself but, in this case, where the criminal is apprehended.

CESAR LAUREAN

A typical example of how our extradition system works to change how we pursue murder cases is that of Cesar Laurean, who fled to Mexico after committing murder and in so doing prevented any notion of a death sentence even though prosecutors might have wanted to do so.

On August 24, 2010, a North Carolina jury convicted Laurean of first-degree murder in the killing of fellow marine Maria Lauterbach, who had claimed Laurean raped her. In January 2008, Laurean killed Lauterbach with a blow to the head with a crowbar and slit her throat posthumously. He buried her and her eight-month-old fetus in his backyard after attempting to set the bodies on fire.

Laurean made a run for it and escaped to Mexico, where he went into hiding. The case was widely discussed by the media, including the *Nancy Grace* show, *America's Most Wanted*, *On the Record*, and Geraldo Rivera's show on Fox News. Mexican authorities captured Laurean in the town of Tacambaro in the state of Michoacán, and they extradited him back to North Carolina after receiving assurances that he would not face the death penalty. Though the state might have opted to treat this as a capital-punishment case, it was unable to do so because of the extradition requirements. Had American authorities captured him in the United States, the likelihood of seeking the death penalty was at least present.

In the end, our diplomatic relations with Mexico, not our justice system, made the decision of how this case was ultimately prosecuted.

MEXICO AND PAROLE

In October 2001, Mexico's Supreme Court ruled life in prison or any term without guaranteed paroles was "cruel and unusual" punishment. They were denying extradition to the United States if there was not a guarantee there would be some form of parole in the American sentence. Up to that point, American prosecutors cooperated with the no-death-sentence portion of the extradition requirements as long as they could substitute LWOP, but they found the further restrictions so difficult that they often refused to comply with the extradition process if there was the requirement that parole would have to be part of the sentence.

A frustrating example of how the system sometimes worked was the case in Santa Cruz, California, of Miguel Loza who, in 2003, slashed the throat of a seventeen-year-old woman and raped her teenage friend. The murder victim, whose throat was slashed, lost consciousness, went into a vegetative state from which she never recovered, and died six months later.

Loza fled to Mexico, where American authorities found him in a Mexico City jail. Mexican authorities, following the Supreme Court ruling, refused to extradite him unless we guaranteed an element of parole in his sentencing. Prosecutors refused to cooperate on the basis that they did not want a man who was a killer, rapist, and child molester ever to walk free. They left themselves with the fragile solution that we would arrest him if he came back to the United States and then pursue the case in the American court system. Santa Cruz County Chief Deputy District Attorney Ariadne Symons admitted, "It's not much of a plan, but it's all we've got. I think there's a good chance he'll come back, because his family's here."

Fortunately, this unacceptable situation came to an end when, in the face of increased violence throughout Mexico, in November 2005, the Mexican Supreme Court, in a six-to-five decision, overrode the earlier decision and allowed life sentences without parole in their extradition agreements with other countries. In the wake of that decision, they allowed extradition even if there was the possibility of LWOP. However, they still refuse to extradite if there is the possibility of a death sentence.

JULIAN ASSANGE

Julian Assange has two possible legal problems. One is in Sweden, where he faces charges of sexual misconduct involving two women, and the other is the possibility of prosecution in the United States for his involvement in the publishing of classified documents on his WikiLeaks website in 2010. He sought and obtained asylum from Ecuador because of the possibility that if he were extradited to Sweden to face charges, the Swedes might secondarily extradite him to the United States to face espionage charges. If extradited to the United States, he might face the death penalty. There is no problem with his extradition to Sweden because it does not have capital punishment.

Assange moved into the Ecuador embassy in London and has not left there for over two years. The British has strongly condemned this arrangement and even threatened to remove him forcibly on the basis of the contention that they have the right to do so according to Article 41 of the 1961 Vienna convention, which discusses the obligation of diplomatic missions not to impede the legal due process of the receiving state.

Assange has claimed that, as a result of his self-imposed confinement, he developed cardiac and respiratory problems and wants to go to Ecuador for treatment. The British remain adamant that they will arrest him if he leaves the premises, while Ecuador remains equally steadfast in its commitment to his refugee status and his protection.

The interesting part about the fear of extraditing Assange to the United States because of the possibility of a death sentence is that there is no real case against him at all. The Justice Department essentially concluded that it would not bring any charges against him for publishing classified documents because he "published" them and did not "leak" them. This is in contrast to Edward Snowden and army intelligence analyst Bradley Manning, both of whom leaked information. Assange did publish classified documents, but if officials were to pursue him on criminal charges, they would also have to pursue many American news organizations and journalists. The difference between leaking and publishing significantly affects their legal status.

There is, of course, the possibility that the United States might decide to prosecute, but there is real doubt as to the possibility of success given the above considerations. There is no case against Assange at this time, and the refusal to extradite is based on the incredibly remote possibility that he would be sentenced to death.

The current consequence of our death penalty in this case is that we are preventing Sweden from prosecuting this individual for possible sex crimes and causing undo international consternation.

JOANNE CHESIMARD

The ultimate escape to avoid prosecution in the United States is to go to a place that is openly hostile to the US and does not share any extradition agreement. The recent decision to ease relations with Cuba brought this situation to light in the case of JoAnne Chesimard, (a.k.a. Assata Shakur), who has lived in Cuba for forty years after Fidel Castro gave her political asylum when she surfaced there after escaping from a New Jersey prison in 1979.

The state had sentenced her to life imprisonment for the murder of State Trooper Werner Foerster during a traffic stop. She was the subject of a large manhunt for many suspected crimes. Chesimard and two accomplices were in the car when it was stopped, and they fired at the two officers, killing Foerster and wounding his partner. She was also wounded in the exchange and faced trial, where she was convicted and sentenced to life. She escaped in 1979 and became the first woman to make the FBI's most wanted list. Subsequently, she surfaced in Cuba, where she was given asylum and has been living there openly ever since. She was well received there on her stance that she was an American counterrevolutionary and the victim of the shooting and not the instigator.

The recent thaw in relations between the United States and Cuba has brought a new round of demands for her extradition from various sources, including New Jersey Governor Chris Christie, but so far Cuba has given no indication that they intend to cooperate and send her back.

About seventy other known criminals wanted in the United States are living in Cuba, where they remain out of reach to the American justice system. These cases also represent a lesson in the frustration of justice that might occur prior to extradition treaties.

A criminal, who can escape to such a hostile country, or even a non-hostile one that does not wish to deal at all, can—even today—escape justice.

EXTRADITION AND THE DEATH PENALTY

The refusal of non-death-penalty countries to extradite if there is a possibility of a death sentence is another factor that influences how we must compromise our pursuit of capital punishment, in this situation forcing us not to pursue the death penalty in cases in which our current legal approach would deem it appropriate. Other country's laws are then in essence telling us how to pursue justice in this country. Our principles include the concept that the law should be meted out equally to everyone, but this tenet is violated whenever we accept a different path to the pursuit of justice—one based on factors other than the crime. This aspect of the extradition process is just such an element. "Equal justice under the law" does not occur, and we cannot defend the unequal treatment of identical crimes.

The rectification of this inequality will be one more benefit from the demise of the death penalty.

Chapter 18

EXONERATION

O ne of the strongest arguments against the death penalty is the possibility of executing an innocent person, and adding to that unspeakable injustice is the realization after the fact that the condemned
was innocent. Exoneration at that point is almost an absurdity for the individual, although it may have some benefit for issues such as family pride
and an individual's legacy. Our system is really very good at establishing
guilt, but mistakes occur even in the best hands.

Researchers and attorneys at the University of Michigan Law School
and the Center on Wrongful Convictions at Northwestern University
School of Law have painstakingly established a new archive, the National
Registry of Exonerations, which is the most complete catalog of people exonerated after serious criminal convictions. Over the past twenty-three years, over two thousand people were falsely convicted in the
United States. Since there is no official record-keeping system for US exonerations, these academics probed independently and obtained detailed
evidence on 873 individuals. Twenty-four percent of the exonerations involved false or misleading forensic evidence, which is of interest since we
have come to rely so heavily on forensics through the influence of television shows such as *CSI* and media attention on ongoing trials. There are

another twelve hundred for whom there is less data. Four hundred sixteen of the cases were homicides, and in two-thirds of those, perjury or false accusation was the most common factor leading to a wrongful conviction.

Some states have developed entities to review questionable cases in order to ascertain a convicted individual's guilt or innocence. In July 2007 Dallas County District Attorney Craig Watkins established the Conviction Integrity Unit to investigate and prosecute old cases in which evidence might point to additional or different perpetrators. The unit reviewed over four hundred DNA cases with the Innocence Project of Texas (IPTX). This special unit is staffed by one assistant district attorney, one investigator, and one legal assistant and is the first of its kind in the United States.

The Innocence Inquiry Commission of North Carolina was established to review claims of innocence by convicts, and on February 17, 2010, its activities were vindicated when a three-judge panel voted to exonerate Greg Taylor, who was convicted of the 1993 murder of Jacquetta Thomas, a prostitute. Taylor served seventeen years of a life term for her murder despite his persistent claims of innocence. The commission identified various irregularities in the trial, particularly the fact that, contrary to testimony, no blood was found in Taylor's truck. An agent of the state's bureau of investigation ran tests that would have documented this, but that information was never shared with prosecutors at the time of the trial. One witness, who claimed she saw Taylor with the victim, later testified she was not sure of that recollection. Another witness testified to a scenario that was physically impossible.

More and more governmental and private agencies are looking into past cases, particularly with the aid of more intensive review processes and new forensic technologies. Professionals expect more successes in the future.

According to the blog of the Innocence Project, which is an independent, nonprofit institution, since 1989 there have been 337 postconviction

DNA-related exonerations in the United States, and in twenty-eight of those cases, the individuals had pleaded guilty. Some states now require homicide case interrogations be taped, and many other jurisdictions are taking this step voluntarily to prevent coercion and provide accurate recordings of proceedings.

Some reviews have provided happy outcomes even though many years have passed. James Bain was the 247th inmate exonerated by DNA evidence in the United States. He spent thirty-five years in prison on a rape and murder conviction, which was eventually overturned, largely because of DNA evidence.

Henry James spent thirty years of an LWOP conviction in the Louisiana State Penitentiary at Angola for a crime he did not commit. On the basis of DNA evidence, Judge Henry Sullivan overturned James's conviction at the request of lawyers from the Innocence Project and Jefferson County prosecutors. James is among twelve Louisiana inmates cleared by DNA testing, and he served more time in prison than any of the others.

JOSEPH SALVATI

On July 31, 1968, Justice Felix Forte sentenced Joseph Salvati, then a thirty-five-year-old married father of four, to LWOP for a crime he did not commit. Forte sentenced three other innocent men for participation in the same crime. The incredible part of the story is that FBI members knew these men were innocent.

It was the 1960s, when J. Edgar Hoover waged a campaign to rid the mob from crime-infested New England. In the very popular movie *The Departed*, Jack Nicholson played the role of an Irish crime boss who developed relationships with members of the FBI and became an informant who influenced them to "look the other way" in regard to his own unlawful activities. The movie was based on the life of James Joseph "Whitey" Bulger Jr., who recently gained widespread notoriety for his capture in

California after hiding for fifteen years. A second more recent movie, *Black Mass*, starring Johnny Depp, is a biography of Bulger and also documents his relationship with the FBI. Bulger's function as an informant allowed him and his gang to prosper at the expense of rival gangs whose illegal activities he was reporting.

In addition to Bulger, the FBI formed several relationships with other crime figures, in particular Joseph "The Animal" Barboza, whose criminal activities included thirty murders. Barboza participated in the murder of Edward "Teddy" Deegan, who was described as a "local hood," and there was some suggestion his FBI contacts knew the murder was going to happen but did nothing to stop it. This was supposedly part of the FBI's infiltration plan to allow its underworld contacts to function without interference and to ultimately gain the confidence of other criminals.

Barboza admitted to his FBI handler, Special Agent H. Paul Rico, his participation in the crime and fabricated the story that implicated Salvati and three other innocent men. Barboza and his colleague, Jimmy "The Bear" Flemmi, found their way off the hook, all apparently with FBI collusion. As an aside, Mafia hit men killed Barboza in 1976 despite his being one of the first informants to enter the US Federal Witness Protection Program, which had been created specifically for him.

Unfortunately, Joseph Salvati spent three decades doing hard time. Two of the other innocent men, Louis Greco and Henry Tameleo, died in prison. The third, Peter Limone, was released in 2001.

Salvati's implication in this crime likely came from an act of retribution by Barboza because of an incident in which Salvati beat off two of Barboza's strong-armed henchmen who came seeking cash. Barboza threatened to get even, and his mechanism proved to be the implication of Salvati in the Deegan murder.

About ten years into Salvati's prison sentence, a massive bright spot appeared in the form of attorney Victor Garo, who heard about the case and had a long visit with Salvati. After concluding a massive injustice had been done, Garo took on the case and obtained freedom for Salvati despite huge odds and institutions working against him. Garo figures he spent thirty thousand hours on the case, all *pro bono*. He obtained the assistance of lawyer and television personality Dan Rea, who provided substantial, powerful ammunition by broadcasting details of the case on his WBZ show.

The case had far-reaching effects, including intervention by Indiana Republican Congressman Dan Burton, who oversaw a multiyear investigation as chairman of the House Committee on Oversight and Government Reform. Burton successfully took on Republican administration attorneys to obtain Department of Justice documents they had tried to keep from Congress on the grounds of "executive privilege."

Massachusetts Democratic Representative Bill Delahunt introduced a bill imposing criminal sanctions on federal authorities who hid evidence. In July 2007, Judge Nancy Gertner awarded the innocent defendants a total of $101,750,000 in damages in part of their civil rights violation claims against the government. Though it was expected the Department of Justice would appeal, it did not. No charges were brought against anyone in the FBI.

JUAN MELENDEZ

Juan Melendez spent seventeen years, eight months, and one day on Florida's death row for a crime he did not commit. Since his release, he devotes his life to the cause of repealing the death sentence and lectures all over the world on this subject. I had the pleasure of attending one of his engaging lectures, at Northwood High School in California in May 2010.

Melendez was born in Brooklyn, New York, in 1951 but as a child fled to Puerto Rico to escape his abusive stepfather, returning to the United States when he was seventeen. In 1974 Melendez went to prison in Florida for armed robbery and served over six years. He went back to his life as a migrant farmer until FBI agents arrested him for the murder of beauty-salon operator Delbert Baker. At the time of his arrest, Melendez spoke very little English and did not have an interpreter. He proclaimed his innocence and stated that he did not know the victim. There was no physical evidence to tie him to the crime, and he had an airtight alibi corroborated by four witnesses that he was with a woman named Dorothy Rivera at the time of Baker's murder.

This conviction lay largely on the testimony of David Falcon, a police informant, who, according to witnesses, had a grudge against Melendez. A codefendant, whose cooperation reduced his own sentencing from death to two years' probation, also testified against Melendez. Juan stated in his 2010 lecture that authorities suggested he could have the same "deal" and receive a reduced sentence if he were to implicate his codefendant. Melendez did not take the offer, but his codefendant did. The Florida Supreme Court upheld Melendez's conviction through three appeals. Melendez was coming to the end of the appeals process when his new attorneys reviewed his file and found a taped confession to the murder by Vernon James, who admitted he and an accomplice committed the crime. This confession was recorded one month before the start of the Melendez trial. The lawyers also found a statement by inmate Roger Mims, who claimed Vernon James admitted to a sexual relationship with Baker and to the crime. There was also a statement from a witness who saw James and his accomplice at the crime scene that very evening. All of this information was omitted at the trial.

With the surfacing of this new evidence, Justice Barbara Fleischer declared Melendez was entitled to a new trial, but the prosecution declined since original informant Falcon was dead and another witness had recanted his story. Melendez left the Union Correctional Facility on January 3, 2002, and received compensation of $100.

MUSINGS ON THESE EXONERATION CASES

These cases demonstrate so many things that can go wrong with our legal system. Deceit, poor defense, overly aggressive offense, outside influences, and faulty maneuverings are all present in these cases and can have truly terrible effects on the lives of a number of people and their families. The Joseph Salvati case is a "poster child" for the advantages of LWOP over the death sentence for obvious reason. If the judge had sentenced him to death and it had been carried out, Salvati's subsequent exoneration would have amounted to a pathetic joke.

Somewhat ironically, the inefficiency of our death-penalty system helped Juan Melendez because, were it expeditious, we would have, by dispatching an innocent man, realized the most feared end result for a flawed capital-punishment system. Melendez paid a heavy price and spent, as he often says, seventeen years, eight months, and one day on death row, but at least he is living out the rest of his years in freedom.

MIND-SET

Particularly poignant is the frustration of these men, all of whom were innocent but realized they were going down a terrible path. For those who believe in American justice, it is hard to grasp that this could happen in our system. Can you imagine the helpless frustration in the minds of Joseph Salvati and Juan Melendez when they realized their lives were being taken away even though they were completely innocent? These injustices should not happen here, but there are also reasons to regain faith.

A noble warrior, in the figure of Victor Garo, fought tirelessly and without pay to obtain justice for Salvati. He not only demonstrated his client's innocence but also did battle with the FBI and Department of Justice. This had to appear an almost impossible task, but this inspirational hero took on this Don Quixote–like quest against impossible odds—and won. Competent attorney representation turned up the information that revealed Melendez's innocence.

FAMILIES OF THE INNOCENT

Not to be forgotten in such tragedies are family members and friends of the wrongly accused. They, too, suffer deprivation and frustration, particularly when they believe in their loved ones' innocence.

In her March 2008 *Reader's Digest* piece, "The Exonerated," investigative journalist Jan Goodwin beautifully spotlights this aspect of suffering in the Salvati case as her article catalogs shocking facts in the story and also beautifully documents the love, bravery, and unyielding support of Joseph's wife, Marie, and the rest of his family.

INTIMATE-PARTNER BATTERING

The case of Brent Louis Vangsness illustrates how changes in legislation can affect prison terms and sentences. Vangsness, now forty-four, was released from prison after serving twenty-six years of a seventeen-to-life sentence for a second-degree murder conviction for killing his roommate in 1984. Vangsness, then seventeen, killed Scott McNaughton by stabbing him more than thirty times with a steak knife and a wood chisel. Vangsness testified that McNaughton had made sexual advances toward him in the past and, on this particular occasion, had held a knife against Vangsness's throat and wanted to sodomize him.

During his incarceration, Vangsness's attorneys appealed his conviction several times, but all were turned down as were several bids for parole.

Since then, however, new laws led to Vangsness's release. Defense attorneys now can contest a murder charge on the basis of the negative psychological impact inflicted by a victim on the killer. Among these changes, "intimate-partner battering" is now a legitimate defense, which carries a maximum sentence of manslaughter. Because of this, on June 7, 2010, in Superior Court in Santa Ana, California, defense attorneys went ahead with a guilty plea to the lesser charge of involuntary manslaughter and, with that, reduced the maximum sentence time for Vangsness. A sentence of voluntary manslaughter carries a maximum of thirteen years imprisonment, and since Vangsness already served twenty-six years, he was freed.

This case brings up the issue of possible exoneration on the basis of new laws that are enacted now and in the future. Intimate-partner battering did not exist as a defense when Vangsness was convicted, but it does now. A reduced sentence is not quite the same as total exoneration, but it has the same effect in that a convicted person can now walk free.

More new concepts might come from the minds of inventive defense attorneys, and if so, they will likely have profound effects on the lives of those on trial or already convicted, as in Vangsness's case—but that is only possible if they are still alive and not executed.

WEST MEMPHIS THREE

In this famous case, three men were convicted of the 1993 murder of three second-grade boys in the woods in West Memphis, Arkansas. Shortly after the bodies were found, police brought in Jesse Misskelley Jr. and questioned him for eight hours. Misskelley confessed to the crime, implicating Damien Echols and Jason Baldwin as well. Misskelley is mentally handicapped, reportedly with an IQ of seventy-two, and was not represented by counsel during the arduous grilling. He recanted his story the next morning, indicating he had broken down under the questioning and therefore admitted to the crimes. His testimony remained as the only evidence for the convictions, even though he recanted it, was not properly represented, gave contradictory statements, and probably was not competent.

Even though they proclaimed their innocence before, during, and after the trial, the jury found the three guilty of the murders. Jurors sentenced Echols to death, and Baldwin and Misskelley to life imprisonment. The Arkansas Supreme Court upheld the convictions in 1996, and it seemed their fates were sealed. Echols's execution date was set in 1994, but that was stayed.

Very soon after the convictions, independent individuals on the outside took interest in the case and started the process of questioning the legal decisions. They questioned the validity of the case's basis, which was the confession of a mentally challenged young man who claimed he broke down under duress, primarily, to end the session. Supporters looked at background information and discovered that the vicinity had, for years, been alive with rumors of satanic-cult activities and rituals. Damien Echols stood out in this Bible Belt community because he dressed in black, listened to heavy metal, and dabbled in Wicca. Jason Baldwin also listened to heavy metal and had several black T-shirts. These factors were enough to allow the prosecution to accuse Echols and Baldwin of the murders as part of a satanic-cult ritual. That was the complete body of information presented. There were no witnesses who tied them to the scene, no implicating physical evidence, and no DNA evidence available at that time in that jurisdiction.

So local police were confronted with this horrible crime, and that kind of thing just did not happen there. Damien Echols came along, an obvious philosophical outsider. He dabbled in the occult and admitted he tried to take an eye out of another boy. He had spent time in a mental institution and was on medication for his illnesses, which had manifested as delusions and hallucinations, among other things. His condition was so severe that he was placed on total disability in the Social Security system. This was a very troubled young man, someone who could easily be a front-row candidate for having committed this crime. This view of the case was obviously negative for the defense, but the interpretation ignited a growing following.

Reports of new methods of obtaining DNA evidence from old crime scenes sparked intense interest, and no evidence of any DNA material was found from any of the three men. More important, investigators *did* find evidence that a hair found in a knot used to bind a victim belonged to the stepfather of one of the murdered little boys.

Public interest became so intense that several books were written. Probably the most influential was Mara Leveritt's *Devil's Knot*, but all caused widespread interest and scrutiny, several celebrities even joining the chorus for finding justice. Echols married while in prison and his wife, Lorri, was influential in forming a group called Arkansas Take Action. In August 2010, supporters jammed into Little Rock's auditorium. The assemblage included Eddie Vedder, Natalie Maines, Johnny Depp, Patti Smith, and other celebrities. Subsequent to that, the Arkansas Supreme Court set a December date for a hearing to decide if the trio deserved a new trial. But then came a largely unprecedented move by attorneys on both sides. The men would be set free if they pleaded guilty to reduced charges of murder through a controversial maneuver called the "Alford plea," in which the defendant maintains innocence but acknowledges the prosecution has enough evidence to possibly convict and impose a more stringent sentence. In other words, each accused pleads guilty to a lesser offense while maintaining his innocence for the first-degree offense, thus avoiding a more ominous sentence such as life in prison or the death penalty. But he still has to admit to a lesser offense with its accompanying lighter sentence. The West Memphis Three each made this plea and were released for time served.

The Alford plea essentially ended the case, but it left a cloud of uncertainty over the question of whether these men were innocent or guilty, and a second trial might have brought a more satisfactory and definitive answer. It appears the state had no solid evidence and that a large segment of popular opinion lay with the defendants, but this unsatisfactory solution is not what we ordinarily expect from our jurisprudence system. Were these three guilty or not?

One provision of the Alford plea has to do with understanding that the state has enough evidence that *might* lead to a more serious conviction. The defendants already experienced maximal sentencing and knew what was on the line if they went to trial and failed. On the other hand, did the state really have sufficient evidence? Did the defense believe the prosecution had such evidence? A court of public opinion and stringent case review indicate the state did not.

So, why did everyone agree to this gray-area solution? For the West Memphis Three, the decision might be interpreted as acknowledging their innocence since they are released. For the state, the interpretation might be more toward guilt since the three did plead guilty and already spent several years in the state prison.

Both sides, then, could claim some kind of victory. For the defendants, the battle for freedom was over, and they were free to go without any fear of future incrimination. For the state, this closed the books on the case and, importantly, carried with it the proviso that because they admitted guilt, the West Memphis Three could not sue for wrongful incarceration or civil-rights violations. Thus, financial practicality played a large role in the decision on the part of the state of Arkansas. It avoided an expensive, time-consuming, and very public second trial, and also what could have been even more expensive later litigations for wrongful incarceration and civil-rights violations.

Jason Baldwin had a problem with this solution, refusing to admit guilt to a crime he continually proclaimed he did not commit. And this was in light of the knowledge that the state did not have any new evidence and that old evidence in the first trial was so seriously challenged as to make it almost completely ineffective. He claimed he would rather remain incarcerated than agree to this halfway situation, but lawyers convinced him to agree to the deal because Echols would continue to live on death row if they all did not agree to the plan.

The West Memphis Three case points out several issues. First, there appears to have been a rush to judgment in convicting these men of the crime. Later, attorneys for both sides decided on a dubious solution. The case that started out with a rush to judgment ended with a rush to freedom.

All three left prison, with Echols and Baldwin vowing to continue the fight, to find the real killer, and to prove their innocence. We will not know if they are really guilty or not until we find absolute previously undiscovered, definitive evidence for their innocence—or the real murderer.

Again, this represents the possibility of one of the most feared consequences of the death penalty—the conviction of an innocent man. Echols was on death row and might have been executed if not for the public outcry.

In a black-and-white world, the case would have had a more satisfactory endpoint through a second trial that decided on a definite innocent or guilty conviction. But the Alford plea represents another method for exoneration in certain cases that do not lend themselves to a more definitive ending.

The Alford plea, in this case in particular, demonstrates another frailty of the death sentence, because it would have done Damien Echols little good if the state had proceeded with his scheduled execution in 1994.

PLANTED DNA

With the scientific specificity of DNA, proponents of the death penalty feel the chance of executing an innocent person is extremely unlikely when genetic evidence comes into play. A recent development in Omaha, Nebraska, however, might forever change the way we look at DNA evidence. David Kofoed, chief crime-scene investigator for Douglas County, has a reputation for solving crimes others could not. Across a decade he put away hundreds of criminals, often on the basis of cold, hard, scientific fact. On March 23, 2010, Kofoed was convicted of planting blood evidence during a murder investigation.

David Kofoed's work came under the spotlight after the 2006 murders of Wayne and Sharmon Stock, a Cass County couple. Prime suspects were a nephew and cousin, and detectives obtained a confession from the nephew, who retracted it the next day. Investigators were unable to find any physical evidence and carefully went over a car linked to the suspects. A day later, Kofoed reevaluated the car and found a drop of blood belonging to one of the victims. The suspects were charged with murder and spent seven months in jail before being released after prosecutors found the confessions did not fit the facts. A Wisconsin couple later admitted to the crime and was sentenced to life in prison.

The now-cleared nephew filed a lawsuit alleging civil-rights violations, and this brought the FBI in to investigate David Kofoed's role. FBI investigations led authorities to charge Kofoed with evidence tampering, and he was convicted. Cass County District Judge Randal Rehmeier brought up a second murder case that was similar in that there was a confession but no physical evidence until Kofoed found a drop of blood.

Prosecutors carefully stated that they thought Kofoed planted evidence only in the case for which he was tried and that no such activity seemed likely in previous cases they reviewed. Logically it's feared this case might prompt appeals from many others in which DNA evidence was useful in convictions. There is already another case in which Kofoed's work is being challenged.

So now we come to an intersection between the highly specific, well-established science of DNA evidence and the old-fashioned criminal activity of planting evidence. The question that remains is this: What implications does this have for the many cases already decided, at least partially, on the basis of DNA evidence? Is this problem isolated, or is there a potential for it to be widespread and further contribute to the nightmare of reviewing previously decided cases?

This case casts doubt in what has become one of the most trusted types of forensic pathology, not because of the inaccuracy of the testing but because of questionable methods and motivations of those who gather the material. So far, there is no overwhelming wave of such cases, but the possibility exists in more than simply theory since we have a case in which an officer is convicted for this crime. Granted Kofoed is appealing the conviction, but even if he eventually gains exoneration, a small cloud of doubt has risen over the issue.

SCIENTIFIC MISCONDUCT

There is no perfect method for investigating cases, and forensics is no exception. Everyone understands mistakes can be and have been made, but a disturbing possibility is the issue of misconduct by scientists. The Innocence Project offers a few examples.

Fred Zain, a former director of the West Virginia State Police Forensic Laboratory, testified in many cases in twelve states, including dozens in West Virginia and Texas. New evidence, including DNA testing, demonstrates that Zain fabricated results, lied on the stand, and withheld evidence from his reports.

Pamela Fish, Chicago lab technician, is accused of giving false and misleading court testimony that contributed to convictions of nine men. Subsequent DNA testing exonerated three of these men and raised questions about the other four.

A two-year study that ended in 2007 showed evidence in Houston's crime lab was mishandled and results were misreported.

DR. CHARLES SMITH

Another disturbing case is that of Dr. Charles Smith, a Canadian pediatric pathologist. While practicing at Toronto's Hospital for Sick Children, Dr. Smith performed over one thousand autopsies and gained a reputation for his expertise in the field of pediatric pathology and forensics. An Ontario coroner's investigation into forty-five cases revealed he made questionable conclusions in twenty of those, which were instrumental in leading to thirteen convictions. Justice Stephen Goudge led the investigation, and in October 2008, he concluded that Smith actively misled superiors, made false and misleading statements in court, and exaggerated his expertise in trials.

Smith testified that he saw himself as a member of the prosecution team and that his job was to help convict the accused. To that end he lied under oath, misled courts, and "lost" evidence that would have been helpful to the accused.

CONCLUSIONS FOR EXONERATION

There are numerous reasons for exoneration. Human error, misguided advice, deceit, professional malfeasance, changes in the law, witness frailty, and new evidence can all change the definition of guilt or innocence, the level of guilt, and the severity of sentencing. Commissions and attorneys that pursue these cases often come up with surprises, sometimes shock, and even reopen cases thought to have been ironclad. The obvious point is that exoneration is a fiasco if a convicted individual is already executed.

LWOP!

Chapter 19

SNITCHES

A jailhouse snitch is an individual who shares with authorities information he obtained from a fellow prisoner in regard to the latter's criminal case as it pertains to his guilt or degree of guilt, more officially known as "confidential or criminal informant" (CI). Classically, a snitch is motivated by the possibility of the betterment of his own situation while incarcerated, usually a reduction in his charges or length of sentence.

SANTA CLARA ATTORNEY KATHLEEN RIDOLFI

The argument against relying on snitches is that it can violate the defendant's Sixth Amendment right to counsel. Santa Clara law professor and cofounder of the Northern California Innocence Project Kathleen Ridolfi commented, "If they're planting the informants or the government has any role in placing them, then essentially the questioning of the defendant, picking their brains, is almost as if the police themselves were in the jail cell. It's equal to legal interrogation and you have a right to counsel."

SNITCHING GRAY AREA

The determination, then, of the legal weight of an informant's activities rests with the concept of whether or not he is acting as an agent of the government. One can imagine this concept might be somewhat indeterminate and lend itself to subjectivity and interpretation. Both ends of the spectrum are relatively straightforward: (1) the individual, who presents for the first time such information without any previous contact with any official, is acting legally and (2) the informant who had previous contact with an official and arranged to obtain information is acting as an agent of the government, and therefore, his snitching activities are not admissible.

LEGAL SNITCHING

Jailhouse snitching is not illegal in itself. It becomes "illegal" when it is determined that the snitch is acting as an agent of the state, such as the sheriff's department or district attorney's office. In that case the informant is acting as though he were a policeman, and the defendant has the right to counsel, a condition similar to what we understand as Miranda rights. In the unlikely situation where the informant admits to the defendant he is acting as an agent of the state and the defendant passes on self-incriminating information, in essence giving up his right to legal representation, that information could be used and would be admissible. Confessing to aspects of a crime and supplying information that would be injurious to one's own case is called "admission against interest."

If an informant acts as an agent of the state without full disclosure to the defendant, obtaining potentially useful information and passing it on to the police, anything discovered as a direct result of that information is not admissible in court against that prisoner. For example, if an informant obtains information from a prisoner, who is a drug dealer, that the dealer hid a large quantity of heroin in a certain location, and the informant passes this information on to authorities, whatever is found at that location is not admissible against the dealer. If police find drugs and other things that might implicate the defendant, such as fingerprints or other traceable possessions, none of that information is admissible in court and is referred to as "fruit of the poisonous tree." Information about the location of the drugs, however, might be useful in that the police could destroy it, as they are obligated to do. But armed only with the in-custody informant's information, they cannot, in court, link the defendant to the drugs.

SNITCHES AND THIRD PARTIES

Informant information obtained from a prisoner can, however, be used in regard to a third party. Suppose an informant obtains information from a prisoner that a party on the outside robs banks. The police may act on this information and, as long as they do not illegally trespass, conduct themselves in a way to observe the third-party committing or about to commit a robbery. They may then apprehend him, and whatever information they obtain is useful in court.

IMPLICATIONS OF ILLEGAL SNITCHING

The determination that specific instances of snitching are illegal can have dramatic effects on our legal system. In the case of Daniel Wozniak, Scott Sanders brought up the issue of improper use of a jailhouse snitch, who was known as "Informant F." Prosecutors defended their action because this informant was not a government agent when he collected the information, and therefore that information is admissible in court.

INFORMANT F

On October 12, 2011, Scott Dekraai entered the Salon Meritage, a beauty salon in Seal Beach, California, and shot to death his ex-wife and seven others. He confessed to the crime in May 2014 and was convicted of first-degree murder.

Assistant Public Defender Scott Sanders, who represented Dekraai, accused Orange County prosecutors of illegally using jailhouse snitches, in particular Fernando Perez, known as Informant F, who reportedly was instrumental in other cases as well. He apparently wrote to a deputy and asked to be moved closer to certain individuals so he "could work these dudes." In a separate missive he allegedly wrote, "Garcia, I love my little job I got." According to the complaint, authorities placed Perez in a cell adjoining Dekraai so he could more easily obtain statements about the defendant's role in the massacre and report that information, including claims Dekraai bragged about the shootings.

Prosecutors stated that Informant F came forward of his own accord because of the nature of the murders and not for his own considerations, even though he was facing the possibility of a three-strike sentence for drug violations, street terrorism, and weapons charges. Prosecutors also used what one might call an "electronic informant" in the form of a planted device that supplied 132 hours of continuous recording.

Sanders filed a lengthy motion to have the death penalty removed as an option because of the illegal use of jailhouse informants. Instead Superior Court Judge Thomas Goethal removed or recused the Orange County District Attorney's Office from the death-penalty phase of the trial and turned it over to the California Attorney General's Office.

The ultimate irony here is that all the machinations in the use of Informant F are in play to keep Dekraai off death row, where he would reside until he dies of natural causes, and put him with the general prison population to die of natural causes. Of course, the real result is for this case to drag out to a totally unacceptable degree as we misuse our institutions, everyone involved in the process, finances, and time.

Once again, one person (among other family members in this case) who seems to have a personal understanding of what this means is Bethany Webb, sister of shooting victim Laura Webb. Bethany's statement highlights the tortuous prolongation of this trial in the framework of how it affects the family of the victim: "The worst possible thing [the judge] could have done for the families is [to] extend this another year before we even get to trial."

Informant F might have added some information for authorities, but it was totally unnecessary because evidence against Dekraai was insurmountable and he had confessed to the crime. The final paragraph in the story should be the immediate removal of Dekraai from society into a life of imprisonment, an endpoint that hopefully will be commonplace in similar situations when we eliminate the death penalty.

LWOP!

SNITCHING IMPLICATIONS

Determination that snitching in this case was illegal had a profound effect on its outcome, and it might be a factor that eliminates the death sentence, once again not because of the crime but because of a technicality.

Sanders brought up the issue of improper use of Informant F in the murder case of his client Daniel Wozniak, who faces the possibility of a death penalty. Prosecutors defend this claim because, at the time he collected the incriminating information against Wozniak, Perez was not a government informant.

Prosecutors are defending their use of the very same snitch because his activities were carried out when he was not considered an agent of the government. Whether or not the defense will be able to show otherwise remains to be seen, but it is of some interest that the same informant's information can be treated differently depending on whether or not he had a previous relationship with a government official or employee.

LEONEL VEGA

Leonel Vega, a Santa Ana, California, gang member, was convicted in 2010 of chasing down and killing a seventeen-year-old rival gang member by shooting him in the head. His original sentence was LWOP, but this was reduced to fifteen years because it was found prosecutors used jailhouse informants to obtain information. On the basis of his plea deal, Vega could be released by 2019 since he is given credit for time served. This sentence change has nothing to do with the crime but with the process of obtaining information. One can understand why family and friends of the victim might be upset or even terribly irate.

There is reaction on both sides of the "snitch" situation. An example is commentary from Orange County Superior Court Judge Dan McNerney, who characterized the reduced sentence as a "black eye" for county prosecutors and the sheriff's department. On the other hand, Susan Kang Schroeder, district attorney's chief of staff, said it was an example of how far the DA's office would go to police itself in an attempt to mitigate damage. Still, she admittedly understood why the victim's family was upset that Vega did not receive the entirety of his original punishment. She further commented, "Sometimes, when law enforcement makes mistakes, the tie goes to the defendant."

"TIE" REACTION

This statement demonstrates the lengths law enforcement will go to correct itself. We are so deeply committed to protecting the rights of the defendant or criminal that we go far more than halfway when trying to correct perceived wrongs in our judicial process. Use of the word "tie" usually indicates two equal phenomena, but that is certainly not so in this instance. Shooting someone in the head is *not* equivalent to questionable information-gathering techniques by law enforcement.

This case demonstrates how profoundly the snitching issue can affect our jurisprudence system, benefit criminal defendants, and frustrate prosecutors.

RENÉ "BOXER" ENRIQUEZ

Being a jailhouse snitch is a very valuable tool for the inmate who wants to use this technique to lessen his own sentence and possibly even gain freedom. The California parole board considered the case of former Mexican Mafia boss René "Boxer" Enriquez, recommending he be set free on February 22, 2015, on the basis of his activities as one of the state's top jailhouse informants. Enriquez claims he has killed more people and committed more crimes than he can remember, and he is serving three consecutive life sentences. He is currently housed in a secret federal facility, where he translates intercepted communications from the Mexican Mafia. He states that he has turned his back on his former Mafia associates. Grand jury transcripts indicate he earned $50,000 over five years and that his family received $1,000 a month in compensation. Enriquez served as an expert witness several times and apparently provided valuable testimony. Orange County Deputy District Attorney Erik Petersen cited his value as a witness in "Operation Smokin' Aces," which was a multiagency raid in 2013 that allegedly removed forty-eight Mexican Mafia members from the streets.

Enriquez is very articulate and has become an author. In his 2002 biography *The Black Hand*, he describes himself as a regular Joe, "clawing my way out of a dark evil abyss and back into the grasp of humanity." He has also coauthored a book on street terrorism with former Orange County, California, district attorney investigator and University of California Irvine (UCI) professor Al Valdez. He is well known to police throughout the country as a valuable and knowledgeable snitch, and he has lectured via Skype at UCI.

One quote from an unnamed member of the parole board was this: "You['ve] been able to demonstrate to this panel that you've…changed and that you've engaged in positive rehabilitation." Among the documents the board considered in recommending Enriquez's release was a letter from Deputy District Attorney Petersen, who cited his invaluable aid as an informant. Although he also had similar letters of support from other law enforcement people throughout the state of California, others question his motivation and many, such as Orange County District Attorney Tony Rackauckas, oppose his release.

Rudy Loewenstein—a Tustin, California, attorney—also opposes his release, indicating Enriquez was the most manipulative and devious individual he ever met in his thirty-six years of practicing law, and he questions Enriquez's motivation for cooperating with authorities.

GOVERNOR BROWN

Late on February 20, 2015, Governor Jerry Brown ended the debate by halting the scheduled parole, on the basis of the fact that Enriquez's history indicated he would be "an unreasonable danger to society."

The governor's decision to halt the scheduled release of René Enriquez was one he almost *had* to make on the basis of Enriquez's history and the fact that, subsequent to his release in 1989 from the California Correctional Institution (CCI) at Tehachapi, he ordered a murder and committed another. Granted, his services as a snitch have been invaluable. And one would think his ability to control anyone in the Mexican Mafia would be impossible because of the negative impact he has had on that organization. Nevertheless, there is no way to know whether he might still be accepted by certain members of the Mexican Mafia or other crime organizations or possibly even go back into a life of crime independently—although that seems unlikely on the basis of his successes in authorship and in cooperation with law enforcement. Still, Governor Brown had to act in a way he felt was the best approach in protecting the public and Enriquez.

Regardless of which entities he has offended by his assistance to law enforcement, there is little doubt someone holds Enriquez in extreme disfavor. If those entities were to break through the secrecy of the Witness

Protection Program and eliminate him, the parole board and Governor Brown would have to bear some level of responsibility. At this time, Enriquez's life is probably better than if he were living in the general population, and considering his past deeds, this is probably as good as it will get for him.

As discussed earlier, differing factors contribute to our handling of criminals who commit essentially the same crimes. Enriquez's current circumstance, which is better than being in the general population, is based not on his murders but on his subsequent actions. Another individual who had, for the sake of argument, committed the exact same crimes would not receive the benefits he has. This is not to say officials are not doing the best they can to eliminate crime, and if that requires dealing with people with whom they would otherwise not deal, they have to make decisions that are, in the long run, the best toward that goal of eliminating crime and protecting the public.

Another issue is that of Enriquez's rehabilitation. One argument for the abolition of the death penalty is that people can actually change and do some good. Some counter that argument with the point that it is very challenging for an incarcerated individual to change. While that might be true, Enriquez offers an example of how an individual can benefit society, regardless of his motives.

SNITCHING AND EXONERATION

Exonerate: to relieve, as of a charge or blame resting on one; to clear of an imputation of guilt; to declare or prove blameless
(Webster's Unabridged Dictionary, 1979, p. 642}

The release of Enriquez would not have been because we exonerated him from his crimes because we now think he is innocent. There is no question of his guilt, and even Enriquez admits to his crimes. The parole board certainly has the right to recommend the release of an individual on the basis of their evaluations of his current status, but the release of Enriquez would have brought up something of a philosophical dilemma in that becoming a jailhouse snitch could be another potential way of obtaining benefits and freedom akin to exoneration.

Family members of victims could understandably interpret such a release as a means to negate the murder. After the governor's decision, one family member, expressing that side of the equation, said, "I felt defeated and now I feel victorious, not personally, but that the right thing happened for all the victims and all the families. I'm just relieved and happy really. I feel grateful to the governor's office for doing what's right. People change, but that doesn't erase what you did and the people's lives you affected."

Enriquez appears to have reached something of a zenith in the snitch profession in that his testimony is received as gospel by the authorities. As an intelligent and trustworthy informant and witness, he is taken very seriously and with little question of his veracity. This is in juxtaposition to the concept we have of the jailhouse snitch who is the cellmate of a defendant on trial and whose testimony brings with it a degree of doubt in the minds of the jury.

This is not so with Enriquez, whose activities almost gained him his freedom. This, of course, leads to the legal and ethical dilemma in that we have an individual whose crimes were such to have earned him three life sentences but whose testimony and assistance in various ways have proven to be such valuable instruments in the battle against crime that we actually considered the possibility of granting him his freedom. There is no question about the denial of liberating an individual who committed his same crimes but did not become such a valuable tool.

Several members of law enforcement feel his assistance has been so valuable that we should essentially forgive him for his crimes. If we do that, we ignore one principle of our system—to represent the murder victims. We are obligated to remember them. Enriquez brings us to a very gray area.

If Enriquez had been sentenced to death in a quick aggressive and efficient capital-punishment system, this debate would never have happened, at least in regard to him personally. Whatever his motivations, his "snitching" activities have been to our benefit, and obviously we would never have seen them had he been executed.

"SNITCH" MUSINGS

Since time immemorial, police departments have made use of informants of all kinds, including the "jailhouse" variety. The rationale for using snitches is clear in that it is a method to obtain information that might be difficult or even impossible to obtain otherwise. Supporters argue that it is a valuable tool in the fight against crime and that significant curtailment would hamper our pursuit of justice. Naturally, criminals generally want to avoid detection and do not go out of their way to provide information that might be injurious to themselves. This often makes it difficult to associate criminals with their crimes and obtain appropriate convictions. Officials reason that if snitches provide the only way to obtain the needed information and take criminals off the streets, so be it. Snitching might have negative connotations, but with certain criminal elements, we are already dealing with individuals and conditions that are less than savory. Although there are exceptions, even the most ardent supporters of the use of snitches would be opposed to it if it contributed to obtaining convictions that are not warranted.

In wake of the discovery of the use of snitches in several instances, including the Dekraai murder case, the Orange County, California, District Attorney's Office performed a thorough in-house investigation on the use of in-custody informants and its effects on the rights of defendants. This resulted in increasing personnel, adopting guidelines for the use of informants, and appointing a committee headed by District Attorney Tony Rackauckas to evaluate the use of in-custody informants in criminal cases. The District Attorney's Office established an independent, external committee, the Informant Policies and Practices Evaluation Committee (IPPEC), which investigates these practices and makes recommendations for future improvements.

SUMMATION ON SNITCHING

The use of in-custody informants is not an illegal activity, the US Supreme Court so decided in the 1967 case of *McCray v. Illinois*, citing, "The informer is a vital part of society's defensive arsenal." In acknowledging the legitimacy of the use of informers, California law provides protection to those who give information to law enforcement and has codified a long-standing legal privilege protecting the identity of informers in the *People v. McShann* 1958 decision.

On the other side of the coin, there must be protection for criminal defendants on the basis of their constitutional rights. The purpose of on-going investigations is to allow legal use of informants, offering guidelines for this invaluable tool and balancing the need for justice with defendants' rights.

Chapter 20

REHABILITATION

The issue of rehabilitation relates to the persona of the individual who is eventually executed for a crime. Suppose a convict really does change and becomes a much better person than the one who committed the crime years before. Allowing that individuals can fake rehabilitation for their own benefit, let us consider the individual who genuinely changes for the better. The person we execute is in many ways not the same person who committed the crime.

There are several reasons for someone to change for the better while in prison, at least theoretically. "Finding religion" is a commonly used expression for people who embrace some form of road to salvation, usually through involvement with an organized religious group. That certainly can happen on the "inside." We speak of people in prison as "doing time," and their every day is a constant reminder of what got them there. That sometimes causes circumspection, leading to a sense of contrition and, perhaps, a desire for a prisoner to become a new and improved version of himself. Obviously many are so truly deranged that this could never occur, and there also are those who feel they should not be in prison for one reason or another. Both are on the defensive and will not come to any acknowledgment of personal failing and need for improvement.

Removal from the long list of negative influences that promoted antisocial and violent behaviors provides the opportunity to step back and engage in internal reflection that can lead to better choices in lifestyle. Aging is a life changer for all of us. No one has the same approach to life and its challenges at fifty as at twenty. Time alone produces changes in the killer, and the aggressive behaviors that got him into trouble in his younger days are no longer anywhere near as virulent. This in itself is a kind of change or "rehabilitation."

People who are rehabilitated can have a positive influence on those on the outside by dissuading them from activities that might get them into trouble and showing by example the terrible consequences that can ensue. If serving LWOP, there is no need to fake rehabilitation to avoid death; therefore, beneficial changes in prisoners are more likely to be genuine.

One of the most storied cases involving rehabilitation is that of Karla Faye Tucker, who was discussed earlier in this book in relation to forgiveness from the victim's family. To all external appearances, Tucker did rehabilitate herself. She became a model citizen and born-again Christian. Widespread support for her developed, and high-profile ministers Pat Robertson and Jerry Falwell were among those who urged mercy for her. But Governor George Bush refused to commute her sentence, and Tucker was executed. There is always the other side of the coin, as many felt her execution was justified. Victim Deborah Thornton's husband was among those who did not share the wave of emotion to spare Karla's life. He lived through the horror of his wife's slaying and all the appeals, delays, and notoriety for the murderer.

Cases like this bring out many arguments. There is the contention that sympathy for the killer in some ways denigrates the victim by minimizing that loss, and perhaps time is responsible for some of those emotions. On the other hand, Americans do not embrace the death penalty with great vigor. Executing anyone, despite their past actions, is somewhat abhorrent for us. It is not in our fabric to embrace the factual part of an execution in which the condemned is helplessly strapped down on a table, and this is especially true if that individual is now a changed man, not the killer who was sentenced years before.

An immediate sentence of LWOP would have obviated the fifteen years of the appeals process that occurred between the sentencing and execution of Karla Faye Tucker. Family, friends, and supporters of the victim could have had closure that much sooner, and Tucker would have gone on to her rehabilitation and positive influence on others without the massive controversy.

Pro-death-penalty people present a strong and understandable argument that those who commit heinous acts deserve their fate. For those who hold that philosophy on the subject, there is no contention that rehabilitation changes a person sufficiently to rethink a death-penalty sentence.

Rehabilitation, with its meaningful influences on the individual and possibly on others, is a powerful life-changing event possible for all prisoners at any time in their lives. Its possibility is yet another argument against execution.

Chapter 21

STORIES THAT TELL
THE STORY

TWO SIDES OF THE CHARLES WARNER STORY

The state of Oklahoma executed Charles Warner on January 15, 2015, for the rape and murder of his girlfriend's eleven-month-old daughter. Warner's execution had been delayed following difficulties with the Lockett execution, in which the IV came out of the vein in his groin.

During the infusion of IV fluids and drugs, Warner is reported to have said, "It hurt[s]. It feels like acid." Apparently, the procedure went on without any further observable problems.

The reactions to this case were numerous and sometimes vitriolic but worthy of note because they define two opposite poles of the issue. The first is the reaction of Justice Sonia Sotomayor. The case was referred to the US Supreme Court, which decided on a five-to-four basis that the execution should proceed. A minority opinion was written by Justice Sotomayor, who is an avid proponent of the abolition of the death penalty. She first suggested midazolam as potentially inadequate, and other people supported this position and referred back to the death of James Woods, whose execution took two hours (though observers said he was not suffering and was not awake during that time). Sotomayor also challenged the validity of using only one expert to appear before the court on the subject of the efficacy of midazolam. The more striking part of her argument, however, was her cruel and unusual punishment reference: "The Eighth Amendment guarantees that no one should be subjected to an execution that causes searing, unnecessary pain before death."

The other side of the coin came from the January 16, 2015, *John and Ken Show* on KFI radio out of Los Angeles. The hosts, John Kobylt and Ken Chiampou, expressed revulsion at the crime and had absolutely no sympathy for Warner. In fact John expressed that the intravenous death was far too easy and that he would have preferred to have beaten him to death, slowly, with a hammer, starting with the lower extremities and gradually working his way up.

These two completely opposite approaches are not unique. They are found in practically every case in which there is evidence of extreme cruelty toward helpless victims and practically any case that reaches national notoriety.

John and Ken expressed a very understandable human desire to avenge the unspeakable, and ideas of violent retribution help people alleviate their own discomfort over the thought of such acts, such as the unbelievable crime of raping and murdering an infant.

People in Justice Sotomayor's camp feel capital punishment in any form is barbaric and oppose it on every front. There is no question Sotomayor's motivations stem from benevolence, even though her sentiments make pro-death-penalty people's blood boil. She stands behind her interpretation of the six words of the Eighth Amendment that refer to cruel and unusual punishment, and interpreting the Constitution and its amendments is her job.

Americans are reluctant to execute anyone, regardless of the crime, except in some people's thought processes to alleviate their discomfort. Most, however, would probably not object to executing Warner for his crime but would like to see it done as humanely as possible. Correctly dosing and infusing midazolam would certainly be totally acceptable. It is possible the higher dosage Oklahoma used might cause discomfort at the IV site. The lower dose used in the Locket execution is still much more than is needed for even prolonged operations, would be totally effective, and may well eliminate this minor issue of pain at the IV site. Remember, the Lockett case went awry because a good IV was not maintained; it had nothing to do with the dosage of midazolam.

How, then, do we defend not executing someone such as Warner, who committed a crime that makes us cringe. The most significant defense comes from his mental aberration, which, by the definition of the man in the street, is unquestionably that he was insane. We do not know if that was temporary, perhaps supported by some type of intoxicant, or if he has a permanent psychotic disease, but we all realize his actions were so out of line with what is considered normal that nonprofessionals would agree he is insane. There are other considerations, such as the time and money spent on a case like this, but when dealing with a crime that horrendous, those issues seem to pale. We do not consider an individual who would commit such a horrible deed sane, and as a general rule, we do not want to execute people with that level of sickness. Granted, there are many who disagree with this and feel that, sick or not, such individuals should face death.

This case allows us to explore the polar opposite opinions of the death penalty and the fact that people on both sides defend their positions aggressively. We go from the extremes of those who feel capital punishment in any form is abhorrent to the other side of the coin wherein people feel our current mode of relatively painless death is not sufficient punishment.

There is the understandable feeling for vengeance but also the realization that the defendant is sick. Balancing all this out is a very difficult undertaking, but a sentence of LWOP is the most efficient and reasonable approach. Enormous resources used in these kinds of cases are much better spent in more constructive areas.

RICHARD RAYMOND RAMIREZ

On Friday, February 6, 2015, an Orange County, California, Superior Court judge sentenced Richard Ramirez to death for the second time for the 1983 murder of Kimberly Gonzalez, whom he raped and stabbed to death behind a bar in Garden Grove. A previous jury sentenced Ramirez to death in 1985, but because the jury foreman did not disclose the fact that he was an FBI candidate, the verdict was overturned twenty-three years later in 2008. A second trial was held in 2013, and that jury also found him guilty but deadlocked over the issue of the death penalty. The judge declared a mistrial. This led to a third trial, and in November 2014, the third jury decided on the death penalty for Ramirez.

Family members were relieved to understand they had come to the end of the ordeal of reliving the horror of Kimberly's final moments repeatedly over three trials. Her sister, Yvette Mejia, said, "It has been an emotional roller coaster for us. Hopefully this is the last chapter."

Kimberly's mother, Mary Hernandez, said, "I'm thankful to God that he let me live to see this day."

Defense attorneys argued for a life sentence for Ramirez in lieu of the death penalty, pointing out his dysfunctional childhood in a household dominated by a violent alcoholic father and that he had been driven to drug abuse in his early teens. Judge Gregg Pickett denied the request, citing the egregiousness of the crime and previous rape conviction in which Ramirez assaulted the victim and threatened to cut off her baby's legs. The jury foreman, identified as Larry K., remarked that jurors were not swayed by the history of a difficult upbringing. He said, "It isn't an excuse. He still had a choice."

The jury foreman identified the issue of what laymen understand about the common-man definition of insanity. We know someone has to be "insane" to rape and then stab someone twenty times until she dies. But Larry K. pointed out the key element in the need for significant punishment—the murderer's free will. *He still had a choice.*

Other obvious victims in this case are family members who had to go through thirty-two years of our capital-punishment system. There never was a question of this man's guilt, but we insisted on dragging the family through years of undeserved pain. Those of us who do not have a good understanding of the law question why someone's application to the FBI has anything to do with the sentence at all and why it took until 2008 for this to become a significant issue. This should not be relevant, but it was, because of the possibility that the defense might have rejected him because of his affiliation with a law enforcement institution.

Kimberly's mother expressed relief that the trial was over and that her daughter's murderer was sentenced to death, but he really was not. In that regard, we've lied to Mrs. Hernandez. Ramirez will go to death row, but in California, no one is actually executed.

Victimhood applies to the rest of us who endure this process and support a journey over three decades long in which there was never a question of the defendant's guilt. Ultimately our institutions are *our* institutions, and we are responsible for effecting positive change in them.

JOSÉ GONZALEZ

On November 21, 1977, José Gonzalez, with the aid of two accomplices, bludgeoned to death James and Essie Effron in the basement of their San Diego clothing store. Mrs. Effron was diagnosed with cancer, so the couple decided to sell their store and hired Gonzalez to help them with a going-out-of-business sale. Mrs. Effron found it necessary to fire him because of rudeness to customers. Operating with the motives of robbery

and revenge, Gonzalez and his two associates took the couple to the basement, tied them up, and beat them to death with metal pipes. A jury
convicted Gonzalez of two counts of first-degree murder in 1978, when
California had neither a death penalty nor LWOP. The jury sentenced
Gonzalez to life but *with* the possibility of parole.

The parole board, in its ninth hearing on the case, recommended parole be granted to Gonzalez, now fifty-nine, primarily on the basis of his
behavior while behind bars. In 2008 California Supreme Court rulings
significantly eased stringent parole restrictions and ordered officials to
consider issues other than severity of crimes, such as inmates' records and
behavior, including issues like any volunteer work they might have done,
while incarcerated. Under that umbrella, the parole board recommended
Gonzalez's release.

California is one of just four states that gives the governor final authority over parole board decisions, and Governor Jerry Brown, under
the more lenient parole requirements, affirmed 82 percent of the board's
decisions, resulting in fourteen hundred lifers being paroled. About 80
percent of those released were murderers, and the rest were largely in the
category of rapists and kidnappers. Governor Arnold Schwarzenegger,
who governed from 2003 to 2011, approved 27 percent of decisions by the
parole board, resulting in the release of 557 such inmates, and Governor
Gray Davis, 1999 to 2003, approved the release of only two.

Michael Beckmann, Gonzalez's lawyer, said he was remorseful and
had the right to be released under state law, since he served over thirty-
seven years and satisfied his legal requirements.

Cheryl Effron and her brother Gary, the children of James and Essie,
are opposing the release, citing the enormity of the crime and their strong
conviction that he might kill again.

This case again brings up the possible divergence of the rights of victims versus the rights of murderers. The parole board feels Gonzalez
served sufficient time and is rehabilitated to the point he should go free.

But murder victims will never walk free, and they have no voice except that of their family and friends.

VICTIM VERSUS SOCIETY

We now leave in the hands of the parole board and governor the power to decide if a criminal has satisfied his debt to society. Before the Supreme Court eased the requirements, a debt to society was much harder to pay. Now that the court has changed things, it is acceptable to let more people out of prison through a more lenient decision-making process. Should "society" be the proper arbiter for this decision, or should it be the victim, who never will be free? Do we overstep our bounds when we make such decisions involving someone else's supreme victimization?

DALE EATON

The state of Wyoming found Dale Eaton guilty of murdering eighteen-year-old Lisa Kimmel (a.k.a. Lil Miss) and sentenced him to death by lethal injection in March 2004. He initiated his crime on March 25, 1988, when he abducted Kimmel, who was on her way to visit her boyfriend in Cody. Eaton abducted her at gunpoint as Kimmel stopped in a restroom along the highway. He took her back to his property, where he held her captive in an old school bus that lacked electricity and running water. He raped her numerous times and tortured her. He struck her on the back of the head with such force that it caused a four-inch skull fracture, and he stabbed her six times. Eaton then dumped Kimmel's body into the North Platte River, where two fishermen found her a week later.

DNA findings at the crime scene implicated Eaton, and a search in 2002 found Kimmel's car, with the license plate "Lil Miss," buried on the property. At the time of the discovery of his implication in the crime, Eaton, an ex-felon, was serving time in a Colorado prison for illegally carrying a firearm. He was also facing the possibility of an involuntary manslaughter charge related to the death of a fellow prisoner.

The murder of Kimmel was regarded as a shockingly brutal case and gained immediate widespread attention, including multiple television shows and a heartbreaking book by her mother documenting the story of her loss and grief.

Despite the shock and sympathy for the victim, on November 20, 2014, the US District Court for the District of Wyoming vacated the death sentence but upheld the conviction, resulting in a life term for Dale Eaton. Eaton's new legal team argued that his original defense was flawed primarily because of an inadequate job investigating his life, mental instability, and family history and that these factors might have stood for mitigating evidence that could influence the jury to avoid the death sentence. They also argued that the prosecution failed to reveal that an inmate who testified against Eaton was in line for a reduced sentence for cooperating. The hearings went on for several weeks and included testimony from psychiatrist Dr. Kenneth Ash, who indicated Eaton suffered from bipolar disorder, which is characterized by extremes of depression and hypomania. The doctor's testimony weighed heavily toward the impetus to reduce the sentence from death to life in prison.

Mental instability had a great deal to do with the reduction of the sentence from death to life in prison, but it required the defining of a specific diagnosis by a psychiatrist to influence the new defense team and the district court.

JAMES HOLMES

July 20, 2012, James Holmes, armed with multiple weapons, opened fire inside a suburban Denver movie theater, killing twelve and wounding seventy. Aurora police apprehended him in the parking lot immediately after the event.

Preliminary hearings for Holmes's trial began in 2013. On March 27, 2013, in a move to avoid the death sentence, his defense team made an offer to plead guilty in exchange for an LWOP sentence. Arapahoe County District Attorney George Brown Brauchler felt the enormity of the crime was such that death was the appropriate sentence and rejected the guilty plea. On May 31, 2013, defense attorneys changed the plea to not guilty by reason of insanity. Also, because of the enormity of the crime, preparations for the trial were such that the three-month jury-selection process did not begin until January 2015, and the trial finally began on April 27, 2015.

Psychiatrists testified that Holmes's schizophrenia was responsible for his actions and that he was psychotic at the time of the killing. The prosecution argued he was sane because he made fairly meticulous secretive plans for the attack, amassed the ammunition and weaponry required, and behaved normally in every other facet of his life prior to the killings.

Psychiatrists pointed to the fact that he indeed was psychotic by virtue of schizophrenia and that this was the cause of his actions. The prosecution went back to 1843 and argued he was sane because he knew what he was doing was wrong and tried to hide his plans. They argued that his ability to make plans proved his sanity. Psychiatrists and psychologists are fully aware that delusional people are able to make even extensive plans and also know that what they are doing is wrong on some level.

In the end, the jury did not find Holmes insane, and that defense, as is usually the case, failed, even though psychiatrists understand those arguments for sanity are flawed.

On July 16, 2015, after an eleven-week trial, the jury found Holmes guilty of first-degree murder and other charges. On August 7, 2015, the jury sentenced him to LWOP, which came as a great surprise because most people expected a death sentence. The life sentence was imposed, apparently, because one juror felt she could not sentence him to death because of the severity of his mental illness. This is something of a turn of events since the jury had already decided Holmes was sane. This particular juror, however, understood the gravity of his illness and embraced the philosophy that we cannot execute anyone who is so sick as to commit such a crime.

The irony is that this almost two-and-a-half-year legal exercise resulted in the same sentence that could have been obtained without it had the prosecution accepted the guilty plea back in 2013.

JAMES HOLMES AND INSANITY

The James Holmes case is a perfect example of why the insanity defense is so outrageously flawed. The term "crazy" is politically incorrect, but it is a good intermediary between the legal term "insane" and psychiatric term "psychotic." Second, experts on the subject, psychiatrists, told the jury Holmes was schizophrenic, psychotic, and delusional and that these conditions were the basis for his actions.

What we try to do in a jury trial when bringing up the notion of "insanity" is determine if the defendant's mental impairment or sickness caused his actions. In the James Holmes case, this was clearly the reality. Nonprofessionals know it, and mental-health professionals know it. Unfortunately this does not translate well to the legal understanding of mental illness in the term "insanity."

JAMES HOLMES, REALITY, AND PRACTICALITY

There was never a question of Holmes's guilt. If we could suppose King Solomon was a totally reasonable and just person, and we could resurrect him and put him in charge of our justice system, the James Holmes case would have been over in minutes. Understanding and balancing the enormity of the act and pathology of the mind, Solomon would have immediately removed him from society into a life of confinement. Colorado

Governor John Hickenlooper, as well as other governors, has said he will not allow anyone to be executed while he's in office. The result is that all the usual machinations ensure the immediate application of the death sentence will not happen.

LWOP!

Chapter 22

PRO-DEATH PENALTY

The essence of this book by necessity incorporates arguments against pro-death-penalty concepts. One of the most interesting death-penalty proponents is Professor Robert Blecker, whose understanding of the frailties of our punishment system puts him in many ways philosophically in sympathy with death-penalty opponents who also are concerned about some of the same weaknesses.

ROBERT BLECKER

Robert Blecker is a noted pro-death-penalty protagonist, who has great experience with related issues, including a period of over twelve years of walking freely inside Lorton Central Prison, where he probed the lives of street criminals and gained tremendous expertise in this area. In his book *The Death of Punishment*, he presents the argument that our sentencing and methods of punishment for murderers are not severe enough when contrasted with the crimes. It is very hard to disagree with his cogent arguments when he juxtaposes descriptions of the heinous murders committed and current prison lifestyles, which include athletics, other forms of organized socialization, color televisions and Internet, shopping at the commissary, and fairly liberal visitation rules.

Blecker selects what he calls "the worst of the worst" and claims he would sentence them to death. He is taken aback by the fact that some of our worst murderers wind up with some of the best conditions, and he finds those situations not compatible with real justice. Part of the problem lies with the practicality of how we deal with prisoners on a day-to-day basis, and Blecker interviewed a warden who admitted there was nothing in it for him to make it tougher on his prisoners and, in fact, that was not his job. Giving some privileges to prisoners made controlling them easier and safer for his personnel.

Although Blecker's primary goal is execution for those who have committed terrible crimes, he would accept a compromise, a much more severe form of incarceration in a separate facility that consists of a life of privation Blecker has dubbed "permanent punitive segregation." This form of punishment excludes athletics, color televisions, visitation, and commissary privileges and limits exercise to work-only situations. These prisoners do not have to fear execution but instead live a life of deprivation. This requires reeducation and changes in our correctional facilities, but arguably it is a much harsher sentence than death because, as we see in our current system, the inmate sentenced to death looks forward to improved conditions of death row with a minimal chance of execution far down the timeline.

Professor Blecker, in arguing that death by lethal injection is too easy, suggests death should be by firing squad or some other constitutional method and not medicines.

In arguing that we should separate out "the worst of the worst" and subject them to execution, Blecker presents a strong case on the basis of the pathologic cruelty murderers perpetrated on their victims. His descriptions of the crimes starkly contrast with the comparatively easy lives of murderers and are cogent arguments for the notion that this is unjust and totally inappropriate.

One problem is in determining who are "the worst of the worst." How do you draw the line? Any murder, particularly in the first-degree category, is reprehensible, but the professor is correct that some murders are so outrageously cruel they stand out from the rest.

There are people on both ends of the spectrum, but there is a large gray area in between, and who determines how we handle those people in that middle ground? How would we determine what level of cruelty falls into the category that demands the death sentence? It is difficult almost to the point of impossibility to determine, for instance, that we should execute murderer A for his crimes but not murderer B because his crimes were just slightly less heinous. The legal maneuverings by attorneys on both sides would be mind-boggling. They would, of course, get involved in mitigating factors and levels of sanity, as we do in the penalty phase of most murder cases currently, and this would get us involved in areas of subjectivity, powers of persuasion, and the vagueness of trying to determine levels of cruelty.

This whole discussion also incorporates the fact that the man in the street knows anyone who could commit a terribly heinous murder is not sane, and since we really do not want to execute the mentally ill, we cannot take these deranged people and terminate them.

Sentencing people to capital punishment would probably do what Professor Blecker does not want to see in that "the worst of the worst" would have a better life on death row than other murderers have in the general prison population. Defense attorneys would keep them alive for years, and the arguments about their mental aberrations, poor upbringings, and other issues propel these cases into the interminable, endless cycle.

The better approach is to rapidly and efficiently segregate sick people from society permanently. Even though the descriptions of heinous cruelty in some murders make the blood boil and calls for severe retribution, the realities of the pathology of murderers and the practical functioning of our jurisprudence system point to the fast and efficient application of permanent incarceration as by far the best solution.

Chapter 23

DEATH TO DEATH

* **There is no real death penalty.** Twenty-eight executions as opposed to fifteen thousand murders do not constitute a viable institution.
* **Costs are enormous.** Every aspect of a death-penalty case is more expensive than those of a noncapital case. The trials are more expensive, housing on death row is more expensive, and the appeals process is very expensive. These costs are bad in jurisdictions that can afford them and can be financially devastating to those that are less well off financially.
* **Victims' families are treated very poorly.** They are dragged through multiple reminders of their tragedies and rarely see the execution promised them as our concept of ultimate justice.
* **The system is a huge waste.** Our professional personnel, courts, money, and time would all be better utilized elsewhere.
* **There is so much capriciousness in the system that it makes it illogical and unfair.** The commission of identical crimes can lead to a death sentence or not, on the basis of varying state laws, attitudes toward the death penalty, how aggressive local jurisdictions are, and the political climate in regard to

"tough on crime" stances. Apprehension in and extradition from a non-death-penalty country assures the murderer will not face the death penalty. Wealth and fame both play heavily in the diminution of chances for a death sentence. The skills of the defense team are critical, and the poor are at a distinct disadvantage since they cannot afford the high-priced talent the rich can.

* **African Americans represent a far greater percentage of death-row inhabitants.** A black man has a much greater chance of receiving the death penalty if he kills a white person as opposed to his killing a black person. White victimhood is the most predominant factor in determining who goes to death row and who is executed.

* **Women are treated with more leniency than are men**.

* **Our current capital-punishment system has no deterrent effect.**

* **There is fear we might execute an innocent person**. Even though our current forensic advances make that less likely, it still remains a distinct possibility. Despite precautions, malfeasance occurs, and we have incarcerated and even executed the wrong people.

* **We really do not want the death penalty.** Physicians and drug companies refuse to participate, and though Americans still *say* they are pro–death penalty, they do not want to participate in the actual process of execution. Attorneys are reluctant to participate, particularly in the appeals process. There are several examples of judges' negativity when they use their judicial prerogatives to hamper or prevent death sentences.

* **The abolition movement is well on its way.** Fewer states participate in the death-penalty system, and we have already eliminated most reasons for the death penalty.

* **The death penalty can be a service to the murderer.** It can afford a better lifestyle for the inmate, a means of suicide for the mentally deranged, and a promotion of extremism.
* **The jury panel is not made up of peers.** The reason is that we eliminate the 40 percent of Americans who are against the death penalty.
* **Obviously any chance for exoneration or rehabilitation is eliminated** after an execution.
* **The appeals process is totally out of hand**. Although it is intended to ensure justice and to avoid executing the innocent, it has gotten totally out of hand. It is repetitious and goes on forever, and we have the difficult-to-impossible task of providing adequate representation for the murderer.
* **The insanity defense almost never works.** Definitions vary between professions, and communication verges on the impossible level. The layman has his own understanding of insanity in that anyone who can commit an horrendous murder is insane, but the fact the murderer acted out of free will closes the argument on his culpability, the need for him to answer for his crimes. More support is needed for the psychiatrists and psychologists who attend to those with potentially treatable psychiatric conditions within the framework of incarceration. The insanity defense is almost as flawed as the death penalty.
* LWOP!

POSTSCRIPT

Feel free to continue this discussion by visiting our blog, deathtodeath. net. The death penalty is far from dead, and your comments on either side of any of the issues are encouraged.

AUTHOR

B ob Dolan is a retired surgeon who resides in Fullerton, California
with Marianne, his wife of forty-eight years.

BIBLIOGRAPHY

Associated Press. "Condemned Man's Choice of Meals." News. *Orange County Register*, September 23, 2011, 3.

—————. "Inmate Dies of Natural Causes." News. *Orange County Register*, July 19, 2009.

—————. "San Quentin Prepares for an Execution." News. *Orange County Register*, September 22, 2010.

—————. "States Running Out of Execution-Drug Supply." News. *Orange County Register*, January 29, 2011, 3, 8.

Banks, Sandy. "Death Penalty? No, It Isn't." *Los Angeles Times*, July 19, 2014, A2.

Banner, Stuart. *The Death Penalty: An American History*. Cambridge, MA: Harvard University Press, 2002.

Bedau, Hugo, and Paul Cassell. *Debating the Death Penalty*. New York: Oxford University Press, 2004.

Bharath, Deepa. "Inside the Minds of the Twisted." News. *Orange County Register*, October 24, 2012, 1, 12.

—————. "Moving Past Her Pain to Help Other Victims." Life. *Orange County Register*, February 28, 2015, 9.

Biesecker, Michael (Associated Press). "Judge Commutes Three Death Sentences." News. *Orange County Register*, December 12, 2012, 15.

Blatchford, Chris. *The Black Hand: The Story of Rene "Boxer" Enriquez and His Life in the Mexican Mafia.* New York: HarperCollins, 2008.

Blecker, Robert. *The Death of Punishment.* New York: Palgrave McMillan, 2013.

————. *The Death of Punishment: Searching for Justice among the Worst of the Worst.* New York: Palgrave MacMillan, 2013.

California Penal Code. "Of Imprisonment and the Death Penalty." Thomson Reuters, 2014, 1006–1303.

Carl, Traci (Associated Press). "Villagers in Mexico Say Fugitive Marine Drew Attention." News. *Orange County Register*, April 12, 2008, 4, 5.

Cassidy, Jon. "A Couple of Photos Link to Forward Missing Women." *Orange County Register*, March 17, 2010, 1, 7.

Chandler, Kim (Associated Press). "Inmate to Be Freed after 30 Years." News. *Orange County Register*, April 3, 2015, 10.

Chemerinsky, Erwin. "How Disabled Is Disabled Enough to Be Executed?" Local. *Orange County Register*, June 4, 2014, 11.

Committee on Deterrence and the Death Penalty. National Research Council. *Deterrence and the Death Penalty.* Washington, DC: National Academies Press, 2012.

Death Penalty Information Center (DPIC).

Dray, Phillip. *At the Hands of Persons Unknown: The Lynching of Black America.* New York: Random House, 2007.

Editorial staff. "Companies Won't Sell Execution Drug to Kentucky." News. *Orange County Register*, January 19, 2011, 7.

————. "DA Drops Death Penalty against Mumia Abu-Jamal." News. *Orange County Register*, December 8, 2011, 11.

————. "DNA Evidence Frees Man Jailed in Girls' Deaths." News. *Orange County Register*, August 5, 2010, 7.

————. "Kentucky Judge Halts Murderer's Execution." News. *Orange County Register*, September 11, 2010, 10.

————. "The Limits of the Death Penalty." *New York Times*, April 16, 2008, A24.

————. "States' Death Row Populations Fall." News. *Orange County Register*, December 18, 2009, 13.

————. "Virginia Executes Killer Who Bragged." News. *Orange County Register*, March 19, 2010, 6.

Egelko, Bob. "Murderer's Execution Cleared." *San Francisco Chronicle*, September 25, 2010, 1.

Elias, Paul (Associated Press). "Execution Try Fails after Court Setbacks." News. *Orange County Register*, September 30, 2010, 17.

———. "Judge Tosses States Legal Injection Procedure." News. *Orange County Register*, December 17, 2011, 22.

Emery, Sean. "Jury: Santa Ana Mother Was Sane When She Drowned Child." Local. *Orange County Register*, February 10, 2015, 2.

Erickson, Nicholas. "Juan G. Silva, Dad Who Took Rap for Son's Hit-and-Run to Leave Prison." *Journal Sentinel*, July 27, 2015.

Gerber, Rudolph, and John Johnson. *The Top 10 Death Penalty Myths*. Santa Barbara, CA: Praeger Publishers, 2007.

Graczyk, Michael (Associated Press). "Texas Executes Killer." News. *Orange County Register*, August 6, 2008, 4.

———. "Texas Running Out of Execution Drug." News. *Orange County Register*, August 2, 2013, 18.

Greenhouse, Linda. "After a 32-Year Journey, Justice Stevens Renounces Capital Punishment." *New York Times*, April 18, 2008, A20.

Greenhut, Steven. "No Recession-Driven Crime Wave." Commentary. *Orange County Register*, July 4, 2010, 1–2.

Hardisty, Greg. "Mom Gets Five Years after the Newborn Drowns in Toilet." Local. *Orange County Register*, September 28, 2011, 1.

Hare, Robert D. *Without Conscience: The Disturbing World of the Psychopaths among Us*. New York: Guilford Press, 1999.

Hernandez, Salvador, Scott Schwebke, and Vik Jolly. "Promise Me the Death Penalty." News. *Orange County Register*, September 18, 2013, 1, 12.

Jolly, Vik. "High Court Reverses OC Death Sentence." News. *Orange County Register*, February 3, 2012, 11.

———. "Mother Sentenced to Five Years for Toilet Drowning of Baby." Local. *Orange County Register*, October 22, 2011, 2.

Jones, Ashby. "Texas Almost Out of Execution Drug." *Wall Street Journal*, March 16, 2015, A6.

Katz, Jonathon, and Erik Eckholm. "DNA Tests Exonerate Two Convicted in 1983 Murder." *New York Times*, September 3, 2014.

Keegan, Kyle, and Tony Saavedra. "Jail Informant Won't Go Free." Local. *Orange County Register*, February 3, 2015, 1, 10.

Kiehl, Kent A., and Joshua W. Buckholtz. "Inside the Mind of a Psychopath." *Scientific American Mind*, September/October 2010, 22–29.

Koerner, Claudia. "Families Say Justice Restored." News. *Orange County Register*, February 26, 2013, 1, 9.

———. "Imprisoned 'Night Stalker' Serial Killer Dies of Natural Causes at Age 53." News. *Orange County Register*, September 10, 2013, 22.

———. "Prisoners Getting a Second Chance." News. *Orange County Register*, February 26, 2013, 1, 9.

Liptak, Adam. "Supreme Court Allows Use of Execution Drug." News. *New York Times*, June 29, 2015, A1.

Locke, Mandy (McClatchy Newspapers). "Innocence Panel Frees Prisoner." News. *Orange County Register*, February 8, 2010, 8.

McCaffrey, Shannon (Associated Press). "Clemency Denied for Condemned Killer." News. *Orange County Register*, May 6, 2008, 7.

Mickadeit, Frank. "Alcala's End Game at Next Court Level." Local. *Orange County Register*, January 7, 2010, 2.

———. "Alcala Gives a Weak First Impression." Local. *Orange County Register*, February 3, 2010, 2.

———. "Alcala Swansong as Weak as His Defense." Local. *Orange County Register*, March 10, 2010, 2.

———. "DA Has One More Shot at Alcala KO" Local. *Orange County Register*, February 11, 2010, 2.

———. "Former Alcala Judge Calls In." Local. *Orange County Register*, February 17, 2010, 2.

———. "Not the Analogy Alcala Wanted." Local. *Orange County Register*, March 5, 2010, 2.

———. "Photos Don't Help Image." Local. *Orange County Register*, February 12, 2010, 2.

———. "Other Victims' Kin Rally at Trial." Local. *Orange County Register*, February 25, 2010, 2.

———. "Whither 4th Hawks Killer?" Local. *Orange County Register*, April 22, 2009, 2.

Montgomery, Dave (McClatchy Newspapers). "Texas Set to Defy Treaty with Mexican's Execution." News. *Orange County Register*, August 5, 2008, 6.

National Center for Constitutional Studies. *The Constitution of the United States*, 2014, 1–34.

New Yorker. "Weighing Costs of Death Penalty Cases." *Wall Street Journal*, January 28, 2008, B5.

Ortiz, Jean (Associated Press). "Planted Evidence Paves Way for Appeals." News. *Orange County Register*, March 25, 2010, 6.

Peltz, Jennifer (Associated Press). "Alcala Arraigned in New York Slayings." News. *Orange County Register*, June 22, 2012, 8.

———. "Serial Killer Faces New York Charges." News. *Orange County Register*, June 21, 2012, 8.

Puente, Kelly. "DA: We Erred but Not Enough to Be Off Dekraai Case." News. *Orange County Register*, March 15, 2015, 1, 3.

———. "Racking Up Years on Death Row." News. *Orange County Register*, November 12, 2014, 1, 6, 8.

———. "Their Parents' Killer May Go Free." Local. *Orange County Register*, March 16, 2015, 1, 6.

Rohde, Stephen. "Put Down the Death Penalty." *Orange County Register*, July 9, 2006.

Saavedra, Tony. "Informant Battles Derail Another Case." News. *Orange County Register*, March 20, 2015, 1, 14.

———. "Killer Turned Snitch Poised to Go Free." Local. *Orange County Register*, February 12, 2015, 1, 16.

————. "Previous Parole Ended in Murder." News. *Orange County Register*, February 17, 2015, 1, 9.

————. "State AG Appeals Dekraai Ruling." News. *Orange County Register*, March 21, 2015, 1, 10.

Schwebke, Scott. "Orange County Is among Nations Highest for Death Penalties." Local. *Orange County Register*, October 6, 2013, 8–9.

Sforza, Teri. "Bill Would Abolish State's Death Penalty." News. *Orange County Register*, July 8, 2011, 1, 3.

Sherman, Mark (Associated Press). "No Death Penalty for Child Rape." News. *Orange County Register*, June 26, 2008, 4.

Skutch, Jan. "Troy Davis' Final Day." *Savannah Morning News*, September 21, 2011, 1.

Stacy, Mitch (Associated Press). "Florida Man Exonerated after 35 Years behind Bars." News. *Orange County Register*, December 18, 2009, 11.

Stevenson, Mark (Associated Press). "Execution Barely Fazes Crime-Weary Mexico." News. *Orange County Register*, August 7, 2008, 9.

Temkin, Moshik. "How to Kill the Death Penalty." *Los Angeles Times*, May 27, 2014, A13.

Thompson, Don (Associated Press). "Bill to End Death Penalty Stalls." News. *Orange County Register*, August 26, 2011, 14.

Turnbeau, Gary. "California's Death Row Is a Mockery of Justice." Local. *Orange County Register*, December 2, 2009, 9.

Urbina, Ian. "In Push to End Death Penalty, Some States Cite Cost-Cutting." *New York Times*, February 25, 2009, 1, 19.

Walters, Dan. "Death Penalty Lethal for Brown?" Local. *Orange County Register*, October 18, 2010, 5.

Wasserman, Barry. "Seal Beach Shootings: 'An Eye for an Eye.'" Local. *Orange County Register*, October 22, 2011, 14.

Webster's New Universal Unabridged Dictionary. New York: Simon and Schuster, 1983, 642.

Welborn, Larry. "Alcala Claims He Does Not Remember Four Murders." Local. *Orange County Register*, March 5, 2010, 2.

———. "Alcala Says He Has an Alibi." News. *Orange County Register*, February 3, 2010, 1, 2.

———. "Alcala's Extradition May Help Bring Closure." Local. *Orange County Register*, February 10, 2012, 7.

———. "Alcala Suspected in Bay Area Killing." News. *Orange County Register*, March 8, 2011, 1, 7.

———. "Alcala Testifies He Never Met Victim." Local. *Orange County Register*, February 12, 2010, 2.

———. "Conspirator Gets Death." Local. *Orange County Register*, May 2, 2009, 1, 3.

———. "Convicted Killer Tells Jury about Own Abuse." Local. *Orange County Register*, June 25, 2008, 1, 3.

———. "Death Penalty Trials Make a Comeback." Local. *Orange County Register*, January 3, 2013, 1, 2.

———. "Defendant Questions Victim's Mother." Local. *Orange County Register*, January 26, 2010, 1–3.

———. "Detectives Identify Some Proposed for Alcala." Local. *Orange County Register*, April 11, 2010, 1–2.

———. "Jurors Want Judge to Sentence Supremacist to Death," Local. *Orange County Register*, October 30, 2009, 1, 3.

———. "Jury Deadlocks in Penalty Phase of 1983 Bar Slaying." Local. *Orange County Register*, June 4, 2013, 3.

———. "Jury Selection Begins in Serial Slaying Case." Local. *Orange County Register*, January 6, 2010, 4.

———. "Killer Filed Claims over Candy, Playboy." Local. *Orange County Register*, April 2, 2010, 2.

———. "Killer Says He Doesn't Care If He Gets Death or Life." Local. *Orange County Register*, October 28, 2009, 9.

———. "Killer's Trial Enters Third Penalty Phase." Local. *Orange County Register*, October 12, 2011, 4.

———. "Murderer Gets Wish for Death Penalty." News. *Orange County Register*, November 24, 2009, 1–2.

———. "New York Seeks Extradition of Killer." Local. *Orange County Register*, January 28, 2011, 1, 3.

————. "New York Slayings May Be Added to Orange County Case." Local. *Orange County Register*, March 8, 2009, 6.

————. "No Orange County Murderers on Execution List." Local. *Orange County Register*, November 9, 2010, 2.

————. "Ocala Defense Leaves Many Questions." Local. *Orange County Register*, February 16, 2010, 1, 3.

————. "Pain, Memories Still Haunt Relatives of Alcala's Victims." Local. *Orange County Register*, April 4, 2010, 2.

————. "Prosecutor Calls Alcala 'Predatory Monster.'" Local. *Orange County Register*, February 24, 2010, 8.

————. "Prosecutor Seeks Death for Convicted Murderer." News. *Orange County Register*, October 29, 2009, 3.

————. "Questions Surround Alcala in 1977 Slaying in New York." News. *Orange County Register*, July 18, 2010, 18.

————. "Sentences: California Executions on Hold." News. *Orange County Register*, September 17, 2009, 2.

————. "Serial Murder Suspect Cites Insanity for Sex Slayings," Local. *Orange County Register*, November 3, 2009.

————. "Survivors to Speak during Alcala Penalty Trial." Local. *Orange County Register*, March 2, 2010, 1, 3.

————. "Suspected Serial Killings to Be Tried in OC." Local. *Orange County Register*, June 13, 2008, 17.

————. "Woman's Killer Gets Death." Local. *Orange County Register*, January 21, 2009, 1, 3.

————. "Woman Standing Up for Murdered Sister." News. *Orange County Register*, September 17, 2012, 1, 10.

Welborn, Larry, and Srisavasdi Rachanee. "Man Who Killed Roommate to Be Freed." Local. *Orange County Register*, January 9, 2010, 1–3.

Welborn, Larry, and Vik Jolly. "Veteran's Widow Weeps for Killer." *Orange County Register*, December 17, 2011, 2.

Wesson, Gail. "Death Row Inmate Dies in Prison Hospital." News. *Orange County Register*, March 24, 2015, 1.

Will, George. "Feel Safer? Thank Prisons." News. *Orange County Register*, June 22, 2008, 1, 5.

Williams, Carol, and Maura Dolan. "A New Strategy on the Death Penalty." *Los Angeles Times*, February 24, 2009, B1, B7.

Williams, Juliet. "Death Penalty Support Falls." News. *Orange County Register*, September 13, 2014, 1, 20.

Williams, Mary. *The Death Penalty: Opposing Viewpoints*. San Diego, CA: Greenhaven Press, 2002.

Wisckol, Martin. "Expediency Stocks Death Penalty Vote." News. *Orange County Register*, October 14, 2012, 9, 10.

Wolf, Richard. "Supreme Court Refuses to Ban Controversial Method of Execution." *USA Today*, June 30, 2015.

www.ingramcontent.com/pod-product-compliance
Lightning Source LLC
Chambersburg PA
CBHW062201270326
41930CB00009B/1604